Russian Political Institutions

BY

DEREK J. R. SCOTT

FREDERICK A. PRAEGER, *Publisher*
New York

BOOKS THAT MATTER

Published in the United States of America in 1961 by
Frederick A. Praeger, Inc., Publisher
64 University Place, New York 3, N.Y.

© Derek J. R. Scott, 1961

All rights reserved

Library of Congress Catalog Card Number: 61-15896

First published in Great Britain in 1958 by
George Allen and Unwin Ltd.
Second edition published in 1961.

RUSSIAN POLITICAL INSTITUTIONS is published in two editions:

A paperback edition (U-509)
A clothbound edition

This book is Number 94 in the series of
Praeger Publications in Russian History and World Communism.

Manufactured in the United States of America

Russian Political Institutions

PREFACE

I was told that if the lectures on the Russian way of conducting political life which I at present deliver in the course in political institutions in the University of Manchester could be converted into an appropriately inexpensive little book even undergraduate students of politics might read it. The result of the conversion is perhaps a little longer than was envisaged because of the comprehensive nature of Russian politics and the opportunities which literary creation offers for fitting in a variety of things which for lack of time or cloudiness of mind do not get said in the lecture.

The book offers little information which has not already been published in English, and such as there is comes almost entirely from the more readily accessible organs of the Soviet press. The aim is rather to draw together the body of information which we have and to present it in a form suitable for the first approach of the serious student to the subject. Most of the reasons why books on Russia, including this one, are the peculiar products which they are form a necessary part of the course in understanding the Russians, and so belong in the introduction, which people are supposed to read, rather than in the preface. It should, however, perhaps be mentioned here that by a peculiarly unfortunate piece of timing this book was in proof, and the author in West Africa, when between December 1956 and May 1957 Mr. Khrushchov's ideas of the way to organise the management of economy began to change the administrative shape of Russia. While the book's main arguments are not affected, readers are entitled to expect the structure described to bear some resemblance to that which they read about in their daily newspapers, and accordingly I have made such changes as the rigid limits of page proofs and the lack of concrete information on the changes permit. References in the text to 'the present time' or 'now' are believed to be true as to the date of this preface, though often based on material of 1956.

I confess myself greatly indebted to Professors W. J. M. Mackenzie and D. P. Costello and Mr. Peter Campbell of the University of Manchester, for reading and commenting upon this book in the course of its evolution. Of course, they must be discharged from all responsibility for any violence to the facts and the English language and for any outrageous opinions that remain. More than gratitude is due to my aunt Mrs. W. Pevalin, whose successive typed drafts provided a most elegant background for successive layers of authorial scribble.

In this second edition corrections and amendments have been made only where statements in the original version were known to be misleading as descriptions of the situation existing at the date of this note. Statements which declare their dates and are believed still to represent adequately the present position are, for the restraint of costs of production, left unchanged.

D.J.R.S.
Manchester
15*th September* 1960

CONTENTS

	pages
PREFACE	5

INTRODUCTION: SCOPE OF THE ATTEMPT — 15
Difficulties of Russian Studies — 15
Method and Plan — 17

I. WHAT RUSSIAN POLITICS ARE ABOUT

Material Inheritance — 21
 Territory and natural endowment
 Foreign contacts and expansion of the Russians
 Late development

Administrative Tradition — 23
 Absence of representative institutions
 Absence of local self-government
 Peasant emancipation and the rural commune
 Alexander II's local-government reform
 Judicial reform
 A country of poor peasants

Attitudes — 29
 Peasant discontent, rural and urban
 Lack of firm body of support for the regime
 Disruptive force of the intelligentsia
 What is national character?
 Russian national character before the revolution
 Military defeat precipitates revolt of 1905
 First acceptance of liberal democracy

Doctrinal Equipment — 32
 Why Marxism appealed to the Russians
 Difficulties and organisation of the early Russian Marxists
 Lenin's Russification of Marxist doctrine
 What belief in Marxism has changed in Russia

The Manner of Seizing Power — 41
 The prepared 'October' revolution of 1917
 The issues remaining to be solved
 The lessons to the ambitious

The Issues — 42
 Who shall rule?
 Economic priorities

CONTENTS

pages

    The frontiers and security
    Particularism
    Local alliances in the centralised state

The Periods   45
    War communism and anti-bolshevik threats
    The N.E.P. and the succession to Lenin
    Planning and the consolidation of Stalin's power
    Unbridled Stalinism
    Unstable oligarchy

The Participants   53
    Citizens
    Followers of politics
    The political society
    The sovereign decision-making body

II. SOVIETS, UNION AND CONSTITUTIONAL STATE

The Invention of the Soviets   56
    Marx on the Paris commune
    The soviets of 1905
    Lenin builds them into the Marxist state
    His attitude between 'February' and 'October'
    Congresses of soviets and executive committees
    Addition of a government of conventional type
    By-passing the soviets ('dual subordination')
    Purging the soviets
    Absence of a legal formulation of sovietism

The Union   63
    Nationalist demands and Russian bolshevik response
    Bolshevik acceptance of 'federalism' ('autonomy')
    Its content
    The People's Commissariat for Nationalities
    The formation of the U.S.S.R.
    The Union legislature
    The types of ministries
    Sense in which this is 'not federalism'
    Federal powers over federated units
    A matter of 'subordination', not of limitation
    Utility of Soviet autonomy-federalism
    Promotion to the status of a federated unit
    Autonomous units
    How secure is federal and autonomous status?

Administrative Areas   71
    Economic motive of division, and mutability
    The invention of new areas (1920's)

CONTENTS

pages

The problem of the intermediate level (1930's)
The Stalinist trend to fragmentation and its reversal
Consolidation of 'village' and district areas—motive
What it means in terms of population
Manifestation of urbanisation
Why keep the 'village' soviet?

Collective Administration 78
'Collegiality'
The collective head of state
The ministry 'collegium'
'Collegiality' and 'one-man headship' in industrial management
Collective management of national economy replaced by ministerial management

The Function of Soviet Constitutionalism 81
Why constitutions are made
Soviet Union's lack of pressing motive to adopt a written constitution
The occasions of the three constitutions
The manner of making of the 1936 constitution

Contents of the Constitution 83
The chapter headings
Declarations of faith (Chapters I and X)
Rights of federating units
Excess of detail in political structure and machinery
Apparent return to the separation of powers
Amendment and interpretation of the constitution
Uniformity of constitutions of federated and autonomous units

Utility of the Constitution 88
The constitution as record
Supplementary evidence
The constitution as ideology

III. CONVENTIONAL STATE MACHINERY

The Representative Bodies—What They Are 90
Size and basis of election of U.S.S.R. Supreme Soviet
Supreme Soviets of union and autonomous republics
Local soviets
Soviets no longer 'political foundation' of the U.S.S.R.

How They are Formed 93
Unequal representation before 1936
Franchise under 1936 constitution

CONTENTS

pages

    Method of voting
    Electoral commissions
    Registration
    Nomination and constituency conferences
    Practice of open voting
    Cases and causes of failure to secure election
    Some functions of Soviet elections
    Product of the elections (party membership, etc.)
    Pattern of composition of 1954 Supreme Soviet

What They Do   100

    Rules and practice on frequency of meetings
    Verification of mandates
    Officers of the Supreme Soviet
    Standing commissions of Supreme Soviet
    Local standing commissions
    Separate and joint sessions of houses of Supreme Soviet
    Nature of discussion
    Official categorisation of Supreme Soviet business
    Business performed by 1954 Supreme Soviet
    Business of a local soviet
    Soviets as vehicle of criticism of local administration
    Lobbying in the soviet system
    Soviets as briefing conferences
    Soviets as schools of government
    Why people attend soviets

The Inner Bodies—How They are Formed   111

    Nature of executive committees, praesidia, bureaux
    Praesidium of a Supreme Soviet
    Executive committee of a local soviet
    Selection of members of an executive committee
    Type of person selected
    Councils of ministers
    Quality of the ministers
    Other members of the Council of Ministers
    Praesidium of the Council of Ministers
    Ministers and Supreme Soviet
    Councils of ministers of union republics

What They Do   120

    Acts of the councils of ministers
    Acts of the Praesidium of the Supreme Soviet
    Meetings of the councils of ministers and praesidia
    Their part in the system of hierarchic supervision
    Work of a local soviet executive committee
    An urban local soviet executive committee
    Acts of executive committees
    Meetings of executive committees
    Supervision over supervision
    Reconciliation of myth and practical needs

The Ministries and Departments   127

    The ministries at federal level
    The ministries at union-republic level

CONTENTS

                                  pages

    Ministries and administrations of autonomous republics
    Departments and administrations of local executive committees
    Internal structure of the ministries
    Ministerial acts and authority
    The minister and his collegium

IV. THE PARTY

Structure   136

    Relations of the party structure to the state structure
    Party rules and designations
    Structure of primary organisations of the party
    Representative machinery of the party
    Committees and central committees
    Bureaux and secretaries
    Congresses of the C.P.S.U.
    Central Committee of the C.P.S.U.
    Plenary meetings of the Central Committee
    Former bureaux of the Central Committee
    Praesidium of the Central Committee
    Bureaux of republican party central committees
    Secretariat of the party
    The First Secretaryship since Stalin
    The junior secretaries
    Central checking ('revision') commission
    Committee of party control
    Advancement at the top

Staff   152

    Changing principles of organisation of party staff
    Party schools
    Party groups; party work in ministries and armed forces
    Party work with youth

Membership   157

    Principles of recruitment
    Party strength in 1917
    Recruiting drives
    Exclusions and restrictions
    The party in the period of purges
    Recruitment rules and practice from 1939
    The post-war membership policy
    Composition by nationality
    Composition by sex
    Composition by occupation
    The party and its allies in the state machinery
    Interlocking of party and state deliberative bodies

CONTENTS

pages

What Membership Means — 167
Duties of membership
Rights of membership
Financial and social burdens of membership
Dangers of membership
Incentives to seek membership
Influence of members
Influence and obligations of office-holders
Paid officials
Advancement in the party

The Party as Administrative Machinery — 175
The task set the party
How the party works in the administration
Party oversight
Party responsibility for agriculture
Party responsibility for staffing ('cadres')
The 'nomenklatura' in party staffing work
Principle of abstention from detail
Shortcomings of party officials
The cost of party oversight

The Party as Organised Faith — 184
Ideology
The utility of ideology
The cost of ideology
Party self-education and propaganda
Distinction of propaganda and agitation
The Central Committee department of propaganda and agitation
Party control of the press
Members' neglect of ideological work

The Party as Symbol — 190
Embodiment of the revolutionary tradition
Embodiment of internationalism

V. THE WEB OF MANAGEMENT

Organisation in Industry — 191
'Subordination' of industrial enterprises
The links with the ministry

The Men in the Machine — 193
Recruiting and establishments in industry
Posting
Powers of the manager
Unauthorised managerial methods

CONTENTS

Agriculture — 198
   The ministerial pattern
   The constitution of collective farms
   The management of collective farms
   Checks upon the management
   State farms and collective farms
   The collective-farm member's incentives
   Machine-tractor stations
   Disposal of produce

Organs of Detection and Regulation — 205
   The banking system
   Audit
   State control
   Police
   The procuracy

Organs of Adjudication — 210
   Arbitration
   The judicial system
   Civil business of the courts
   Criminal business of the courts
   Other punitive jurisdictions
   Pressures on the judges
   The quality of Soviet judicial work

The Armed Forces — 217
   The citizen's experience of the forces
   The officers
   Political influence of the military

Education and the Educated — 220
   The general education system
   Higher education
   The content of Soviet education
   The learned institutions and their task
   Assignments, incentives and limitations of the Soviet educated
   The scholar and politics

Further Lines of Control — 228
   Trade unions
   The press
   Specialised societies, churches, etc.

VI. DECISION AND PERFORMANCE

Top-level Decisions — 233
   What is the sovereign decision-taking body?
   What sort of matters does it decide?

CONTENTS

	pages
Planning and Budgeting	234

    The economic plan—a general order
    The instruments of planning
    Their preparation
    Budgets
    The process of budgeting
    Heads of revenue
    The revenue of local soviets
    Responsibility for expenditure

Low-level Decisions   240

    Occasions for general consultation of the public
    How to get things done from below
    The field for private agreement and initiative

Securing Performance—Economic   242

    Financial incentives to plan-fulfilment
    Negative side to emphasis on plan-fulfilment

Securing Performance—General   244

    Absence of freedom from supervision—its results
    Penal system
    Economic motive in penal system
    Incentives to the ambitious
    The stimulus of general well-being
    The sense of national danger
    The sense of national power
    The fiction of the enemy
    Consequences of absence of party conflict

BIBLIOGRAPHY   251

INDEX   257

INTRODUCTION

Scope of the Attempt

Difficulties of Russian Studies

It is difficult to approach the study of anything Russian in the same frame of mind as we are accustomed to bring to the understanding of other societies. The Russian authorities present the experience of their country as of universal application, and the foreign observer is apt, in the same spirit, to take it as an example, good or bad. Moreover, the world is now much involved in Russian affairs, and its ability to see them dispassionately is affected by a reasonable desire to know what Russia is going to do next. But both polemic and prophecy, particularly tempting in the field of politics, are remote from the study of political institutions. These are the more or less conventionalised processes by which the divergent wills of individuals in a society are, in fact, reconciled into acceptance of courses of action taken in the name of the society as a whole or of recognised associations within it. We seek in this book to understand the process where the individuals involved are Russians, as we are already accustomed to do where they are Americans or Frenchmen. Our concern is with the very recent period of history which we call the present, though this is not to be understood without some reference to the remoter past.

We have to face at the outset the problem of the terms in which to discuss Russian politics. Many of the institutions which we traditionally accept as keys to the nature of political systems—the legislature, elections or the head of state—exist, but are of little significance in the real process of politics as we define it. Others—the government or the party—although important are something very different from the institutions similarly designated in the systems with which people in this country are more familiar. Other terms useful in political discourse—the civil service or central and local government, and the different balance between them—are inapplicable because of the virtual absence in the Russian system of the distinctions which they imply. The total field of study is itself different. If we decide (as to make his subject manageable the political scientist must) to consider as politics only such adjustment of wills as is effected by means of some formal machinery, such as meetings in particular places, established and obligatory procedures and a systematic apparatus of coercion, we find ourselves obliged to take account of many activities in Russia which in lands of liberal tradition are not politics. What crops the cultivator is to plant, how much of his resources the factory manager is to put to investment, what research projects are to be undertaken in the universities, are all not merely relevant questions. Without them much of the system has no purpose.

We are also notably less well supplied with detailed and reliable information than in the study of most other countries. The motives of individuals' action are the stuff of our studies, and we cannot reach the individuals. Russia produces no memoirs and only the personages of approved national legend have biographies. The examples of Soviet citizens presented by Russian sources are improbably uniform if one considers that theirs is a very large country with still imperfect communications. Lack of personal contacts makes it difficult to know the relative reliability of different sources of information and to fill in any missing detail so as to complete a picture which will satisfy our standards of realism. The view is obscured by a systematic secretiveness maintained by severe penalties for disclosure of information not elsewhere considered as of vital importance. The official picture is black and white. There is a clamour of self-praise; there is also much denunciation of faults, though these are normally either past or exceptional and always individual or tactical rather than consequent upon the grand strategy of the system; but the normal, the adequate performance, the reasonable settlement, are rarely shown, since they teach no lessons. There is little which looks like objective assessment from within. Outside there are no witnesses or commentators whom all, friends or opponents of the regime, are prepared to accept as factual and unbiased. Eyewitnesses are either visitors on an officially conducted tour or refugees with a sense of grievance. Their bona fides is certain to be questioned, however unjustly; it was usually questioned even in the days of the Tsars. Finally, despite recurrent waves of official advocacy of collective leadership, more rests upon a few individual personalities than perhaps in any other country, and these are largely unknown.

The system neither claims to be, nor is, permanent. According to the official creed, political as well as other social institutions are a superstructure of which the foundations are economic forces, the ultimate result of which is determined beyond human power to alter it and in face of which there is scope for wisdom only in knowing how to conform to and assist them and to avoid the stresses of wrestling with the inevitable. The superstructure is determined by the foundations, though only the initiates know how, and even they, it seems, can rarely explain before the event. Whatever the theoretical background, it proves in practice very hard to be sure that what we think we know of the position in the Soviet Union yesterday is true of today. Administrative areas, the system of government offices and their competence, the departmental structure within them, the legislation for the time being in force, even the identity of the participants in the central counsels of the system, are in a state of perpetual flux.

All this is distinctive of Russia only in degree. The political institutions of any major power are habitually discussed with reference to their supposed magical properties as secrets of greatness; this has been true of British practices and still evidently affects assessment of those of the United States. No administrative corps can resist the temptation to preserve its mysteries from the vulgar eye of the observer, and that of the United Kingdom perhaps less than most. Russia differs only in that the administration is more comprehensive. There are countries with which, for geographical and other reasons, direct contact is as difficult. But probably in no country of comparable general interest, except China, are the obstacles in the way of understanding so many.

Method and Plan

Recognising these limitations, we may nevertheless seek so to arrange the information which we have as to form a picture more or less corresponding to that which presents itself to the Soviet citizen when he takes a decision on his relations with his fellow-citizens. In so doing we must recognise that the decisions are taken on the basis of material circumstances and traditions which can never be fully described. The context differs for each individual engaged in the process, for Russians, like other people, lead lives of their own. At best we can give a rough sketch of an aspect of the whole which needs to be filled in with knowledge of the geography, history, literature and other aspects of the life of the country.

Also, as with other countries, but, for the reasons suggested, especially in the case of Russia, we must in our capacity of political scientists beware of passing avoidable judgments. It is not a question relevant to our work, whether we should like to live under such a system. In our personal capacities as residents in the same world we may be concerned, lest the tendencies of the system be such that we might have to. But communism as developed in Russia would, upon transfer to this or any other country, either be further modified to accord with the recipients' associations and ideas of what is reasonable or it would be imposed by force. This is so with the transfer of any political system from one country to another, and a system forcibly imposed is bad whatever its origin. We study Russian political institutions as we study any institutions of any society, as part of the study of man, in order to understand what it feels like to be another person in other circumstances —to know, as far as we may, the reasons others see for acting as they do. We cannot hope to refrain entirely from judgment, since it is in human nature to judge. It is therefore well to have reasons for our judgment. This book rests on the assumption that a judgment is acceptable only in so far as its standards are Russian, a reasonable estimate of what Russians, in Russian circumstances, would find more or less satisfactory. Placed as we are in respect of access to detailed information, we can hardly assess any particular institution. Even for better documented countries it is difficult to say how far any part of the system can be changed without changing the whole. On the system as a whole it is possible to comment without being entirely unscientific.

The documentary means of access to the experience of the Russians are the daily and periodical press, published texts of legal instruments and commentaries upon them, and the official textbooks intended for the use of various classes of students and officials. The legal texts are defective. The gazette of the acts of the Supreme Soviet (*Vedomosti Verhovnogo Soveta*),[1] or, in fact, since the Supreme Soviet meets rarely, mainly of its Praesidium, is now almost a weekly, but contains little but honours and awards, changes of administrative areas, agencies and ministers, and postings of ambassadors. A comprehensive collection of acts of the Council of Ministers (*Sobranie Postanovleni i Rasporjazheni Soveta Ministrov SSSR*), containing mainly administrative instructions, and the greatest in volume of the classes of rules

[1] The principles of transliteration followed in this book are: to avoid it wherever possible, to use as few letters as possible, and to respect generally accepted conventional spellings of proper names in frequent use where consistency would produce an unfamiliar form. The letter 'y' is always a vowel, the letter 'j' is used to represent the consonantal 'y' sound. After the vowels 'i' and 'y' at the ends of words it is omitted. The hard sign (separating two sounds) is represented by an apostrophe. The letter 'e' is to be understood always to have a consonantal 'y' sound before it without any indication (one exception will worry only those who already know the Russian form). The Russian 'h' sound is represented by the letter 'h' (the exception for proper names preserves the now familiar initial of Mr. Khrushchov's surname). 'Zh' has its conventional sound. The Russian 'e' as in Mr. Khrushchov's name is transliterated according to sound; the adjectival ending in 'go' (as here) according to sight. Terms quoted in parenthesis in the text are always given in the singular if capable of being so used. Where used in the plural in the text they are given the English form of plural in 's', however badly it fits.

which Russians have to obey, has not been published since August 1949. We are dependent for direct information on such measures upon various special editions and handbooks. Recent comments in the Soviet press on the inconvenience resulting from the unsystematic publication of party and government decisions[1] suggests that there may soon be some improvement in this. In any case, decisions and decrees not themselves divulged have consequences which must be divulged, and we can read much of the legislation in this indirect fashion in the press. The press is itself an imperfect source. Apart from material of a Court-circular character and international news consisting largely of formal exchanges of messages between governments, it is concerned primarily with exhortation, self-congratulation and the denunciation of shortcomings. Much of this praise and blame is evidently justified. In the statements of fact there is probably little falsification, though there is much suppression. The textbooks are mostly highly legalistic and give little indication of the practice of politics, but they are useful as indications of the official approach. In addition, among the works published outside Russia we get a fair volume of memoirs and travellers' tales which, though subject to the bias which we have mentioned, contain much information which fits in with what we already know. A knowledge of human nature enables us to spot the more notably tall stories.

Since to write about Russia is to be suspected of bias, certain assumptions must be admitted at the outset. It is assumed that though revolution and Marxist indoctrination have modified the motivation of the Russians, the change has not been so far-reaching as to render inapplicable what we think we know of human nature elsewhere, or of Russia before the revolution. It is assumed that the answers which post-revolutionary experience together with approved pre-revolutionary thought provide to the problems of life are not so complete as to obviate the necessity for drawing upon the experience accumulated from the centuries of the nation's life. Also, lest value judgments be detected, the author must admit to holding that while all government is bad in that through its operation the individual feels frustrated by forces outside himself, that is least bad in which the occasions of such frustration are fewest. Another assumption is that, in general, efficiency is good, that a political system should be operated with the expenditure of the least amount of time of the smallest number of people, and that

---

[1] E.g. *Kommunist*, No. 12 of 1955, p. 9. F. Burlatski, in *Kommunist*, No. 8 of 1956, p. 57, states that in recent years many decrees of the Council of Ministers have not been published at all. Two edicts of the Praesidium of the Supreme Soviet confirmed at the Supreme Soviet session of February 1957 had not previously been gazetted.

the achievement of any of its purposes should not render more difficult the achievement of the rest.

Chapter I is intended to suggest some of the experience, practical and theoretical, upon which Soviet politics draw, and the nature of the purposes which it is their function to reconcile. Chapter II treats of the manner of the invention of the institutions claimed to be distinctive of the Soviet state—the soviets, the Union and collective administration —and of the place in this original creation of the highly unoriginal instrument formerly known as the Stalin constitution. Chapter III examines the organisation and functions of machinery familiar in liberal states but functioning there to rather different purpose; elected bodies, the inner bodies elected by them, and the administrative departments headed by members of some of the latter. Chapter IV concerns the party, its organisation, membership and manner of operation. Chapter V examines the structure which under the ministries discharges their main function, the operative management of the fully nationalised economy, and other systems of control, including the judicial system and the armed forces, which with the party and Soviet system make up the intricate web of Russian administration. In Chapter VI a brief attempt is made to explain how priorities of tasks are decided upon, obligations determined and performance of them secured.

CHAPTER I

What Russian Politics are About

Material Inheritance
The territory of the U.S.S.R. in itself has sufficed to make the political experience of its people very different from that of western Europe. The area of the country is 8,512,000 square miles. No part of this vast area extends into latitudes farther south than those of the continent of Europe, and part of the mainland extends some eight hundred miles north of the Arctic circle. Moscow has four or five months of frost in the year, and even the northern parts of the Crimea have three or four. In some 47 per cent of the territory the soil below the surface to varying depths remains permanently frozen. Distance from the sea produces an extreme range of temperature, extending in part of eastern Siberia from a monthly mean of $-60°$F. in January to $60°$F. in July, and in exceptional seasons more than half as much again in either direction. Over large parts of the territory summer is extremely short and winter conditions such as to prevent agricultural work. Only parts of the Crimean and Baltic coasts enjoy a temperate climate. The soil includes, in the black-earth belt, extending from the Ukraine south-eastward, some of the best grain-growing land in the world, and some well-watered valleys in the Caucasus and central Asia are fertile, but in general the country is poorly endowed for agriculture. Much of the Asian south is desert, and more than half the country to the north has poor soil added to an unfavourable climate. In most parts the rainfall is poor or unreliable. The mineral resources, rich in the country as a whole, are scarce in European Russia. Mountains defend most of the southern frontier but present little obstacle to internal movement, though forest, frost and flood make for poor overland communication across the Siberian plain. Rivers provide better natural routes, but few in any part of the country are naturally navigable by vessels of economic size or provide an outlet to an ice-free sea. In the south the east-west communications by land are good. To the north-west the land frontier in its natural state was blocked by forest and marsh, and the extent of northern coastal waters navigable for any considerable part of the year

was, until recently, narrowly limited. The best communications with Europe lay down the rivers running south to the Black Sea.

The first Russian state, centred on Kiev, on this southern river system, derived its Christianity, in the Greek form, and its considerable early civilisation from the Eastern Roman Empire of Constantinople, thus adding cultural to physical isolation from western Europe. The open plains to the south-east brought invasion by the Tatars, which in 1240 put an end to Kiev as the Russian capital, and for some five centuries cut Russia off from the Black Sea as well. It was left to the principalities of the northern forests, among which Moscow took the lead, to reassemble, resettle and expand the country. In 1547 the Prince of Moscow was crowned Tsar (Caesar), and in 1589 the Metropolitan of the Russian Church, who had settled there in 1326, was at the Tsar's instance raised to the status of Patriarch, the two titles implying a claim to the succession to the Roman-Byzantine inheritance, vacant since the fall of Constantinople to the Turks in 1485. At the accession of Peter the Great (1682 as joint Tsar under a regency and 1689 as effective ruler) Russia was still without an outlet by sea to Europe either to the north—otherwise than round the North Cape—or to the south. During his reign, however, both routes were opened, and the former was safeguarded by the foundation of St. Petersburg, to which the capital was transferred; the route to the south was again lost. The move to the east into northern Siberia, which may be dated from 1578, met with very little resistance from the scattered tribes, and by the middle of the seventeenth century it brought the Russians to the Pacific. The land acquired, however, was not inviting to the voluntary settler, and the expansion was a venture of the Tsars for the sake of the tribute in furs paid by the native tribes. Another motive was early found in the utilisation of the territory as a penal colony, and this continued, with subsequent differentiation between convicts and exiles—the latter usually quite leniently treated—almost without interruption up to the revolution. Free settlement was early encouraged but not very successfully, and reliance was put mainly upon plantation of crown serfs and cossacks. In the south, where resistance was stronger, systematic garrisoning and settlement led the way and slowly gained ground against Tatar resistance. The progress culminated in 1783 in the conquest of the Khanate of the Crimea. There followed a rapid expansion into the Caucasus at the expense of the Turks and into central Asia; the latter ended in 1884 with the capture of Merv on the Afghan frontier, and British dissuasion from further advance.

The restrictions on development set by distance and natural obstacles were overcome only with the spread of railways in the second half of the nineteenth century, centrally organised, like much in Russia, as a military operation. The trans-Siberian railway, which after long delays set out from the Urals in 1891 and by 1904 formed, by way of the Chinese Eastern Railway, a continuous route to the Pacific, first made the exploitation of the resources of southern Siberia a practical proposition. Even in their earlier stages the railways began to open up some of the best agricultural land in both European and Asiatic Russia and to make possible the full utilisation of Russia's scattered mineral resources. An expansion of the economy resulted, which, though belated, was rapid, even if by the time of the revolution it had not yet attained the rate of growth of western Europe. Such forces of growth were reflected in a marked acceleration of the increase of population which allowed of a rise in Siberia alone from 1,540,000 European inhabitants to 9,500,000 within a century (1816–1914), while the population of old European Russia, supported by industrialisation and the influx of food from the new lands, was itself trebled. The population of the whole empire in 1913 stood at about 165,700,000; the population of the U.S.S.R., after the recovery in the Second World War of an area more or less equivalent to the losses of territory suffered in the First and in the upheaval of the revolution, had by the census of 15th January 1959 risen to some 208,827,000. Of these some 114,508,000 were Great Russians, now widely dispersed throughout all republics of the Union. There were some 36,981,000 Ukrainians and 7,829,000 Belorussians. Of the non-Slavonic peoples the largest group were those of Turkic speech, who numbered almost 23,000,000, including 3,581,000 Kazahs, 4,969,000 Tatars and 2,929,000 Azerbaidjanis.

Administrative Tradition

Isolation from Europe gave Russia a distinctive administrative tradition. Preoccupation with defence, national consolidation and colonisation of territories, of which the vastness threatened further disintegration, made it markedly military in character. The Tsar was, as his full title proclaimed him, an autocrat.. Such possible germs of representative institutions as there were in Russian tradition vanished in the seventeenth century. The Tsars' original body of advisers, the *Duma* of boyars, was soon turned by the expansion of the state into a turbulent assembly of formerly independent nobles imperfectly reconciled to their subjection to Moscow. Its power for evil or for good was, however, weakened by the increasing dilution of the traditional nobility with administrative and other servants of the Tsar, and Ivan IV instituted in opposition to it a wider assembly, the *Zemski Sobor*

(Assembly of the Land), which included not only the members of the Duma and the ecclesiastical synod but also representatives of the Tsar's administration and of the merchants who were his fiscal agents. The 'time of troubles', the period of disputed successions, violence and foreign intervention which followed upon his death, and the insecurity of the first Tsar of the house of Romanov which emerged from it, gave to the *Zemski Sobor* temporary importance and something of the character of a parliament in which for a time even the peasantry was represented. The mere size of the country, however, was inimical to such a development; to some meetings of the *Sobor* the provincial merchants were not invited at all. Moreover, the rapid advance of serfdom in the first half of the seventeenth century cut at the roots of popular representation, and the absence of any general positive desire to oppose representative institutions against the authority of the throne allowed of the decline of the assembly as soon as there was again a Tsar sufficiently firmly established to exercise that authority. From the time of Alexei (1645–76), the second Tsar of the house of Romanov, its meetings became rare; for the last twenty-two years of his reign and the six years of his successor it did not meet at all, and it was last convoked by Peter the Great in 1698 to pass judgment on his sister, the former regent Sophia, for plotting rebellion against him. The reforms of Peter put an end both to the *Zemski Sobor* and to the *Duma*, which had throughout continued to lead a more or less real existence apart from the larger body. His Westernising tendencies looked not to the parliamentarianism of the European maritime fringe of his day but to the relative administrative efficiency of central Europe.

The central machinery of government as it reached the nineteenth century contained organs with names suggesting representation, but the terms were misleading. Peter's Governing Senate was an appointed tribunal which by that time had become merely a supreme appeal court. The Council of State, instituted in 1810, was a form of nominated legislative council. Its membership (which included all the ministers) was entirely under the Tsar's command, but even this form of legislative procedure was found inconvenient by the autocracy. It relied rather on a smaller body, the Committee of Ministers, which was set up in 1802, but by reason of the responsibility of each of the ministers directly and severally to the Tsar was never allowed to grow into a cabinet. A measure passed by this body was not in name a law (*zakon*) but had equally binding force, as did any measure issued in the name of the Tsar. Both bodies showed a tendency to inflation of membership. In 1861 there was instituted a Council of Ministers, as distinct from the Committee, but this was from the first rendered inoperative by the requirement that it should consider only business proposed to it by the Tsar. It remained open to him to consult informally with such ministers as he wished or, if he preferred, to ignore them all. Among them was the Procurator-General, reputedly described by Peter as 'the all-seeing eye of the Tsar'[1] and combining the normal duties of a Minister of Justice with a general supervision over the whole administration. The administrative work of the ministries might be duplicated at will by the Tsar's private secretariat, and for the greater part of the nineteenth century the police work was so duplicated.

Local administration until the late nineteenth century was under firm central control. The country was divided by Peter the Great into areas under appointed governors (*gubernator*). The number of these governorships (*gubernija*) had risen to seventy-seven by the beginning of the twentieth century, in addition to a number of unincorporated areas known as regions (*oblastj*). The governor was assisted by an advisory council of departmental heads, including the agent of the Procurator-General, but whatever their influence at the centre their advice locally was not binding on him. The strength of the governors made it difficult to induce the nobility to participate in local administration. One of the principal reforms of Peter the Great was to build up a new nobility obliged to life-long state service, military or civil, and open to all attaining an appropriate rank in such service, the higher ranks—down to major and its civil equivalent—conferring hereditary nobility, the lower a personal status of noble. In recompense for their obligations, and as a further manifestation of the same rigid national discipline, the institution of serfdom, which during the proceeding century of insecurity had been increasingly imposed upon the peasantry, was systematised by the registration of serfs, and in the course of the eighteenth century it was even intensified and further extended. Under Peter's successors the nobility was able to obtain a relaxation of the conditions applying to it, and in 1762 it secured from Peter III its release from all obligations to state service. The peasantry, being less well placed to press for favours, had to wait another century to get rid of its share of the burden. Meanwhile the authority of the lord over his serfs extended to transportation to Siberia and to sale, including sale apart from the land until the practice was forbidden in 1798. Catherine II in 1785 acceded to the demand of the nobility for greater exclusiveness by raising the ranks in state service which should confer hereditary or personal noble status. She also sought to utilise the nobility in local administration by the creation of assemblies of nobles for the several districts and for the governorships within which they

[1] Quoted by M. Kovalevsky, *Russian Political Institutions* (1902), p. 128.

were grouped. Their powers extended beyond the regulation of the affairs of their own order, and the appointment of their own marshals of the nobility, to matters of general concern, including the nomination of judicial and police officials in their areas. In general, however, the nobles declined to be interested in affairs outside their own estates. The institutions of urban administration established at the same time were similarly unsuccessful, although more broadly based.

The reorganisation of the system of local government in the reign of Alexander II was dependent upon the reform for which he was best remembered: the emancipation of the serfs in February 1861. This provided for the privately owned estate serfs to be given their freedom without, in principle, any compensation to the lords, although the owners of the poorer lands who had taken to utilising the labour of their serfs in non-agricultural pursuits, including new industrial departures, were in fact recompensed for the loss of value by the substantial overvaluation of their land at the peasants' expense. Of the cultivable land the landlords were to retain between a third and a half according to the quality of the soil, while for the rest they were to be compensated by an advance from the state, of which the emancipated peasants were to pay off the greater part by redemption dues over a period of some fifty years. Emancipation without dues but with only a quarter of the normal allocation of land was offered and about 6 per cent accepted. For the payment of their redemption dues and taxes the peasants were made collectively responsible through the already existing general village assembly of householders, or *mir*. This assembly elected its own elder, and in addition to its fiscal reponsibilities was given general authority to regulate village affairs, including the periodic repartition of the land where this traditional form of tenure was retained. Increasingly, as government support was withdrawn from it, such tenure gave way to individual ownership, though not necessarily to consolidation of individual holdings, and the *mir* lost this function. There remained at village level, and at the higher level of the *volostj* (the traditional groupings of villages which had remained among state serfs and which were now reintroduced to the former privately owned villages), a curious form of local government based on inverted class discrimination. Only the members, the emancipated serfs, participated, but the powers of general regulation extended to all persons in the area other than the landed gentry. Opinion soon developed in favour of the replacement of this by an all-class institution, but this was only achieved at the level of the *volostj* in 1917, when it was too late.

At the level of the governorship and district (*uezd*) there was a system of local government providing representation for all owners of real property, not equally but on a scale heavily weighted in favour of wealth. To the land assemblies, or *zemstvos*, instituted in 1864 for thirty-four governorships, three categories of electors—individual owners of land or factories of a certain value, individual urban house and property owners, and peasant communes—elected their representatives for a term of three years by means of three separate electoral colleges. This was probably as liberal as the system could be made, while the conversion from serfdom was still incomplete. The *zemstvos* were not given freedom to select their own chairman; the marshal of the nobility for the area was to act as such *ex officio*. The length of their session was limited to twenty days at the higher level and ten at the lower. Between sessions their functions were entrusted to an 'administration' (*zemskaja uprava*), elected by them subject to the governor's veto and paid, as the members of the *zemstvos* themselves were not. After the general fashion of continental Europe, these inner bodies were obliged to act as agencies of the central authorities and under their supervision, as well as on behalf of their own *zemstvos*. In 1890, however, in the reign of Alexander III, this relative liberalism was modified. Representation was put on a class instead of a property basis. The nobility became an electoral category on their own, other private landowners, such as the new capitalist who was buying up the estates, joined the townsmen in a single category, and the weighting in the nobles' favour was increased. The peasant class lost its direct representation altogether; the *volostj* meeting was now to put up two candidates of whom the governor should select one. The elective principle was from the first qualified by the representation granted to the agents of the central ministries and to the church. Yet something was achieved; from 1873 the *zemstvos* began to acquire the power to make by-laws for the regulation of local affairs, and rendered useful service despite their lack of financial resources and the veto left to higher authorities. In the field of education especially they made good progress, and in the more fortunately placed parts of the country gave promise of the early extinction of illiteracy. Much is said to have been done for the improvement of local statistical services and for hospitals and other health services. A means was at last found of engaging the services of at least the minor nobility in work for the public good, and employment increasingly became available in the new administrations for the intelligentsia.

In the towns there were comparable developments. A municipal law of 1870 provided that the town *dumas* should be elected by property owners and taxpayers with weighting, after the Prussian or Austrian fashion, in favour of the richer among them and the further election of the *uprava* by these bodies. In 1892 the weighting for wealth was dropped in favour of election by wards, but the tax-payers were excluded and the qualifying holding of property was raised, particularly for the larger towns, so that less than 1 per cent of the urban population then had the vote. Half of the *uprava* remained in office from one four-year term of the Duma to the next, so that the incoming Duma elected only half the membership of the effective governing body. Powers were similar to those of a *zemstvo*, though with greater freedom from the governor's veto, and the *uprava* was, like those of the *zemstvos*, utilised by the central authorities as part of the bureaucratic hierarchy of administration.

The judicial system also underwent in 1864 a drastic reformation, making it one of the most liberal in continental Europe, with a jury system, an independent judiciary and an unpaid magistracy after the British fashion. This system, however, was soon eroded; various classes of cases were withdrawn from trial by jury, and the local procurator was in 1884 given the power of veto over the appointment of jurors. In more than half the governorships, it seems the new system of courts never came into being. The Justices of the Peace were abolished outside the towns and replaced by a new official combining the functions of a magistrate with administrative supervision over the peasant local government of the *volostj*. Above all, nothing was ever done to reform the police, which remained inefficient, multiple in structure and virtually unchecked in the exercise of its powers. In an article published in 1883 denouncing the country's prison system Prince Kropotkin asserted 'not that the principles of Russian penal institutions are worse than those applied to the same institutions in western Europe. I am rather inclined to hold the contrary. . . . In Russia, however, principles are always ruined in application.'[1] The opinion could be given a wider extension.

The late development and industrialisation of Russia was reflected in the lack of towns. The medieval growth of urban life, like so much else in Russia, was stunted by the country's preoccupation with military security. In the middle of the nineteenth century there were only thirty-two towns of over 20,000 people, but by 1900 there were sixty-five, and of these nine had over 150,000, a standard which at the earlier date was reached by only the two capitals. Even so, many of them differed little from villages in the density or form of construction of their buildings, in their possession of the amenities of urban life, or in the occupations and outlooks of their inhabitants. Even in the early years of the twentieth century probably a majority of urban workers—of whom these were in all under 3,000,000 in 1917—still held some land, and in other

[1] Prince Kropotkin, 'Russia's Prisons', *The Nineteenth Century*, January, 1883, pp. 27–8.

ways maintained their connection with the villages. As there was hardly any proletariat, so also there was hardly any bourgeoisie. The merchants and craftsmen of the country towns, such as there were of them, lacked the cohesion and self-assurance of that class in western Europe. The new industrialisation was slow to produce a conscious group of Russian businessmen. Development was largely by foreign capital and partly by foreign skill, and at the cost of the accumulation of a heavy burden of foreign debt, and of the export of the country's increasing but still scanty supplies of wheat, which the peasant could himself rarely afford to eat.

Russian agriculture, on which the whole edifice rested, remained highly inefficient, with far lower yields than in Western countries, and this was true of the holdings of the gentry as well as of their former serfs. To the traditional incompetence of Russian landowners at estate management the emancipation added a serious shortage of labour, as the peasant, though barely able to wrest a living from his own land, refused to work that of his former master. Despite the provision of credit on favourable terms to the nobles, they found it increasingly difficult to make farming pay. Already by the late 'eighties it was reported that a quarter of the noble estates left by the emancipation had been mortgaged to the land bank and another quarter sold. Sometimes the purchasers were foreigners; often they were the more enterprising of the peasants. In the opening years of the twentieth century the substantial yeoman with a holding of several times the size of those of his neighbours and with the resources to employ the labour of others became a new feature of Russian rural society. But if some succeeded, many failed, sliding hopelessly into debt.

Attitudes

Despite their increasing acquisitions from the nobles and the possibility of expansion into the new areas of the empire, the demand of the peasants for more land remained the principal disruptive force in Russia throughout the period from emancipation to the revolution of 1917. The emancipation settlement had assigned to the landlords land which the peasants felt to be their own, and the fact that they could have made more efficient use of what land they had did not diminish the sense of grievance. There remained also the question of status. The emancipation of 1861 had left the peasants—the great majority of the population—still less than full citizens. They were bound to their villages no less than before, not to their lords by obligations of service but to the *mir* by the collective obligation for payment to the state. They remained subject to a separate system of courts applying a separate rural customary law. Collective responsibility for obligations was gradually eroded and in most places abolished in 1903, and in the following year official concern at the rising waves of rural unrest and violence brought the cancellation of much of the burden of debt for redemption dues as well as other relaxations. It left little time to build the peasants into the social structure before Russia had to face a world war. Discontent was increasingly manifested also among the urban workers. It was, in fact, the same discontent, for the workers were peasants and their grievances went with them into the towns. Industrial strikes had already started in the 'seventies, and became increasingly frequent. The opinion of their employers, too, as it developed, came to distrust and resent a system of government which, while it offered protection against foreign competition, had little regard for the opinion of those engaged in practical business. The nobility itself was by no means to be relied upon as a pillar of the existing order. The reluctance of the autocracy to entrust it with any effective responsibility for public affairs, the exclusiveness which it had itself sought and the gulf set between it and the people by recent serfdom and illiteracy, had left it with very little belief in its own powers of leadership. In so far as this generally serious and well-intentioned aristocracy looked abroad for the intellectual stimulus which it could not find in Russia, it met with thought which condemned its social position. But the element in Russian society most fitted to detonate the explosive situation created by Russia's many discontents was the intelligentsia, the products of its institutions of higher education. The intelligentsia was a mixture of all classes, including in large numbers the nobility, but by its education it was set apart from all classes of the archaic Russian social system, and unfitted for any employment which Russia's undeveloped economic life and its unintellectual administration had to offer, at least until the end of the nineteenth century. For want of more constructive outlets it was driven to conspiracy as an habitual exercise. Uninstructed and unrestrained by responsibility and the test of practice, it ceaselessly pursued mainly foreign ideas to their logical but often unreasonable ends.

The bias imparted to the dispositions of the generality of persons comprised within a nation by the forces operating at any given time upon them, from the facts of geography to the balance of personalities, may be called the national character. It is a pattern which remains in the formed character of the individual, in institutions and conventional behaviour, in literature, the form of the language, and habits of thought, and in other facts, though it has no permanence or life of its own. The features of the Russian national character at the time of the revolution which struck observers as characteristic arose very obviously out of the country's circumstances. Among 'the people' (*narod*), which in pre-revolutionary usage invariably meant the peasants, there prevailed a rustic torpor; an unreliability and unpunctuality, reflecting the seasonal cycle of long idleness and short intense effort which the climate dictates; a susceptibility to religious enthusiasm, often of a highly destructive kind; a tolerant but profound distrust of the stranger, the townsman, the educated. Among the last there was a dark awareness of indebtedness to the people, a pride in Russia's peasant power of endurance, often expressed in religious terms as holiness proved through suffering. There was a sense of not belonging to Europe, a consciousness of being materially backward yet of having superior qualities, a desire to emulate the achievements of the foreigner, combined with resentment and distaste for the inhumanity of his ways. Through the society as a whole there prevailed a sense of solidarity, and an acceptance of the necessity of leadership was combined with a critical attitude to particular leaders which, observers thought as early as the Crimean War, might bring down the Tsar himself in the event of a national defeat. And long before the revolution there was a foreboding of change, pronounced even among the nobility.

In August 1905 Russia was obliged to accept defeat at the hands of Japan after an eighteen-month succession of military disasters. It was a shock for the world, the first obvious defeat by an Asiatic power of a power accounted European. For Russia it resulted in a revolutionary fracture of the old regime which, though it left the Tsar on the throne, left him less than an autocrat. This was a complex affair. Mounting agrarian discontent broke in renewed violence in February 1905, its urban and industrial reflection was disastrously handled by the authorities, and general discontent with incompetence and oppression had already led to the assassination of the Minister of the Interior in the middle of the previous year. To these forces there was added an unwonted stirring of political organisation, from the Marxist Social Democrats to the liberal gentlemen of the *zemstvos*.

The disturbances of 1905 culminated in the last few months of the year in a wave of industrial unrest which in St. Petersburg assumed the proportions of a general strike loosely co-ordinated by the Soviet (or Council) of Workers Deputies, and in similar manifestations in Moscow. The conflict led to Russia's first acceptance of liberal democracy as known in western Europe, expressed in the creation of the State *Duma* and the reconstitution of the Council of Ministers into something like a cabinet with a chairman of its own, comparable in position and function to a prime minister. From this opening of the prospect of political life there resulted the appearance for the first time in Russia of political parties which were something other than conspiratorial groups with disruptive aims. A *Duma* directly elected, though on a restricted franchise, was promised by the Tsar as early as February 1905, and as danger advanced the concession was extended to include universal suffrage. In his October manifesto of the same year the Tsar undertook to make no law without its consent, though he retained to himself the power of a veto. A Council of State, reformed to provide for the election of half the members on a restricted franchise, remained as a strong and conservative second chamber. Increasingly as order was restored the Tsar showed reluctance to accept the limitations on his power. Four *Dumas* were called; for two months in 1906, for a little over four in 1907, from 1907 to 1912, and finally from 1912 to the fall of the regime in 1917. Their markedly critical attitude to the administration was indicated in the short lives of the first two and in the changing composition of all four. The attitude of the authorities undermined the majority of the new liberal (Constitutional Democrat) party in the first *Duma* to the advantage of both right and extreme left in the second, and a change in the electoral law diminished the left as well in the third and fourth. The ministers were independent of the *Duma* and responsible only to the Tsar, who could and did maintain ministers not enjoying the confidence of the *Duma*, and even ignored those ministers for unofficial advisers of his own disastrous choosing. Nevertheless, even the last of the *Dumas* remained highly critical of maladministration during the war of 1914–18, and was able upon occasion to force a ministerial resignation. Political life had begun in Russia. But it was late. It needed peace and a wise Tsar; it was given neither. The war which broke out in 1914 brought early losses to Russia more crushing than any other state had to endure. The tender growth of industry and the transport system broke down from neglect, overloading and lack of hands, and famine threatened St. Petersburg itself. The military successes of 1916 were a last effort; thereafter Russia was sustained by the will of her allies rather than her own.

Doctrinal Equipment

The theories of society propounded by Karl Marx early found favour with Russians, and the first translation of his principal work, *Das Kapital*, was into Russian. However, Marx distrusted his Russian disciples and specifically declared his doctrine inapplicable to Russian circumstances. Marx was a Rhineland German and the basis of his

WHAT RUSSIAN POLITICS ARE ABOUT

thought was German philosophy and a practical interest in German politics. To these elements he added an acquaintance with French socialism and British economics, and observation of social conditions in both countries. His appeal to his age lay in the fact that he professed to see as inevitable, and laboriously assembled arguments to prove imminent, what many people felt to be morally right: the emancipation of the new factory workers for whom the traditional social structure seemed unable to provide any tolerable place. This he achieved by his adaptation of the dialectic of Hegel—the process by which an original state generates its own opposite and ultimately clashes with it to produce a synthesis which is neither, yet contains and transcends both. Marx removed it from the realm of ideas, where its conservative inventor had placed it, to that of material—by which he meant economic—facts. He held that the tools or processes used by men at each of the predetermined stages of development—what he called the forces of production—in some way enabled the owners of them to make themselves the ruling class, having control of the state, which, as Marx used the term, meant only the coercive machinery of society, by which to hold down the opposing classes. As such it would wish to hold its advantage as long as it could, but progress could not be arrested. As the economic process outgrew the social structure, so a revolutionary situation would come to fruition to bring in the new ruling class. Factory production, he held, depended upon, and so designated as the appropriate ruling class, the proletariat, which his compatriot, patron and colleague, Friedrich Engels, defined as the class 'whose means of livelihood depend entirely upon the sale of its labour'. This, he held, was the last of all possible classes. With its arrival in power the process would be at an end, and, with no other classes to hold down, the state as he defined it would wither away. This 'dialectical materialism' offered no reason why it would be the last of the classes, why, for instance, the peasantry should not be yet another; it merely assumed it.

This in itself ruled out Russia, with no ruling bourgeoisie to be overthrown, no proletariat to overthrow it and peasants everywhere. Marx, having a practical eye for a revolutionary situation, found Russia interesting and expressed the intention of revising his work to show where that country fitted in, but in fact he did not do so. With the flexibility which was characteristic of his theories he chose to consider that Russia might escape the capitalist stage of development, progressing from feudalism to an agrarian socialism and being carried on from there by the revolution made by the proletariat in the more advanced countries of the West. Accordingly he gave his support against the Russian Marxists to the advocates of a revolution based upon the traditional Russian *mir*. These, the populists (*narodnik*), the principal category of active Russian political opinion in the 'sixties and 'seventies, were not a party so much as a trend, the adherents of which agreed only on the necessity of going to 'the people' to teach them their destiny and, as some held, to learn from them their supposed peculiar rustic virtues. But in 1881 one of the two factions into which the populist movement had lately split effectively put it out of action for the rest of the century by assassinating the Tsar, Alexander II, to whom the peasants, expecting further benefits from their liberator, were still strongly attached. The vacuum which they left gave the Marxists their chance, even without the blessing of Marx. To organise, however, was not easy.

In 1898 there was founded the Russian Social Democrat Party, the name then traditionally adopted by Marxist parties. The founding congress hardly had time to produce a manifesto lamenting the difficulty of its task before the participants were arrested. In 1903, what for continuity's sake was called the Second Congress had to start all over again, meeting abroad. It promptly split into two opposing factions, which, despite attempts to achieve unity in 1905, in order to exploit the advantageous situation of that year, never came together again. By this time populism was back in the field in the form of the Social Revolutionary Party, which was founded in 1902, and by reason of its advocacy of aims and methods comprehensible to the peasants, the seizing of the land for those who tilled it and the use of violence, was now making good progress in the rural parts, where trust in the autocracy had faded. Things were more difficult for the Marxists. Their doctrine had no place for the peasant and his land-hungry small-scale farming, which they considered reactionary, while violence, they thought, could effect little in the working out of the laws of history. Nor in the absence of capitalism and bourgeois domination in Russia could they offer any very inspiring prospect of rapid results. Their first leaders drifted into the school of thought known as Legal Marxism, which advocated the establishment of capitalism, often in terms hardly distinguishable from those used by the liberals, in confidence that having been got into this situation the proletariat would be able to get itself out again. Another wing (which became known as the Economists) favoured a policy of trade-unionist industrial action for immediate benefits without too much regard for the larger issue of the transformation of society. Marxism, like most Western theories, did not get very far in Russia until it had been worked over into a peculiarly Russian form.

This transformation was effected by V. I. Uljanov, who for conspiratorial purposes took the name of Lenin, one of the second generation of Russian Marxists, an intellectual born in 1870 of upper-class parentage, like most of the leaders of the movement at the time. He rapidly made himself the leader of one of the factions into which the Social Democrat Party split on its second foundation in 1903, originally the smaller faction, though happy for accidental reasons in possession of the name of Bolshevik (of the majority), which by his skill in organisation it soon proceeded to justify. Lenin quietly admitted into the doctrine the possibility, which no previous Marxist would have accepted, that one class might make two revolutions, and he subsequently went on to suggest that it might make them without any very considerable interval in between. Moreover, he found a justification for alliance with the peasants, which is best expressed in his pamphlet *Two Tactics of Social Democracy*, written in August 1905, to provide the party with a line for the revolutionary situation developing in that year: 'The proletariat must carry through to completion the democratic revolution by uniting to itself the mass of the peasantry in order to crush by force the opposition of the autocracy, and to paralyse the instability of the bourgeoisie. The proletariat must complete the socialist revolution by uniting to itself the mass of semi-proletarian elements in the population; in order to break by force the opposition of the bourgeoisie and to paralyse the instability of the peasantry and of the petty-bourgeoisie'. The word 'democratic', despite its place in the party's own name, was not at this time used by Marxists in any approving sense. By 'democratic revolution' Lenin meant the revolution believed to be imminent which would 'for the first time make it possible for the bourgeoisie to rule as a class'. However, even with the most elaborate plans for taking the bourgeois horse to the water, there was no certainty that it would drink. It was still not clear how, if the bourgeoisie could not or would not rule, the proletariat was to overthrow it. In 1905 this problem did not have to be faced. The revolution of that year was not from the Bolshevik point of view effective.

The first effective shift in the location of power was that of March 1917, known by reason of the different Russian calendar of that time as the February Revolution. In this the Tsar abdicated, and his designated successor, his brother, refused to take the throne until called to it by a representative constituent assembly. Until this could be arranged effective control of affairs passed to a provisional government under Prince Lvov, the leader of the Union of Zemstvos, and with representation of the Social Revolutionaries in the person of Kerenski, who, on the reconstruction of the government in July, took over the chairmanship. From May onward the Menshevik faction of the Social Democrat Party was also represented in the government, together with minor socialist groupings, but without the Bolsheviks. Marxists agreed that this was the democratic revolution. The question was thus posed of how long they had to wait before its successor. Lenin solved this immediately on his arrival in the capital in April by declaring it already in progress.

Yet if in shaping the course of events Lenin's organising skill counted for more than Marx's analysis, it was not without consequence that the makers of the second revolution of 1917 were trained in Marxist teaching and believed it relevant to their country's situation, or that their successors in power apparently still do. Their beliefs affect their interpretation of events in terms of causes and motives and their estimation of the probable consequences of their own actions, even though for lack of practical guidance in Marx those actions are often applications to their new ends of methods traditional in Russia. The Soviet state is not simply old Russia, and the accepted beliefs are an important part of the reason why it is not. Merely to discern historical inevitability and to know oneself on its side is gratifying, and the knowledge may have added materially to the self-assurance of the Russian leaders. Dialectical materialism, though unhelpful as an explanation of revolutions or a guide to the making of them, remains an influential part of the inheritance, though perhaps for its Hegelian rather than its Marxian elements. The idea of sudden qualitative change was in itself immediately attractive to those discontented with things as they were, which in Russia was an almost universal condition. The idea of contradiction, which is yet no absurdity but part of the order of things, has remained no less attractive to the new regime, which has, by reason of the rawness of its theories and the original nature of the state which it set up, frequently needed to justify changes of front. Stalin's statement of the revised attitude to the withering away of the state is the classical example. 'We are,' he said, 'in favour of the state dying out, and at the same time we stand for the strengthening of the dictatorship of the proletariat, which represents the most powerful and mighty authority of all forms of state which have existed up to the present day. The highest possible development of the power of the state, with the object of preparing the conditions for the dying out of the state—that is the Marxist formula. Is it "contradictory"? Yes, it is "contradictory", but this contradiction is a living thing and completely reflects Marxist doctrine.'[1] The coexistence of opposites as part of the process of change—though with the end probably envisaged in the terms of the dialectic of Marx in which there is no true synthesis but a simple supersession of one

[1] Report of Central Committee to Sixteenth Party Congress, published in *Leninism* (English translation of *Voprosy Leninizma*) (10th edn. 1934) II. 342.

opposite by the other rather than that of Hegel—may be seen in the current doctrine of the relations between socialist and capitalist states. To see contradictions as the way of history's unfolding was to be predisposed to the creation of contradictions wherever these might loosen an undesired stability, whether to refine the party before the revolution, to subjugate the peasantry in the early years of the new regime, or to undermine the potentially hostile alliance of foreign powers. In general, a disposition to see things in terms of conflict does not make for conciliatory or trusting policies, even where these are objectively possible. To see history in terms of self-initiating stages of social development to a pattern and towards an end prescribed in the nature of things is not conducive to belief in the historical significance of the individual.

If Marx's emphasis on the economic causation of history was an embarrassment to his Russian disciples, while they were seeking in his name to overthrow the Tsarist state, it was a source of strength to them when they found themselves in power with an accomplished revolution behind them and a new state to build. Industrialisation was the prime need of Russia if it was ever to play a leading role in the world in competition with the powers of the West. They were not the first to see this. A systematic policy of industrialisation might have been pursued had there been no revolution. It is less likely that it would have been given prominence had the revolution been made under the leadership of the Social Revolutionaries or others committed to the interests of the peasant. But there was none so disposed to give attention to this necessity and to the economic factors generally as those who were accustomed to speak in terms of factories and the social product, and of whom self-respect demanded that they provide with all due speed the causes for what had already happened. This was not the Marxism of Marx, which in fact it stood back on its Hegelian head, making the material, in Marx's economic sense, dependent on the human will, but it was an almost inescapable result of the application of Marxism to Russian circumstances. In its immediate effects the revolution retarded development, hindered the recovery of industry from the disruption of war by impractical ideas of workers' control and extinguished the more economic units of agricultural exploitation by the encouragement given to the peasant allies to seize what they could. But it was from the first unlikely that the followers of Marx would be content so to leave things. Their realisation of the importance of doing something about the economy did not mean that they had at the outset any clear vision of what they ought to do in any given situation, or of the magnitude of the task of management to which they were committing their new state. Lenin completely underestimated the skills required for running the economy once capitalism had laid the foundations and provided the means of communication. For the most part, he held, they amounted only to the 'simple operations of registration, recording and checking ... quite within the reach of all literate persons'.[1] But Lenin himself was no man to be deterred by the possibility of the unseen obstacle. Looking back in 1923, he quoted with approval the dictum of Napoleon, 'On s'engage, et puis on voit', and instanced the New Economic Policy as one of the successful pieces of improvisation produced in the course of the engagement joined in November 1917.[2]

Engels declared that 'So long as the proletariat uses the state it does not use it in the interests of freedom, but in order to hold down its adversaries, and as soon as it becomes possible to speak of freedom, the state as such ceases to exist'. This last dimly envisaged event was remote from the practical considerations of the more effectual of the Russian revolutionaries long before Stalin provided his ingenious dialectical explanation of the neglect of it. More originally, Stalin added that the state would be needed even when the ultimate classless society called communism should have been reached, so long as there were still capitalist powers around to threaten it. There remained of Engels' declaration only the justification for strong government. The purpose of the communist cannot be to put checks on the power of the state, as seemed to the American Founding Fathers and the nineteenth-century liberals to be the wisdom of the constitution-maker, but to see that the right class wields it. Marxist belief thus made for a continuation of authoritarian rule no less than did Russian lack of experience of anything else.

How far the makers of the revolution were also committed by their Marxist faith to a dictatorship of the party over and through the proletariat was not at this time clear beyond dispute to the Marxists themselves. Marx was not very helpful. He asserted that in preparing the revolution the communist element in working-class politics, being the most advanced and resolute and having the advantage of knowing where it was going, 'pushes forward all others', but about the post-revolutionary phase he had nothing to say. It was all rather remote, and he was a practical man. Even Lenin, whose contribution to the elaboration of Marxism consisted largely in the development of the theory and practice of the party, had little to say about this later phase. But in practice the Russian Marxists, drawing upon the conspiratorial party tradition of the days of autocracy and not the parliamentary

[1] V. I. Lenin, *The State and Revolution* (1917), in his Works (Russian edn.), Vol. 25 (1949), p. 392.
[2] Lenin, *Our Revolution*, Works, Vol. 33 (1950), p. 439.

experience which became available only in the time of the *Duma*, fell naturally into the assumption that they must continue to 'press forward' by their party's own direct action and not merely through participation in the working of constituted machinery. After the revolution Lenin resisted the wish of Trotski and others to make a specific declaration in favour of party dictatorship, but in practice it was assumed that, like the state itself, this other regrettable necessity must continue for so long as there was still opposition to be beaten down.

For anything as specific as the organisation of the party it was useless to look to Marx. Already by the time of the revolution, however, the matter had been actively debated among the Marxists for some time, and the dominant Bolshevik faction was equipped with a firm tradition mainly of Lenin's making. His trust was in the disciplined striking force. It must, he said, contain 'chiefly people whose occupation is revolutionary activity', and, in direct contrast to the more familiar trade-union type of workers' organisation, it must be 'not very broad and as secret as possible'. It must have its members in the factory but, in virtue of their profession of revolutionaries, under orders of the party committee, not in virtue of their employment as industrial workers. For 'broad democracy' within the party he had little use, and he specifically rejected an 'immoderate use of the elective principle'. These means were related to the pre-revolutionary situation; the secretiveness was justified by Lenin on the ground of the necessity to exclude the prying eye of the police, but it was possible to argue that in the period of continuing insecurity much of the same sort of care was still needed. By the time of the revolution this attitude had become the distinguishing mark of the Bolshevik against other factions.

This does not mean that Russian communism was narrowly lost for democracy. Lenin was more thorough, more ruthless and more far-seeing than his Menshevik adversaries, but they hardly differed from him on specific issues. At the time when they were still in the ascendant they were even more strongly convinced than he of the inadmissibility of the expression by members of dissenting opinions, and Trotski, who to his own undoing combined the hardness of the Bolsheviks with the doctrinal inflexibility and personal attachments of the Mensheviks, seems to have been earlier than Lenin in making his claim for 'the leadership's organised distrust of the members, a distrust manifesting itself in vigilant control from above over the party'.

A name for the principle on which the party was organised was found in a resolution of the Bolshevik conference of December 1905 held at Tammerfors in Finland, which declared 'democratic centralism' to be 'the indisputable basis of party organisation', though without explaining what it was. In the following year Lenin provided the definition: 'The principle of democratic centralism and of autonomy of the local units means full and reciprocal freedom of criticism so long as unity in a specific action is not destroyed thereby, and the inadmissibility of any criticism whatever which undermines or makes difficult unity on any action decided upon by the party.'[1] In practice, difficulty was found in agreeing whether at any given moment the party had made up its mind or not. Lenin at the time of providing this definition was seeking to reverse a decision which the Mensheviks, who in principle accepted his formulation, wished to preserve. He was able to raise the issue not because the decision was in some way provisional, but because he was Lenin.

Marxist discourse contrasts such 'democratic centralism' with 'bureaucratic centralism', in which orders are passed down from the centre without preliminary sounding of opinion below. It was the principal criticism of the Titoists against the school of Stalin that, though bureaucratic centralism was a necessary element in a socialist state— in the army, in the security services and in a situation such as that of the early days of the Soviet regime when there were large areas of the country without proletariat or communist sympathisers—it was the duty of the communist regime to build up democratic centralism against it. In Russia, they claimed, on the contrary bureaucratic centralism had itself been made into a system.

An important feature of the background of the party which seized power at the revolution, though much the same would have been true of any other of the Russian conspiratorial parties, was the importance which it attached to theory. Right conduct, it held, stems from right belief, and a heterodox explanation of a social situation was presumptive evidence of a disposition to improper courses of action. To express views which could be paralleled in the writings of the discredited, in Bakunin or in Blanqui, was to be discredited oneself; and, conversely, to fall from favour with the majority or controlling group in the party was to stand convicted of heterodox views. This was the pure spirit of the Russian intelligentsia, as of any school of thought which, deprived of the possibility of direct observation of action, is obliged to infer it from principles. Again, the attitude survived into the post-revolutionary situation in which the circumstances which produced it no longer obtained. It has, however, elements of practical utility. The myth of orthodoxy in application of the teachings of Marx and Engels and their legitimate successors to situations which they could not foresee has

[1] Lenin, *Freedom of Criticism and Unity of Action*, Works, Vol. 10 (1947), p. 409.

been one of the principal props of the new regime. To oblige their opponents to argue their cases in an idiom of which those established in control of the apostolic party are themselves the acknowledged masters has throughout been a source of great advantage to the latter and a valuable means of discipline. In 1955 Stalin's views on the stage reached by the revolution, his clarification of a distinction between communism and a state of socialism prior to it, which was not in Marx at all, could be brought into action to remind Mr. Molotov that he was not invulnerable, and of recent years the authority of Lenin could be called to the aid of the party in dissociating itself from the more malodorous aspects of Stalinism.

The Manner of Seizing Power

In contrast to the largely spontaneous outbursts of 1905 and March (or February) 1917, exploited by the extremist parties but not of their own creation, that of November (or October) 1917 was deliberately engineered by Lenin and made possible by years of careful preparation of the party. Lenin was himself on the spot, as he had not been at the start of either of the previous developments, having been enabled by the Germans to reach Petrograd at the beginning of April. By exploiting the fluid situation of a country which had undergone a change of regime and committed itself to the reformation of its administrative system in the middle of a disastrous war, by building up the power of the soviets and the congresses of soviets against the provisional government, and raising all the disruptive issues which the latter wished for the time being to keep quiet, he created a situation where power could be seized without the need to fight for it. The peasants were doing his work. The troops at the strategic points were on his side. There was little resistance in Petrograd, some in Moscow and a few of the garrison towns, none anywhere else. There was also not much seizure of power anywhere else, but the capitals once conquered in centralised Russia, the rest could be expected to follow. Many issues still remained to be sorted out. Stalin, who surveyed these events from the editorial office of the party newspaper, later named 'peace, the agrarian revolution and freedom for the nationalities' as the three principal factors out of which the bolsheviks built up their support.[1] In fact, peace was not to be obtained except on the most humiliating terms, the surrender at Brest-Litovsk on the 3rd March the following year of all the western borderlands, conquered since the time of Peter the Great, except the northern

[1] J. Stalin, 'The October Revolution and the National Policy of the Russian Communists', Works (Russian edn.), 1947, V, p. 113.

outlet to the sea. Even from that it was felt advisable to withdraw, and the capital returned to its ancient seat at Moscow, where it has ever since remained. Even Brest-Litovsk did not guarantee peace, for its effect was to trigger off among the Tsarist generals, the Czechoslovak former prisoners of war and Russia's late allies an armed resistance which might have otherwise been postponed. The new regime had to continue the fight up to the latter part of 1920. The agrarian revolution was achieved on terms which Marxists could not possibly allow to become permanent, and freedom for the nationalities was also to prove at variance with their principles. Nevertheless, as an example of technique, the seizure of power taught lessons to those who were able to learn. It was an example of what might be achieved by temporary alliances based upon the moods of the moment, and it showed that the advantage in such manœuvres lay with the party least involved in loyalties to temporary allies. It was an example of the advantage of organisation, of self-confidence, of knowing what you want when others do not. It was a lesson to the ambitious within the party, and it was Stalin, the Georgian whom Lenin had recruited as his expert on nationality problems and agent in the underground who, comparatively small though his part in the event itself had been, showed the subtlety of mind to follow it most consistently.

The Issues

The Russian revolution, like any revolutionary movement, left no clear heir to the power which it overthrew, and in the politics of Russia since the revolution the motive of retaining power, enlisting support and eliminating rivals, has always been predominant. The Marxists, as specialists in revolution, had studied the precedents and in particular the lessons of the French revolution. They knew that the first organisers of change might themselves be overthrown by others more extreme if they were not vigilant to frustrate and outbid them. In particular they were aware of the danger of a Bonaparte, and the necessity to keep the military power amenable to orders though strong enough for action. Russian political life from the bottom to the top has been penetrated by realisation of the danger of the unguarded moment.

Next to this motive has been that of economic priorities. The economic bias of Marxism has made the Soviet Union into a single vast firm with the consequent problems: finding and organising an effective force of managers, keeping them loyal and skilled and interested, rationalising departmental organisation, budgeting and allocating resources. This last has been far from simple. The revolution was made at a moment of opportunity but not of plenty. It was not possible to amass and apply the immense capital required for the development of the resources lately revealed into a solid foundation of basic industry without denial of the desire for a better standard of living which was already emerging and was bound to develop with the further urbanisation which industrial growth implied. Yet there could be no other stimulus to effort except the traditional and tempting Russian method of coercion. The food supply in Russia had always been unreliable for both climatic and organisational reasons, and had been apt to break down in famine, particularly in times of war and disturbance. The new regime had to provide a basic security of food supply while diverting more to its developing towns. It could not do this with such a diminution in the efficiency of agriculture as was implied in its own encouragement of peasant seizure of land. Its traditional advocacy of retention of the large estates by entrusting them to some form of co-operative management by the peasants was bound to seem a more tempting solution. And yet the difficulties which existed without the ill-will of the cultivators could only be increased by incurring it. These have throughout been the topics of a constant debate within the Soviet political system, and most of them are not settled yet.

The traditional concerns about the frontier and security have retained their old urgency. Apart from foreign intervention Brest-Litovsk had stimulated new nationalisms in the territories now cut off from Russia. Moscow was presented with Moscow's old problem of winning them back, and in particular of again forcing back the frontiers of the west. From the timing of the revolution in the middle of a world war there resulted a mutual resentment between the Soviet and the non-Soviet world, intensified by the decision almost inevitable for a revolutionary government to disown Russia's immense foreign debt. The need to prevent encirclement, real or supposed, and to ward off intervention, which at least from the direction of Japan still continued to threaten in the 'thirties, have been prime motives of Soviet Russia throughout its history. Here lay yet another incentive to industrialisation and also to the relocation of industry away from the frontiers. An obvious response to the preoccupation with foreign danger has been, in view of the official doctrine's internationalist associations, the direct appeal to peoples over the heads of their governments. The demands thus made upon foreign communists and their obvious relation to exclusively Russian interests, however, have operated to keep the number of Russia's committed supporters small and to alienate much sympathy which might have been gained among the uncommitted.

Another force with which the regime has throughout had to reckon has been the desire to protect local interests and peculiarities. Before the revolution there had been little divergence on national grounds within the territories to which the Bolsheviks found themselves heirs. Even in the newer territories of central Asia government, though severe, had not been discriminatory, but already with the influx of Russian colonists material interests were beginning to diverge. In particular, the native races were becoming concerned about the shortage of land. Thus when the tight hold of the centre over them was removed by the disorders of 1917 there were many who were willing to seize the opportunity for establishing their independence. This soon came into opposition with the internationalism of the Marxists, which, once the state was found to be necessary, had little to distinguish it from old-fashioned imperialism. Nor was it enough that the former empire should remain united; it must also be uniform. Already before the revolution even the Great Russians, who had previously been remarkably uniform in character and way of life in spite of their wide territorial dispersion, were beginning to develop local differences, and in the *zemstvo* governorships these extended to differences of political practice. But the new society was to be a socialist one, and the binding interpretation of what was implied in socialism was that of Moscow. Its determination of economic priorities necessarily came into conflict with local concern for the balance of the local economy, as well as with conservatism and caution, and its unwillingness to compromise has left it with a permanent burden of discontent and unreliability.

For such and other reasons, notably the professional interests of officials, there has been a tendency to the formation of a variety of local alliances for protection against the centre. Clearly these still persist generally throughout the country, and particularly where circumstances favour them, as in remote areas, areas with a common minority culture and a local language which compels the centre to some reliance on local assistance, or where they are supported by personal relationship. All this is comprised within the sin of 'familyness', which is constantly being denounced in official pronouncements and publications. The term covers much more than nepotism, though that is part of the problem. The leaders themselves for their own purposes have been obliged to create very powerful particular interests, of a different but no less dangerous type. The various corps of officials, who, for lack of popular competence and enthusiasm, and by reason of the very nature of the work, have had to be established, continued or revived to run the machine, are disposed to such offences as 'preserving the honour of the uniform'—covering up the faults of other persons in the same service. The authorities have felt obliged to devote much thought to (again in their own idiom) keeping the line open for 'signals' from below. Often this has meant laying more lines, complicating the administrative structure at a heavy cost in manpower and in convenience of working.

The Periods

The circumstances and issues of politics have changed greatly in relative importance with the passage of time since the revolution. Soviet writers, as Marxists, mark off periods in economic terms, and in general this coincides conveniently with the changing balance of political themes. We need not accept also the myth of consistency which they simultaneously maintain and in which they are often supported by opponents apt to see their worst excesses implicit in their earliest acts. Our distinction of periods, like any other, is artificial.

The first period of the regime, extending to the spring of 1921, is economically described as that of 'war communism', and may politically be called that of the anti-Bolshevik menace. The dominant themes were peace—its conclusion on tolerable terms and its preservation—defence against foreign intervention and the civil war against the few remaining supporters of the imperial family and the more numerous upholders of military ideas of sound government, the maintenance of the food supply and the reversal of the flight from the famine and disorders of the towns, and the working out of the implications of the decree of general nationalisation issued on the 28th June 1918. Lenin and his supporters were possibly led by circumstances to carry their communist principles into effect faster than they had intended. For the successful conclusion of the complex of wars in which they were involved they needed urgently to restore the country's economic life, and their nationalisation may also have been intended to forestall German or other claims to foreign assets. Moreover, they needed to keep ahead of the extremism which in a revolutionary situation can easily mobilise support against moderation. Enthusiasm was high, and ideas such as direct management of all economic enterprises from the centre, or workers' control, or both at once, communal living and the moneyless economy based upon allocation of goods in kind—or the similar idea of the lawless state based on public interest and economic planning—seemed feasible, and died out only over the years. The myth of the coming revolution in western Europe, which would solve most of Russia's difficulties, lived on to the end of the period.

In politics the main concern of the Bolsheviks was to get rid of the Constituent Assembly. Before their seizure of power they had been its strongest advocates in order to embarrass the provisional government.

They could not now repudiate it, yet they could not hope to control it. The elections produced only 175 Bolshevik members out of a total of 707, which included 414 of the Social Revolutionary Party. Lenin took precautions against the Assembly's going the wrong way; he exploited a split among the Social Revolutionaries, and used it to question the validity of their majority; he arranged a meeting of the Congress of Soviets, over which he had already begun to exercise influence, for three days after the Assembly was due to meet. When it met in January 1918, and still proved refractory, he dissolved it by force of arms and prevented it from meeting again. The Congress of Soviets, thus presented with a *fait accompli*, duly declared itself the permanent, instead of, as previously, the provisional, government of Russia. The popular demand for a constitution was satisfied by one of the Bolsheviks' own making approved by another Congress of Soviets in July 1918. In the internal affairs of the party the Leninist standards of discipline, which in the period of revolution and war the Bolsheviks had had to relax, were increasingly asserted. This culminated in the denunciation by the Tenth Congress of the party, meeting in March 1921, of 'deviation' and 'fractionalism'—holding any discussion by groups within the party of views not approved by the leadership—as impermissible, and the prescription of a periodic 'cleansing' (*chistka*)—or 'purge', as it has generally been translated—as the remedy. This measure was at the time conceived in terms of public examination of records leading to reprimand or expulsion of offenders, without its later more sinister connotations. The same congress opened the way to a new period by acceptance of the New Economic Policy (N.E.P.).

The occasion of the N.E.P. was the mounting discontent in the country, caused mainly by realisation that internal peace was not to be achieved as easily as had once been hoped, by continued food shortages and by peasant unrest resulting from the violent methods adopted to remedy these at the expense of the food-producers. They came to a head in February-March 1921 in the expression of specifically anti-Bolshevik —though not anti-soviet or counter-revolutionary—demands by the men of the naval base, and former Bolshevik stronghold, of Kronstadt, which the Bolsheviks felt obliged to beat down by military action during the meeting of the Tenth Congress. The new policy represented an attempt at conciliation; the peasants were to be permitted to sell their produce in the open market after settlement of fixed obligations to the state instead of being subject to arbitrary requisition. In the main this settled their active discontent and enabled many of them to achieve comparative prosperity, but it did not remove their heightened distrust of the towns and their consequent reluctance to supply them with food or to show such agricultural efficiency as might attract a new expropriation, and it did not make the minute holdings resulting from the land redistribution any more economic as units of cultivation. Limited yet substantial revival of private enterprise was permitted in commerce and the greater part of industry, the state restricting its field of monopoly to what, in the military terminology favoured by the Marxists, it called the 'commanding heights' of heavy industry. Foreign capital was again allowed access to Russia under government-granted concessions. Lenin admitted that it was a partial return to capitalism and expressed the hope that state enterprise would prove itself more efficient in free competition. At least it brought some return to law and judicial procedure—though the *Che-ka* (the revolution's secret police) continued active—and to traditional ideas of orderly administration, to increased readiness to make use of officials who had served under the Tsar, and to the abandonment of the Marxist idea of limiting officials to 'workmen's wages'. Willingness to compromise with non-Marxist views, at least in inessentials, was shown also in the admission of federal institutions to the system of government. There was much in all this which many sincere Bolsheviks could hardly have accepted from anyone but Lenin—especially since over much of the field it was not brilliantly successful, for capital was understandably timid—and when the N.E.P. was little over a year old his influence—not moderate but always prudent—was virtually removed. Already at the end of May 1922 a stroke seriously reduced his physical powers, and two more strokes, in the latter part of the year and the beginning of the next, left him paralysed until his death in January 1924. Out of the public eye, the struggle for the succession was already well advanced. Trotski was, after Lenin, unquestionably the most brilliant figure of the revolution, and for his achievements as its military leader the most popular, though not the most judicious. Yet Stalin, obscure, in intellect and in fame, had secured a unique central position, with command of two key departments of the state administration and at the same time of the yet unrealised power of the party's administrative machinery, formally confirmed by his election as its General Secretary just two months before Lenin's first stroke. Lenin distrusted Trotski's judgment, but in his last months he came increasingly to fear Stalin's ambition and dishonesty, and, given time and strength, would probably have sought to break his former protégé. His judgments on both men were proved correct. Stalin triumphed by the means of which Lenin had himself advertised the efficacy, by organisation—though through the office, the personal file and the manipulation of postings rather than through the public meeting and the pamphlet—and by adroit changes of policy. In the wide spread of party opinions he took the safe dead centre. Against Trotski's bold and arduous course of immediate and rapid industrialisation and a firm hand with the trade unions and peasants, for which the country then had little heart, he advocated the more cautious policies of the party's principal propagandist Buharin. He opposed Trotski's argument for more democracy within the party—not even Trotski suggested the possibility of its extension outside the party—which alarmed many with less personal interest in the consolidation of bureaucracy than Stalin had. He enlisted to his cause the general desire for a *détente* in international relations by casting doubt on the safety of his rival's revolutionary zeal. Trotski was manœuvred into isolation, largely by exploitation of his own strong sense of Bolshevik discipline, and expelled from the party in November 1927, and from Russia in January 1929.

The period extending from the Fifteenth Party Congress of December 1927, which passed the directives for the preparation of the first Five Year Plan, to the Eighteenth, of March 1939, which approved the third Five Year Plan—some fourteen months after it had come into operation—has a political unity as the period of determination of the content of Stalinism when the location of power was no longer contestable by political action, and only the use which Stalin was to make of it was in doubt. Within it, however, there is a significant change of subject in the year 1934, which began with the election of Andrei Zhdanov as one of the secretaries of the party Central Committee and closed with the murder of Sergei Kirov. In the earlier part the economic theme was clearly dominant. Without any special experience or original ideas in this field, and without any guidance in the writings and practices of Lenin, Stalin found himself obliged to produce some solution for the pressing problems of economic power more positive and more gratifying to communist prejudices than the discredited N.E.P. Having eliminated Trotski, Stalin was driven to adopt the essentials of Trotski's policies, and in many respects to exceed them in boldness of conception and ruthlessness of application. The first Five Year Plan, which came into operation in October 1928 and was accepted by a party conference in the following April, inaugurated a rapid return to the stringencies of war communism without its wilder idealistic enthusiasms. Though the official claim of its completion in four years was clearly not literally true, its success in its own material terms of increased industrial production far exceeded all reasonable expectation, and, it seems, helped to build up Stalin's own faith in the efficacy of organisational methods to solve all problems and so in his own omnicompetence. Intensive collectivisation of agriculture, for which the Fifteenth Congress had given authority, entered on its full compulsive phase in 1929, and had virtually achieved the complete extinction of the private farmer before, at the end of 1930, Stalin halted it as a product of official excess of zeal. This in part it probably was, but Stalin's magnanimity did not extend to the reversal of its achievements. From 3.8 per cent of the total crop area in 1928 the share of socialised agriculture apparently rose to 98.4 per cent in 1936. Here results in terms of production were less favourable: peasant embitterment and resistance and government reprisals kept output down and cost the country some half of its livestock, but the land was for the first time made substantially amenable to the will of Moscow, and Stalin could hope to make good by mechanisation what had been lost.

In the second part of the period, in the middle 'thirties, the issues of Soviet politics again became more complex, as Stalin sought to impose on others the legend of his own infallibility, of which he had convinced himself, and the personal control of all aspects of the country's life which it justified. In Zhdanov he found the intellectual powers which he himself lacked and which he needed for the manipulation of his subjects' minds. A rigid orthodoxy based upon minute oversight of all aspects of cultural life, isolation from all unauthorised contact with the outside world, suppression and rewriting of inconvenient internal sources of information and the conscious revival of Russian tradition favourable to autocracy, were the main elements of the new policy. The motives for the murder of Kirov, one of the more moderate of the Stalinists, may have been personal and, if political, were certainly muddled, but the motives of Stalin in utilising it as the occasion for a new phase of the process of purges in party and state are fairly clearly related to this development. The process began with a general examination of the records of party members which reduced the total membership between 1933 and the beginning of 1937 almost by half, and from 1936 to 1939 it passed to a wider field in the form of the mass arrests, summary trials, transportations and shootings associated with the name of Yezhov, the People's Commissar for Internal Affairs of the time. In each phase persons who might in some way have stood in the way of the new legend were conspicuously numerous among the victims. These included almost all close associates of Lenin except those notoriously clients of Stalin himself, a very high proportion of other members of long standing or exalted position in the party, the leaders of the Communist Parties of the minority nationalities, foreigners, including foreign communists, and real or supposed friends of foreigners. Zinoviev and Kamenev, Stalin's first allies against Trotski, whose deposition from influence in the party had been contemporary with that of Trotski himself, were brought back under the lights for trial and execution, and their fellows and successors were similarly played off one against the other and in turn overthrown. More tangible considerations perhaps dictated the mass elimination of the loyal but untrained communists in the technical and administrative posts of industry who were obstructing the rise of the new managerial class which Stalin had created, and of the possibly unreliable senior officers of the army, at whose mercy he probably foresaw that he might in the near future be placed by war, for this was the period of the rise to power of Hitler, partly through the misjudgments of the Russians themselves. The party was changed from an arena where a struggle for power was fought out with ideological weapons to a highly specialised instrument of administration. The period concluded with the triumphant Stalin's revision of Leninism at the Eighteenth Congress to provide for the continuance of the state for an indefinite period even after the happy attainment of communism.

The period from 1939 until Stalin's death in 1953 is not marked off by any changes of economic structure such as distinguished those before it. Nevertheless Soviet official opinion seems now to recognise its distinctiveness as the period when Stalin finally got out of hand, when, in Mr. Khrushchov's words, he 'thought that now he could decide all things alone, and that all he needed' (as advisers) 'were statisticians; he treated all others in such a way that they could only listen and praise him',[1] though, on Mr. Khrushchov's own showing, his regard for the opinions of others had been minimal before. Political issues, in the sense of matters for negotiation, hardly existed at the highest level. In another sense, too, the range of politics was narrowed. Throughout the period the scene was dominated by external relations, the opportunities and perils presented by a world at war. Territorial expansion added five new republics to the Union and enlarged three others, and invasion brought a serious danger of the regime's total collapse. During the war of 1941–5 military problems were solved by substantially conventional military machinery and, as in other countries, left little room for the more varied concerns of peace. 'Soviet patriotism', devised in the immediate pre-war years to replace the party's original internationalism, was neccessarily given increased prominence in official propaganda, and its already marked traditional Great-Russian content, the promotion of Great-Russian historical legend, literature, way of life and political influence to the detriment of what remained of the independence of the nationalities, was perhaps intensified by suspicion of the reliability of the latter aroused in Stalin's mind by the defection of some of them in

[1] N. S. Khrushchov, speech in closed session at the Twentieth Congress of the party, 1956 (quoted from text published by the *Manchester Guardian* as *The Dethronement of Stalin*, p. 11—quoted in further references as *D. of S.*).

the days of their first contact with the German invaders. This trend was not reversed on the coming of peace, but there disappeared other trends of the war period, concessions to Western opinion and to necessity, particularly a greater tolerance of breaches of collectivisation in agriculture. The official answer to the immense material and morale problems of the post-war period proved immediately to be a return to rigid planning, collectivisation and control, to extreme measures to stop the gaps in the isolation of the Soviet people from the outside world, and (for some of the nationalities at least) to purges. In general, however, though the regime's repression of opponents remained severe, the purge in the manner of the 'thirties was after 1939 a thing of the past, replaced by an elaborate and constant system of supervision. The end of the war left Russia secure and influential in the world as never before since the revolution, but not apparently more trusting. The Stalin myth was greatly enhanced, probably in his own mind as well as in those of others. It seems unlikely that his participation in military affairs was quite as inept as Mr. Khrushchov seems lately to have suggested, though it may be accepted that his generalship was of no high order. In fact, for whatever reason, the courses of action on which he insisted, such as the defence of Stalingrad, were pursued through to success, much as in the economic battles of previous years. In the post-war years he showed a self-assurance greater than ever before, and amid clamorous adulation laid down the law in a succession of fields in which he had no specialised knowledge whatever. Under his authority Zhdanov's regimentation of Russian thought became absolute. The party had greatly expanded and had a force of new men at its disposal with reputations gained in the activities of wartime, and in particular in the army. Stalin's policy seems to have been to ignore those at the top, who might be dangerous, particularly the generals, whose independent reputations might challenge his own, and to make full use of those lower down who had shown the capacity to be serviceable. Now again the succession was becoming a matter of obvious concern in the top ranks of the party. New rivalries appeared which seemed to centre particularly about the opposition between Zhdanov and Malenkov, Stalin's protégé and deputy in the control of the party machine. With the death of Zhdanov in August 1948 the field seemed open to Malenkov, and his dead rival's retainers were hastily removed from all posts of influence.

In the period which opened in March 1953 and perhaps closed with the plenary session of the party Central Committee of 22nd–29th June 1957 a wide range of political issues again became open. Stalin, as a master in the balancing of men's ambitions, left no acknowledged heir, though Mr. Malenkov seemed designated by the role assigned him at the party congress of the previous October. Yet the situation differed from that at the death of Lenin in the general recent experience of the perils of not being first and the changed character of the party. Apart from this issue of power, Stalin had left urgent problems for settlement in the fields of foreign policy, where opposition had begun to consolidate, and in the economic field, where the contest of repair and development against the provision of incentives remained as ever on the agenda. The early elimination of Beria, who, with the private army and highly developed network of influence of the security services, seemed nearest to supreme personal power, probably resulted from realisation of the need for a balance. That the resentments of the influential against the more obvious instruments of coercion could best be appeased and harnessed by this sacrifice may well have made the decision easier. The subsequent disowning of Stalin suggests that in this respect the sacrifice was found insufficient. The concentration of party and state leadership since the assumption by Stalin in 1940 of the chairmanship of what is now the Council of Ministers was broken up almost immediately after his death, at least in form. Again, however, there were early indications that the leadership of the party machine would prove the stronger. The easing-out of Malenkov from his controlling post in the party in March 1953 was followed by his loss of the leading state post in February 1955, and this led on to his utter undoing in June 1957 at the hand of his successor in party office, Mr. Khrushchov. The leaders' agreements among themselves needed to be buttressed by taking some account of the opinion of the people, or at least of the best people. This gave strength to other potential influences, especially the army. The period saw ventures, mainly literary, to measure the extent of the thaw. Economic policy remained contentious, notably on agriculture and the production of consumer goods. The early months of 1957 were dominated by Mr. Khrushchov's decision, accepted by the party Central Committee in February and given legislative form by the Supreme Soviet in May, to organise the management of the economy on the basis of locality rather than by branch of industry. Probably, also, at a less accessible level of official thought, the latter part of the period was overshadowed by the problem of maintaining influence over the country's client states in the face of their increased manifestation of independence.

The period since mid-1957 has been one of firm return to rule by one man, unfailingly honoured in his appearances, utterances and works and fatal to the political, but not apparently as before the natural, lives of those in whom he has no confidence; an age of persuasion, plastics and peace waged as war.

The Participants

As in any other country, the relative importance of the various issues of politics has been different not only at different times but also for different men. The ordinary Soviet 'citizen', so designated for lack of a claim to the party style of 'comrade', rarely appears in the press, and then usually in a discreditable light. He is found feathering his own nest at the public cost—usually through the inattention of some official 'comrade', who shares in the blame—neglecting his work or otherwise failing in social discipline. Here, as generally, the bias of the Soviet press towards the pathological distorts the picture. We have, however, from other sources enough evidence to form some model of the citizen's world. For him the revolution is a fact, beneficial on the whole; the rightness of his country and the obtuseness of authority are as axiomatic as for his counterpart in any other society; the making or unmaking of ministers and of laws are activities as remote as they were to his grandfather, and verbal conformity and the recognition of influence are senses highly developed as necessary to existence. His concern appears to be to make life as predictable as possible, to live his own life, to avoid officials and to keep out of trouble. In the early days of the new order there were hopes of a dramatic liberation—particularly, among the minor nationalities, hopes of national liberation—but there can be little of this now. Among a section of the youth enthusiasm may still be high, but it soon fades. The same desire for predictability and a little peace is probably the motive of the small official. His 'bureaucracy', which the official organs constantly denounce, is a desire for orderly procedure in which not every case is an exception and the line from higher authority is sometimes silent.

Soviet terminology suggests benevolence but little respect for this class. The 'masses' are always an object, though an important one, rather than a subject—material to be manipulated, to be persuaded and conciliated rather than coerced, but of themselves inert. The 'population' (*naselenie*) which faces the Soviet official is not quite the 'public' of his Western counterpart; usage suggests something more submissive, more in need of protection, less spontaneously disciplined.

A much larger proportion of the population, however, than in most societies—those with ambition enough to interest themselves in the wide prospects which the Soviet system offers, as army officers, managers, leading officials and specialists, 'activists' (regular workers in the party and active supporters of it)—needs to play politics in the sense of basing action on some conscious assessment of the views and motives of government and its agents. They must submit to a much closer supervision than the less ambitious, and the best way to counter it is probably to seek the favour of the well placed. They must advertise themselves, and this generally means undertaking a variety of voluntary tasks, in the permitted social organisations, in the recurrent government drives and campaigns and, above all, in the party, to which closed circle the ambitious man must sooner or later secure admittance. They do not usually, unless they hold or aspire to party office, need to know all the tangled ropes of Marxist philosophy, though, like everybody else, they must accept it, and, unlike the more lowly, may need to make occasional unexceptionable utterances. But especially they must give results in their own fields of employment, perform, secure the performance, or conceal the non-performance of assignments which are habitually a little too big. For people in this position technical incompetence is probably now the only completely irredeemable flaw. Understandably for the generality of them the world revolves around a particular department in the government service; there is little time to look beyond it and its immediate neighbours to see the system as a whole.

For those within the managerial élite who are regularly in interaction with the sovereign policy-makers the position is different. The circle can hardly be considered to extend beyond the twenty members and secretaries of the central directing body of the party, a fair proportion of the sixty or so secretaries of the republican parties and perhaps a few of their associates, ministers of the union government and a few from the government of each union republic, a party secretary or two and perhaps a state official from each of some two hundred non-federal units, together with a few private secretaries and heads of the more frequently consulted specialist agencies—perhaps some seven or eight hundred persons in all. These, though widely scattered, form something like a true political society, with power to advise, and perhaps even to promote policies of their own liking. They need the skill of the politician to sense changes of wind in the upper air and to turn with them in good time, to understand the moods and motives of those below and to secure cooperation from them without committing themselves. They also, like their subordinates, are judged by results, and failure means a rapid return from real influence and prosperity to obscurity. These are the men who must always bear in mind the contingency of a coming purge and how best to avoid it. They cannot allow themselves the safety of silence, but must have the alertness and subtlety to detect what is happening and demonstrate in orthodox terms and with references to texts its rightness and inevitability. Among them are most of the men with a close knowledge of the outside world, and they are kept reasonably well informed of both central decisions and external events. That they are not, in consequence—as probably they are not—a cancer of cynicism at the heart of the Soviet system is probably due to the rigorous process of selection by which they have reached the top, with its implicit emphasis on right ideas as ancillary, but necessary, to material achievement, and to the general human proneness to suppose that what is good for oneself is self-evidently right.

The size of the sovereign decision-taking body—that which needs to consider no limitation on its range of action other than that of physical possibility—has clearly varied from time to time. It is reasonable to say that in the time of Stalin it consisted of one man, with the rest able to do little more than guess, at their own considerable risk, what was going on in his mind. Now there are probably more active participants; and though there seems to be at least one person aspiring to the sole lead, it will probably require a subtlety more than Stalinian to possess it in tranquillity. Such things are more easily done a first time.

We probably have not to suppose that even at this level the practitioners see the system whole, though Stalin may at times have stood back from his work to wonder at his own artistry, and perhaps even Molotov may have reflected with modest pride on the skill which kept him in the safer, if less satisfying, role of the reliable second from prerevolutionary days until his decline and downfall in the ascendancy of Khrushchov. At this level the concern must be to keep the balance of power, to prevent its accumulation in other hands, to appreciate how much is possible with the given material and how that material may be maximised. This obviously requires an intimate knowledge of personality and great skill and tact in manipulation. Such a man must know, as Trotski suggests Stalin did, how so to involve his colleagues in his schemes as to make them feel committed to courses which they would otherwise find distasteful, and yet contrive to look beyond the new ally to his riddance should he seek to become the master.

CHAPTER II

Soviets, Union, and Constitutional State

The Invention of the Soviets

On the form of the socialist state after the revolution Marx was of little assistance. His principal venture into the practical was in 1871, when, for his own short-term advantage in the political manœuvres of the first International, he constituted himself the champion of the Paris Commune, which enjoyed a brief two months of independence upon the close of the Franco-Prussian War. In an address preserved in his writings as *The Civil War in France* he described this creation as according to its constitution it should have been: the representative assembly elected for a short term, the revocability of all deputies, the absence of any separation of powers, the control by local bodies over the police and officials, the restriction of all state servants to workmen's wages, the elective, responsible and revocable judges and magistrates, and the district and national assemblies elected up from the local bodies. He approved the dominance of the towns over the countryside, which, he suggested, secured to the peasants their natural leaders in the urban working men, and he proclaimed the whole a chance-discovered form for the dictatorship of the proletariat. In fact, it was manifestly nothing of the sort, and the declaration of support for violence served only to alarm and estrange the British trade unions and others whose support Marx was seeking. Consequently the attempt was soon forgotten by him and by others, and the work which it produced, though reprinted and from time to time commented upon, was not taken very seriously.

As we have seen, soviets of workers' deputies first appeared in Russia —in St. Petersburg and Moscow, and subsequently in a few other towns —in the course of the troubles of 1905, as co-ordinating bodies among the mass of strike committees. The word 'soviet' in itself is politically neutral, meaning merely 'council', as in the title of the old Council of State. The thing in itself was in 1905 of no one pronounced political complexion. Most of the existing political parties were represented in the St. Petersburg soviet, including both wings of the Social Democrats;

and the dominant figure in it, who exploited most effectively its possibilities for theatrical demonstration, was Trotski, who stood between the two. Even the newly formed liberal grouping, though it did not join, sent a message expressing its solidarity. This soviet was a body of somewhat fluid membership with, at its largest, some 560 members and an executive committee composed principally of Social Revolutionaries and Social Democrats of the two schools. Lenin, who arrived in St. Petersburg during the period of its activity, expressed interest in it and appreciation of Trotski's work, but himself took no part and apparently saw in it no principle capable of further application. Its dramatic appearance on the scene, however, gave prestige to the form, and when subsequently troubles again developed it was imitated. In 1917 soviets began to form, not only among the workers but also in the army and navy and among the peasantry. Their political allegiance was still not certain, though those in peasant areas were dominated almost exclusively by the Social Revolutionaries.

At the beginning of 1917 Lenin apparently began to see new possibilities in the soviets. In an address delivered in Switzerland in January of that year he recalled that in certain towns in Russia they had 'really functioned in the capacity of a new state power'.[1] In March of the same year, by which time they had already reappeared in Russia, he proclaimed the soviets to be a 'new, unofficial, still comparatively weak, workers' government'.[2] A few days after this appeared in print he was on his way home, and on the day after his arrival he first brandished overtly the stick he had devised to beat the provisional government with. In the 'April theses', ostensibly points for discussion in the formulation of party policy, he declared: 'not a parliamentary republic—a return to that from the soviet of workers' deputies would be a step backward—but a republic of soviets of workers', agricultural labourers' and peasants' deputies throughout the country, from the bottom to the top.'[3] His addition to their description accorded with his discovery of the utility of the peasants. In an article in the recently revived party newspaper *Pravda*, in defence of the theses, he proclaimed the authority of the soviets to be of 'exactly the same type as the Paris Commune of 1871",[4] thus placing them in the direct line of Marxist succession. They were to be based not on any parliamentary discussion but on direct mass action and on 'outright seizure', words which, though unspecific, were in themselves attractive to the peasants. The police and army were to

---

[1] Lenin, *Report on the Revolution of 1905*, Works, Vol. 23 (1949), pp. 240–1.
[2] Lenin, *Letters from Afar*, Letter I, Works, Vol. 23 (1949), p. 298.
[3] Works, Vol. 24 (1949), p. 5.
[4] *On the Diarchy*, Works, Vol. 24 (1949), pp. 19–20.

be replaced by the arming of the whole people, who were themselves to maintain order; and officials, in so far as they were retained at all, were to be reduced to the status of simple agents of the people, subject, as in Marx's vision of the Paris Commune, to summary dismissal.

Though Lenin never withdrew his hastily granted recognition of the state of soviets as the form appropriate to the period of the dictatorship of the proletariat, his attachment to the soviets as in fact they existed was intermittent in the succeeding months. The party's April Conference, to which the theses were presented, duly adopted his slogan 'All Power to the Soviets' as a direct challenge to the authority of the provisional government, but in a pamphlet written in preparation for the Sixth Party Congress in the following July he himself urged its withdrawal.[1] The provisional government had for the first time brought itself to take a firm hand with Lenin, driving him into hiding over the Finnish frontier and imprisoning some of his supporters, including Trotski, while the majority in the principal soviets, though ready enough to accept Bolshevik slogans, remained unamenable to Bolshevik control to a degree which threatened the delicate strategy of the minority with disaster. In September he revived the slogan,[2] with equally good cause. At the beginning of that month there had been the first movement of army officers against the provisional government, representing military exasperation with the lack of effective guidance from the capital. The threat was the salvation of the Bolsheviks, the section of the revolutionaries who best knew what they wanted and were prepared to provide firm leadership towards getting it and to throw upon their less resolute rivals the suspicion of complicity with the supposed counter-revolutionary elements. Shortly afterwards they gained for the first time a majority in the Petrograd soviet, where Trotski, now their ally, returned to the chair, and in the soviets of Moscow and other towns. The return at the same time of the peasant soldiers deserting at Bolshevik instigation from the front, and finding in their villages that the Social Revolutionaries had achieved little for them in concrete terms of land, gave them their first control of some even of the rural soviets. The soviets had suddenly become a useful instrument, though not one in the possession of which Lenin could feel entirely secure, even when power was seized in its name in November.

The soviets had already ceased to be purely local. The first All-Russian

---

[1] *On the Slogans*, Works, Vol. 25 (1949), pp. 164–70. In an article published in *Pravda* in the middle of the previous month he was still strongly advocating the slogan (Works, Vol. 25, pp. 134–5).

[2] 'One of the Root Questions of the Revolution,' published in *Rabochi Putj*, 27th (14th) September 1917, Works, Vol. 25 (1949), pp. 340–7.

Congress of Soviets had met in the middle of June. It was not a success from the Bolsheviks' point of view; the 882 delegates included only 105 Bolsheviks as against 285 Social Revolutionaries and 248 Mensheviks, and a Bolshevik motion for the assumption of power from the provisional government was defeated. Like the earliest soviets, the congress resolved to establish an inner executive and administrative body to manage business until the next congress. Even this proved to be as big as 250, of whom in the first instance only thirty-five were Bolsheviks. The Second and Third Congresses of Soviets, though neither provided the Bolsheviks with a majority, were rather better managed by them. The *coup d'état* of November, and the dispersal of the Constituent Assembly of the following January, were staged a few days in advance of the congress meeting, so that the congresses had merely to take delivery of, in the first case, provisional, and in the second, permanent authority as the parliament of Russia, and in this they concurred. In practice it was not the congress but the All-Russian Central Executive Committee, its inner body, which exercised the parliamentary function, in so far as it was exercised at all, and which continued so to do until 1936. But the transfer of power to executive committees was not confined to the congresses, where it could hardly have been avoided, but was found also in the local soviets. The Petrograd (St. Petersburg) soviet of 1917 was from the first managed, and virtually replaced, by its executive committee. Already at the Eighth Congress of the party (to be distinguished from the Congresses of Soviets), held in March 1919, we find a delegate complaining publicly that 'in fact there is a tendency to liquidate the soviets and to convert Russia into a country of executive committees'. Soon there even appeared inner bodies within these inner bodies; and as the functions of the Soviet state became increasingly managerial, this tendency, directed towards the production of agencies of a size and type of membership suitable to such functions, became increasingly pronounced in party, in state, and throughout the system.

In September 1917 Lenin protested against the common interpretation of the slogan 'All Power to the Soviets' as meaning 'a ministry from the parties of the soviet majority', which, he held, would mean leaving in being the whole old official machinery. Instead the people must be involved directly in the whole process of government, including administration. However, Lenin soon brought himself to accept, as from practical considerations it was inevitable that he should, a ministry, though without a majority in the soviets, of which he was himself the chairman. The Second Congress of Soviets, which accepted the revolution of November, resolved 'to form for the administration of the country for the time until the convocation of the Constituent Assembly'—which in the event meant permanently—'a provisional workers' and peasants' government to be known as the Council of People's Commissars'. The choice of title was apparently largely accidental; the Bolsheviks desired to avoid the associations of the word 'minister' and apparently added the word 'people's' (*narodni*) to the word 'commissars', to differentiate them from other commissars already thrown up by the revolution and so named in imitation of the French revolution. The departments entrusted to these officials mostly bore designations familiar in conventional political systems, including, with some peculiarities of terminology, that of Russia—internal affairs, foreign affairs, finance, justice, posts and telegraphs, agriculture, labour, commerce and industry, the army and navy—at first organised as a committee but soon thereafter reorganised into two commissariats—and so on. Thus the ministries were never really in abeyance. The new men took over existing machines, and in the succeeding months the traditional manners of operation of the latter soon reasserted themselves. One of the motives directing events was the desire of the administrators to recover control of their former local branches. In the early days the soviets had been encouraged to seize control of the local offices as one means of disorganisation. With the Bolshevik conquest of power, however, there was a change of emphasis. In December 1917 we find the People's Commissariat for Internal Affairs, while continuing to invite the soviets to seize all government offices, directing them at the same time to co-ordinate their activities with the general decrees of the central authority. It reported that it was itself responsible for unifying their actions and accordingly invited them to submit reports.[1] Soon after the revolution we get complaints of the loss of independence by the soviets and their departments in consequence of the action of officials sent out from the centre.

An ingenious justification was found for this state of affairs in the evolution of the doctrine of dual subordination. By this, departments of lower soviets were to be responsible both to the executive committee, and so the soviet, at the level of which they worked, and also to the corresponding department in their own line of business at the next higher level up to the ministry. The same principle of dual subordination applied to the executive committees themselves, making them, in the terms of Article 101 of the current constitution of the U.S.S.R., 'accountable both to the soviets of toilers' deputies which elected them, and to the executive organ of the superior soviet of toilers' deputies'. In practice the vertical line, as Soviet administrative theory styles it, leading up towards the centre, has proved more effective than the

[1] S. Dobrin, 'Soviet Federalism and the Principle of Dual Subordination', *Transactions of the Grotius Society*, Vol. XXX (1944), p. 269.

horizontal line of control by the local soviets. The device facilitated a return to the administrative state while preserving for the new regime the moral advantage of the new myth of mass political action.

By-passing the soviets, however, was not enough. The centre still needed their services, and for this it had to reorganise them, especially the rural soviets, where, despite the steady drift away from the Social Revolutionary allegiance to the advantage of the Bolsheviks, a conflict of wills still remained. The alliance of the peasantry and the proletariat was one of convenience and not of conviction. Marxists, with their attachment to industrial forms of organisation, were, from the first, disposed to believe in the superiority of collective over individual peasant agriculture, and to favour the retention of the larger estates for use as collective farms. They took over the populist slogans of seizures and redistribution only as a tactical move, necessary for the seizure of power. The necessities of the retention of power, when once they had the towns to feed, drove them no less firmly back to their principles. From the earliest days military revolutionary committees had been posted in the villages to force upon the peasants the surrender of an adequate proportion of their crops. For a more permanent solution they looked to the resentments for which the increasing differentiation, in respect of wealth, of a peasant society offered foundations. To describe and damn the larger peasant, defined as from time to time suited them, they made use of the term '*kulak*', which in its pre-revolutionary usage vaguely suggested sharp practice—from the merchant's giving of short weight to the usurer's expropriation of the impoverished peasant who had increasingly been falling into his clutches. Against him they brought into action the committees of the poor. 'Their main task was to split the village . . .,' Zinoviev explained at the Sixth Congress of Soviets in November 1918, when that task had been completed. 'They are not really elective bodies. They were appointed by visiting representatives of the executive committees or of party organs. . . . There are committees of the poor consisting of a few people—the best people in the village. They hold it under their control although sometimes they are not its elected representatives, and side by side with them there still exist some remnants of the old soviet, a couple of people. . . . We rejected . . . the suggestion that these soviet remnants should be allowed to continue their existence side by side with the committees of the poor as food sections.' The old soviet had been smashed by emissaries from outside the village—in fact from the town. It remained to put something in its place. 'On the transition from the neutralisation of the middle peasant (at the end of 1918) to a policy of establishing a firm alliance with him', the same Congress of Soviets 'passed a decree upon the re-election of soviets with the aim of improving their composition. The immediate conduct of the re-election the congress left to the committees of the poor. On the completion of the re-election at the beginning of 1919 the committees of the poor were liquidated and their function transferred to the newly elected soviets'.[1] The story was repeated in the mass collectivisation phase of 1929-30. Again groups of poor peasants were organised, but this time the village soviets themselves were required to organise them. When many of them failed to do so, and some themselves opposed collectivisation, the authorities satisfied themselves of 'the necessity of re-election, review, examination of personal composition of the backward village soviets which do not manage the new tasks',[2] and acted accordingly.

Three instruments on the powers of village soviets have been issued. Two appeared under Stalin—the first in 1924, and the second, to meet the needs of the period of full collectivisation, in 1930. The third was made by the Supreme Soviet Praesidium of the R.S.F.S.R. in August 1957. The definition of powers is wide, and in the first of these measures included a general competence to provide for all local needs. In the 1930 measure, however, this provision was dropped, and attention was concentrated much more firmly upon the direction of agriculture. The duty of speeding collectivisation was laid upon them; they were given the power to enquire into the internal management of the private farm, and to confiscate the land of people not fulfilling their production plan or their obligation to the state. The latest measure is still unreported in detail, but seems not to go much beyond affirming the soviets' right to receive reports from all farms, both collective and state. Above the level of the village and the town there were until 1936 no directly elected soviets. An order on district and higher congresses of soviets was issued in 1928 giving them power of supervision over the village soviets. When collectivisation had left the village soviets with little to do these higher levels came themselves to be the operative agencies. Their relation as such to the original conception of the soviets was very thin.

---

[1] A. A. Askerov et al. in *Sovetskoe Gosudarstvennoe Pravo* (1948), p. 124. Of the result of the process Lenin admitted at the Eighth Congress of the party (March 1919) that 'The low cultural level brings it about that the soviets—although by their programme they should be the organ of administration by the working people, are now, in fact, the organ of administration for the working people, by the most progressive stratum of the proletariat' (i.e. the party) 'but not by the working masses. Here there is before us a task which we cannot solve otherwise than by protracted education'. His successors were not so much troubled by the fact that the task remained unsolved.

[2] Ja. Berman in *Sovetskoe Gosudarstvo i Revoljutsija Prava*, No. 2 of 1930, pp. 21-2 (periodical quoted in further references as *S.G. i R.P.*).

The 1936 constitution provided for directly elected local 'soviets of working persons' deputies' (no longer of 'workers' in the narrower sense) at all levels of the administrative system—village, settlement or town, district, area, region and territory, and in autonomous regions and national areas—apart from the new directly elected Supreme Soviets in republics. But the state of soviets has never produced a legislative definition of the role and structure of the system of soviets as a whole.

The Union

The losses of territory of the early days presented the Bolsheviks with a major problem of policy. Some Marxist national groupings, confident of early international triumph, professed indifference to vulgar nationalistic desires for self-determination; the Poles, being the most subject to temptation, were particularly austere in their resistance to it. Similar considerations disposed the Russians to be generous. But as experience of independence produced in the former Russian territories a variety of governments, more or less socialist, but mostly such as the Bolsheviks regarded as bourgeois, they could not but desire to see their own form of state prevail. Stalin specifically called self-determination a right of the working masses only and declared that it should be 'a means for the struggle for socialism and subordinate to the principles of socialism'.[1] Lenin was, as ever, more circumspect, but his actions agreed. From the first, aid and pressure were applied from Moscow to that end. In Poland and Finland there was, by reason of the strength of the nationalist sentiments, little that they could do. In the Baltic provinces the same forces, though weaker, were effectively backed by foreign armed assistance. In the Ukraine and Belorussia the situation was very different; there was a general realisation that their interest lay in association with Russia, though, in the fashion of the time, this early took the form of a demand for federation. The first governments set up were not acceptable to the Bolsheviks, and they fell in the latter part of 1918 with the Germans, with whom they had been obliged to ally themselves. Governments of Soviet form and largely made in Moscow took their place and, though not proceeding at once to formal federation, entered into treaty relations with Russia, which involved extensive adoption of Russian legislation and close administrative integration. The recession of resistance and intervention in the Caucasus had similar consequences. Farther east it led rather to direct incorporation in the new Russia.

[1] Report on the national question to the Third All-Russian Congress of Soviets of Workers', Soldiers' and Peasants' Deputies, 15th January 1918—Stalin, Works, IV, p. 32.

As Marxists, the new rulers of Russia were against all forms of federalism. Engels's dictum that 'the proletariat can use only the form of the one and indivisible state' followed obviously from their principles. The proletarians of all lands were, as the Communist Manifesto demands, to unite. Since the state was merely an instrument of a class it was reasonable that this united class should have a united state, and the larger the better. It could work across frontiers drawn against it, but for it to draw frontiers across its own territory would merely play into the hands of the bourgeoisie. 'Federation,' Lenin wrote in a curious definition of his attitude in December 1913, 'means a union of equals depending upon common consent.... We reject federation on principle; it weakens economic links; it is an unfit form for our state.... We are for autonomy for all parts. We are for the right of secession (but not for secession itself for all). Autonomy is our plan for the building of a democratic state. Secession is not at all our plan.... In general we are against secession.... The right to secession is an exception from our general proposition of centralism. This exception is essential in view of Russian Black-Hundred nationalism.'[1] The objection to a union of equals was understandable in one committed to believing that some were right while others were wrong. The objection to any actual secession from a communist state, while recognising the right, followed equally from communist reasoning. The people should readily accept communism when once it was shown to them; from a wish to secede bourgeois motives were to be inferred. Also of interest was Lenin's approval of autonomy, by which, subsequent practice and terminology has shown, he understood freedom from such control of day-to-day operations as is exercised by a head office over a branch.[2] It did not exclude the possibility of such occasional forms of influence as legislation. Subsequently Lenin brought himself to accept the term 'federation', and so made its popular appeal available to his cause, by identifying it with autonomy in his sense. This identification was expressed in the Russian Soviet Federated Socialist Republic (R.S.F.S.R.) established by the 1918 constitution. Despite the name of the new state, the constitution made no provision for federal institutions, but only for certain units designated as autonomous (originally eight autonomous republics and thirteen autonomous regions, to which were later added national

---

[1] Letter to S. G. Shaumjan, 6th December 1913 (new style)—in Lenin's Works, Vol. 19 (1948), pp. 453–4. The black hundreds referred to were the strong-arm bands frequently involved, often with official connivance, in violence against Jews, minority nationalities and intellectuals in the closing years of the empire.
[2] S. Dobrin, op. cit., p. 281.

areas). Stalin even went so far as to extend the term 'autonomy' to cover the relations with Russia of former possessions, such as Azerbaidjan, then ostensibly still independent though in treaty relations with it. The criterion of fitness for the establishment of an autonomous unit within the Soviet state is nationality, which, as it has in practice been defined, means language. The readiness of the authorities in Moscow to recognise the existence of such distinct language groups and to give form to their previously unwritten languages seems to have even exceeded the demand, and the grant of autonomous status which followed has survived even the decline of the people concerned, in consequence of population movements and other forces, into a minority within the area to which it gives its name. The political substance of the award of such status, however, has progressively declined. Thus in the early years of the new state the autonomous republics had within their governments, apart from ministries directly subordinate to those of the R.S.F.S.R., others not directly under any ministry at the higher level, though subject to the All-Russian Central Executive Committee; that is to say, to the central parliament. The latter variety of ministry was designated 'autonomous', thus giving substance to the same word in its Leninist sense in the title of the republics. By the constitution of 1924, however, they lost this distinction, and all ministries of autonomous republics became directly subordinate to some ministry at the next higher level. They differ from the autonomous regions and national areas only in having the titular forms of republics—constitutions, Supreme Soviets (since 1936), ministers, and Supreme Courts. Autonomous regions and national areas differ from purely administrative regions and areas only in the use for official business of their national languages.

The first Council of People's Commissars of 1917, although conventional in pattern, contained already one significant innovation—the People's Commissariat for Nationalities, of which the commissar was Stalin. It was a ragged affair, composed of sections set up as the occasion demanded for the various nationalities in which the Soviet government happened at any given moment to be interested, mainly those of the old Russian Empire, but extending so far as at one time to include a Yugoslav section. The functions of these were wide, extending from cultural affairs to contact behind enemy lines in the period of civil war and intervention. By 1922 the commissariat had become a small government on its own, duplicating, in respect of the territories with which it was concerned, the functions of the other commissariats, particularly those of an economic character, which brought it into conflict with some of the latter. It was consequently abolished in 1923 with the entry into force of the new constitution. But it left behind it the centralising tradition established by its formidable commissar, and also a new representative institution. The Soviet of Nationalities was established in May 1920 as a consultative body, meeting under the chairmanship of the Commissar for Nationalities and including representatives of the several peoples for which he was responsible. With the abolition of the commissariat it was taken within the Central Executive Committee as an equal second chamber.

In December 1922 the R.S.F.S.R., the Ukraine, Belorussia and the Transcaucasian S.F.S.R., newly formed under Russian pressure by the three republics of Georgia, Armenia and Azerbaidjan, agreed to unite into a new federation to be called the Union of Soviet Socialist Republics. The federal constitution was adopted on the 6th July 1923 by the Central Executive Committee of the R.S.F.S.R. in which the other federating units were already represented, and, confirmed by the All-Russian Congress of Soviets on the 31st January 1924. The former body now became the Soviet of the Union, forming together with the Soviet of Nationalities the All-Union Central Executive Committee, or effective parliament of the new federation. The All-Union Congress of Soviets, as the nominal parliament became, remained unicameral. As the constitution also recognised for the first time a further inner body within the Central Executive Committee, the Praesidium, which had, in fact, been in existence for some time, the curious structure was presented of three rings, each elected by that outside it, of which only the second was split into two chambers.

In the manner of the distinction between the two elements of the Central Executive Committee, the American analogy seemed to have counted for something. The Soviet of the Union was to be constituted on the basis of population, after a fashion comparable with the House of Representatives, while the Soviet of Nationalities was to represent the equality of the federated units after the fashion of the American Senate. The product, however, was something very different from the American model. One of its peculiarities was that it provided equal representation, five members each, for all republics—both the four federating 'Union Republics' and the autonomous republics included within the R.S.F.S.R., which were presumably in some sense less than federal. The autonomous regions were to have one deputy each. By the constitution of 1936 this was modified and a distinction was made between Union republics and autonomous republics. The former were to be represented by twenty-five deputies, the latter by eleven, while autonomous regions received five, and the new category of national areas one each.

But in the Soviet Union the representative machinery is always less important than the administration. The 1924 constitution distinguished three categories of people's commissariats, 'all-union', 'unified' and 'republican'. The first, existing only at federal level, provided for the traditionally centralised functions of any federal state: foreign affairs, military and naval affairs, foreign trade—though in this field the republics retained until 1931 certain powers—communications, water transport and post and telegraphs. The second category, renamed in the 1936 constitution 'union republican', contained the majority of the people's commissariats at both levels as well as the Supreme Council of the Economy, the agency supervising the management of state economic activities. The third category, existing only at the republican level, contained the commissariats for internal affairs, justice, education, health and social welfare. Here, in contrast to the arrangement of the representative organs, a distinction was, as we have seen, drawn in the 1924 constitution between the union republics and the autonomous republics. The autonomous republics had ceased to be autonomous, and autonomy had become the mark of the union republic.

The result is not a federal system in the terminology of the non-Soviet world. To say so is not to condemn it. Federalism is a concept evolved mainly for the practical purpose of describing the sort of relations which the central authorities of the U.S.A. maintain with the several component states, and most of the countries to which we are accustomed to apply it owe something to the American example. If we declare that the Soviet Union contains in its constitution a number of obviously unfederal provisions, we imply by this merely distinction from this familiar tradition. Soviet autonomy-federalism recognises no indefeasible rights in the federated units, and prescribes no field of regulation as belonging exclusively to them. Apart from its principal peculiarity, the unified or union-republican commissariats or, as they have been styled since 1946, ministries, it leaves to the central authorities 'the determination of basic principles' in a number of fields for which they are not departmentally responsible. The number of such fields has decreased, but only with the extension of the responsibility of federal departments. Elementary education still remains under the 1936 constitution (Article 14) such a republican power governed by federal 'basic principles'.

The most important of all the federal powers is that to make the national economic plans for the whole of the U.S.S.R., and the consolidated state budget, which includes and provides the means for the budgets of the union republics and the local soviets within them. In addition, the constitution provides that 'in the event of divergence between the laws of the Union republics and a law of the Union, the union law prevails', and decisions and orders of the federal Council of

Ministers are similarly binding throughout the Union (Article 67). No restriction is made in the provisions with regard to the subject of legislation. The Praesidium of the Supreme Soviet of the Union (Praesidium of the Central Executive Committee in 1924) has power to annul the degrees or orders of the Council of Ministers (people's commissars) of a Union republic for illegality. Until 1936 it had the same power over acts of the less productive legislative bodies, the republican Central Executive Committees, and, subject to later endorsement by its own Central Executive Committee), the republican Congresses of Soviets. The list of ministries and their allocation as between the various categories have been left readily variable, and have been frequently varied by administrative decisions at the federal level. Neither constitution of the Soviet Union has provided protection by provisions specially difficult of amendment and subject to interpretation by a body independent of the federal administration. The federal Supreme Court was empowered in 1924 to render decisions concerning the constitutionality of decrees of the union republics upon demand of the federal authorities, but no provision was made for passing judgment on the constitutionality of federal measures, and the power was not included at all in the 1936 constitution.

Non-Leninist federalism implies limitation, acceptance of local and sectional interests. Its presence in a Marxist society would be surprising in view of Marxist ideas of history and state power. Any divergence of the Russian giant-firm state from the implications of the doctrine has not been in such a direction as to make it more probable. It is a unitary structure in which the several elements—administrative units, economic enterprises, etc.—participate not with different rights and interest but with varying 'subordination' (*podchinenie*)—that is, place of attachment to the common frame. Even the national forms of culture accepted in principle have, like all forms, always been held subject to change to accord with changing economic substance. As the directors of all change, economic and otherwise, are Russian by residence and predominantly by origin, there has been a marked tendency to extend the language, literature and mythology of the Russians to the other Soviet peoples. Russian is the general second language in education and administration, and even the minority languages have of latter years been given a Russian aspect by the introduction of the practice of writing most of them in the cyrillic alphabet, even where, as in the Moldavian (Rumanian) language, a latin alphabet was established, or, as in some of the previously unwritten minority tongues, had already been introduced by Soviet scholars. The spread throughout the Soviet Union of a new uniform pattern of life is tending to break up such material conditions for federalism as exist. The primary concern for economic efficiency demands that the boundaries of federal units be habitually disregarded in making appointments to posts, including those conventionally considered political. There seems to be evidence that some regard is paid to the convenience of having a post staffed by a native of the territory concerned but that this motive is of low priority. A variety of organisations and societies, including the party itself, are organised on a basis which factually disregards the existence of the federation.

Soviet autonomy-federalism, however, is not without its utility. It has served, as have federal forms in other countries, to induce divergent communities to associate and to remain together pending the emergence, by whatever means, of a closer union. The early autonomy of the insubstantial nationalities within the restricted area of Russia served for advertisement and persuasion to the larger communities on its frontiers, which were subsequently gathered into the Soviet Union. Even from the point of view of the people themselves, this was at least a process more conducive to happiness than annexation by mere force, though Bolshevik impatience and intolerance led to the frequent use of force as well. The forms of autonomy, and the greater dignity of having it called federation, have probably gratified local pride to some extent. There is advantage in terms of public relations, though there is also administrative inconvenience, in having the local language recognised for official business—and the Soviet Union is not exempt from the rule that good relations make for efficiency. The possession of autonomous status probably confers also some practical advantage on the inhabitants of the minority areas. The qualifying population for establishment of, for example, an autonomous region seems to be lower than that required for a purely administrative region, and the institutions are similar. In a hierarchically administered state this is important. It means that appeals from district decision may be heard not only in the local language and possibly by local men but also probably at a more accessible spot than would otherwise be the case. It does not, however, exclude the possibility of an unlimited amount of interference from higher levels.

From the original four, the union republics have now increased to fifteen. The Transcaucasian S.F.S.R. was in 1936 dissolved into its three component parts and each was admitted as a union republic. In 1925 the Turkmen and Uzbek union republics were created as part of the partition and pacification of Turkestan, formerly an autonomous republic; in 1929 the Tadjik, and in 1936 the Kirgiz, union republics were set up in the same region, and also in 1936 the Kazakh republic was advanced in status. During the Second World War the three formerly Russian Baltic republics of Lithuania, Latvia and Esthonia were reannexed, purged and constituted union republics, and the territories annexed from Rumania and Finland, together with autonomous republics formerly within the R.S.F.S.R., were constituted into the Moldavian and Karelo-Finnish republics respectively, of which the latter was dissolved and absorbed into the R.S.F.S.R. in 1956. Stalin in his introduction to the 1936 constitution expressed three criteria of suitability for the promotion of lower autonomous units to union republican status. They must lie on the frontiers of the Soviet Union, because otherwise it would not be possible for them to exercise the right granted by the federal constitution (Article 17 of the 1936 constitution) freely to secede from the U.S.S.R.; they must have populations of at least one million, and the nationality which gave them their name must be in a majority. It does not seem that all this was seriously meant. The right of secession was declaredly not intended to be exercised, and could not be exercised by some of the present union republics without cutting off others, and even a region of the R.S.F.S.R., from contact with Moscow. Again, it is not clear why it is essential that the name-nationality must be in a majority in a union republic, when this is no longer so of some of the autonomous republics and regions or national areas, and it does not seem that the Karelo-Finnish republic ever possessed this qualification for union status. It seems probable that Stalin was merely seeking to discourage inconvenient demands for promotion, and in his position he did not have to be too particular about the weight of the arguments which he used.

Most of the autonomous republics and autonomous regions and all the national areas are within the R.S.F.S.R. *Autonomous republics* there are the Bashkir, Dagestan, Kabarda-Balkar, Kalmyk, Mari, Mordovian, North Ossetian, Tatar, Udmurt, Chechen-Ingush and Chuvash on the southern and eastern fringes of European Russia; the Karelian (formerly the Karelo-Finnish union republic) on the Finnish frontier; Komi in the north; the Yakut republic covering a vast area of northern central Siberia; and the Burjat (formerly Burjat-Mongol) on the southern frontier. In Azerbaidjan there is the Nahichevan autonomous republic, in Georgia the Abhazian and the Adjarian, in Uzbekistan the Kara-Kalpak. *Autonomous regions* in the R.S.F.S.R. are the Adygei and Karachai-Cherkess in the Northern Caucasus; Gorny Altai, Hakass and Tuva in south central Siberia; and the Jewish in the Far East. The last was a half-hearted Russian alternative to Zionism and is exceptional in that the name-nationality apparently never was, and still is not, strongly represented among its population. Tuva, previously semi-independent, seems to have been formally annexed to the U.S.S.R. only since the war. Nagorny Karabah autonomous region is in

Azerbaidjan, the South Ossetian in Georgia, and the Gorny Badahshan in Tadjikistan. There are ten *national areas*, all in the R.S.F.S.R. Two, for sections of the Burjats detached from the main mass, lie in southern Siberia and four lie along the arctic coast and together extend for some two-thirds of the whole union's length from west to east. One, as vast, is further south in central and one in western Siberia. One is in north Kamchatka, and one at the extreme eastern edge of European Russia. No autonomous or national unit is contained within another. All are subordinate directly to a union republic or to one of the purely administrative subdivisions, though this was not always so.

The federal constitution provides (Article 18 of 1936) that 'the territory of a union republic may not be altered without its consent'. There is no similar guarantee for autonomous republics or for lesser autonomous units either in the federal constitution or in the constitutions of the republics, and in fact five such units were dissolved during the Second World War: the Crimean, Volga German, Chechen-Ingush and Kalmyk republics and the Karachai region. In January 1957 the last three regained autonomy (the Kalmyks as a region until July 1958). Their peoples, and the Balkars, were to be repatriated in two to four years. Union republics have lost territory, by consent or otherwise. Part of the Karelo-Finnish republic was transferred to the R.S.F.S.R. in 1945, and in 1956 the rest of the republic acceded to the R.S.F.S.R., ostensibly of its own freewill, thus extinguishing its union-republican status. In 1955 the R.S.F.S.R. itself ceded the Crimea to the Ukraine, in 1956 the Kazah republic ceded territory to the Uzbek, and in 1957 Georgia ceded to the R.S.F.S.R. its part of the Chechen-Ingush territory.

Administrative Areas

Where there are no claims of nationality administrative areas are based upon considerations of management of the economy and in particular of agriculture, since the greater part of industry has been centrally controlled. The structure therefore is extremely fluid and constantly changes with changing ideas of convenience, unimpeded by the civic particularism which makes alteration difficult in a liberal state. Thus one region in the R.S.F.S.R. which elected its regional soviet with the rest on 3rd March 1957 was abolished on 23rd April.

Immediately after the revolution soviets were set up in the town and village areas of the pre-revolutionary administrative structure, with congresses of soviets at the levels of the *volostj*, the *uezd* and the governorship (*gubernija*), still retaining its old name although now without a governor. It was accepted from the first, however, that more suitable units must be found, and local experiments were early made in the grouping of governorships. The outlines of a new system were accepted by the Central Executive Committee in March 1921, but in April 1923 the Twelfth Congress of the party demanded that development be restricted for the time being to two selected representative regions. By the beginning of the following year, however, change was well under way and continued gradually, though until well into the 'thirties the old and the new units were simultaneously in existence in different parts of the country. The new policy was for larger units than previously: in place of the *volostj* the *raion* (generally translated as 'district'); in place of the *uezd* the *okrug* (usually translated as 'area', though 'circuit' might be a more accurate rendering); and in place of the governorship the *oblastj* (region), supposed to be a unit of distinctive economic character containing both manufacturing industry and agriculture. Certain units of regional status were given the designation of *krai* (territory) by reason of the inclusion within them of units themselves designated as regions. The latter were the autonomous regions included within the R.S.F.S.R. before the war, of which five still remain, and also two purely administrative regions in Khabarovsk territory in the Russian Far East. This local variant was removed in February 1956 by the separation of one of the regions, that of Kamchatka, from the territory, and the abolition of the other. Tuva autonomous region, the recent acquisition, has not been included within a territory. The Primorski (Litoral) territory—between the north-south stretch of the Manchurian frontier and the Pacific—has never contained any units of regional status, and probably owes its designation to the fact that it was formed in 1938 by the division of the former Far Eastern territory, the rest of which became a 'territory' of more normal type. The small 'rural locality'—as the official translation of the constitution renders the Russian term *selo*, the 'village' in the more usual but misleading translation[1]—remained. It was convenient for purposes of control, so long as there were private peasants and a consequent need for the local officials to know them and their resources in detail. In 1924 there was some consolidation, but it was claimed in 1929 that this had been a mistake, unfitting the 'village' soviets for their task, and had been reversed.[2] At about the same time the idea of abolishing the village soviets as superfluous, and giving their functions to the new collective farms gained some currency. The authorities, however, soon decided against it, and it was denounced as Social-Revolutionary in origin—

---

[1] In some parts of the country the latter term, which because of its familiarity we shall use, fits the situation well enough. In others the people live in scattered hamlets, and a single 'village' soviet may cover some dozens of these.

[2] A. Luzhin, *Ot volosti—k raionu* (1929), p. 123.

and also anarcho-syndicalist.[1] The towns remained separate from the surrounding rural areas, with subordination to district or to region (or to republic where there are no regions, and, for the few largest cities, even where there are) according to their size and economic significance, and the largest were themselves divided into districts (*raion*) with their own soviets.

At first only the R.S.F.S.R. was divided into regions and areas, so that elsewhere districts and large towns were of republican subordination. In 1930 the decision was taken to abolish the *okrug* as an unnecessary link in the chain of control. Rather, it was suggested, the *oblastj* should direct groups of districts according to their economic characteristics, without regard for territorial contiguity. Thus Moscow region was reported in 1931 to have divided its districts into five, and subsequently six, groups according to their predominant economic activities: heavy industry, light industry, grain-growing, market-gardening with dairying and animal husbandry, technical crops and crafts.[2] Again, however, the change took some time to carry out, and areas were still in existence in the late 1930s. At the same time there were repeated complaints that regions and republics were finding difficulty in controlling the large number of districts directly subject to them, which in 1930 averaged 129 and reached 585 in the Ukraine and some 230 in the Siberian territory.

In the period preceding and immediately following the Second World War there was a tendency to steady increase in the number of units at all levels above the village, to provide for the constant settlement and development of new areas and also to allow of more detailed management. Already by the outbreak of war the number of regions had exceeded the number of the old governorships, and by the beginning of 1953 there were, apart from the autonomous and national units, 6 territories, all in the R.S.F.S.R., and 144 regions—R.S.F.S.R. 55 (including three in Tatar and two in Bashkir autonomous republics and two in Khabarovsk territory), Ukraine 25, Uzbek 9, Tadjik 3, Kazah 16, Belorussia 12, Turkmen 4, Kirgiz 6, Lithuania 4, Latvia 3, Esthonia 3, Azerbaidjan 2, Georgia 2. By then 26 administrative areas (*okrug*) had reappeared—in the Moldavian, Armenian and Karelo-Finnish republics and in some of the Russian autonomous republics—and there were 4,418 districts, 1,498 towns of varying status, 511 districts within the towns and some 76,000 'villages', of varying local designations, and settlements (*posjolok*) having their own soviets—apparently something under 2,400 of these last being 'workers' settlements' or 'settlements of

[1] Ja Berman in *S.G. i R.P.*, No. 2 of 1930, p. 21.
[2] M. Jurgin in *S.G. i R.P.*, No. 2 of 1931, pp. 89–90.

urban type', with a status somewhat superior to that of an ordinary village.[1] The new administrative *okrugs* and the regional division of Azerbaidjan and Georgia, completed in 1952, were the product of a new acute phase of the persistent concern over effective supervision of districts by higher authorities. In the Baltic republics the administrative structure was not changed from the pre-war pattern to the Russian three-tier system until collectivisation of agriculture had been completed in about 1950, and in Latvia and Esthonia this process of administrative reorganisation continued into 1952. Shortly after the death of Stalin, though it was perhaps due to the organisational fluidity characteristic of the Soviet Union rather than to that event, the *okrugs* began to be abolished again, and none of them is now in existence. Similarly the regions in the Tatar and Bashkir autonomous republics, and in Lithuania, Latvia, Esthonia, Azerbaidjan and Georgia, were all abolished during 1953. In 1955 the Tadjik union republic also abolished two of its administrative regions, leaving only the one geographically most remote from the centre.

The period of these two trends was also one of steady reduction in the number of district and village-soviet areas. Of this the cause is clear. The collective farms, the principal units of the Russian agricultural system, were consolidated at this time, mainly apparently with a view to facilitating control over them. They were reduced in number from some 254,000 to 123,700 in the course of 1950 and 97,000 by the end of 1952, and the result was to make nonsense of the very small village, devised for quite different circumstances and tasks. Cases were reported in 1953 where a single collective farm covered the area of four village soviets, and even one with eight. There were also reported to be places with two village soviets for a single inhabited place, established for different national communities which had subsequently merged. Of the village soviets of this period it is stated that they were normally responsible for only a few hundred people, and had on their territory, apart from the one small collective farm, or part of one, only a primary school and reading hut, a village general store (*seljmag*) and a dressing and midwifery station.[2] It was reported in 1953 that over the last two years the number of village soviets had accordingly been reduced by over 300 in the R.S.F.S.R. alone—though 49 per cent of all in that republic still had under 1,000 inhabitants and some only 200–300,[3] and since then it has

[1] *Izvestia*, 11th January 1953: figure for settlements calculated back from figure for the beginning of 1955, *Narodnoe Hozjajstvo SSSR* (Central Statistical Administration), 1956, p. 26.
[2] Ju. V. Todorski, *Postojannye komissii mestnyh sovetov deputatov trudjashchihsja* (1955), p. 62.
[3] *Sovetskoje Gosudarstvo i Pravo*, No. 8 of 1953, p. 31 (periodical quoted in further references as *S.G. i P.*).

evidently fallen even faster, accompanied by a more gradual continued fall in the number of collective farms, which by the end of 1955 was apparently 87,500 for the whole U.S.S.R.[1] There has been a marked similar trend in the districts, despite a few new creations. Thus at the March 1957 local elections districts were down in numbers to 4,149, together with 432 units of like designation in the towns. Towns stood at 1,596, of which 603 were of higher than district subordination, and 'settlements' having their own soviets at 2,559. There were 121 regions and still 6 territories. There were apparently 50,214 'villages'.[2] The number of village soviets to a district ranged, in the R.S.F.S.R. at the beginning of 1955, from 2 to 31, with the average about 11, and the number of districts to a region from 8 to 60, with the average about 32, though the maximum was by July 1956 down to 57 in Moscow region; the next largest number was 50 in Chkalov region. The Altai territory had 65 districts directly under its administration, and the Tatar autonomous republic had 67. Moscow region had, in addition, 29 towns of regional subordination, and all regions except Omsk had at least 1, though in some cases (Astrahan, Magadan, Kamchatka) it was the only town. The most recently created regions probably indicate the ideal scale which the centre has in mind. Thus the new region of Belgorod, in the R.S.F.S.R., contained 2 regional towns and 31 districts, and Cherkassy, in the Ukraine, 3 such towns and 29 districts; others were much the same. There are a variety of exceptions to the general scheme of subordination. A few village soviets are directly subordinate to region, some others come under towns or the districts within them, while for workers' settlements and the equivalent this latter subordination is, relatively to their numbers, quite frequent. Some towns classified as of district subordination come under towns of higher status.

Population is probably a minor consideration in the formation of administrative areas—and it cannot be decisive in any administrative

[1] *Narodnoe Hozjajstvo SSSR*, p. 128. By February 1956 the number had apparently further fallen to 87,371 (report to party congress, *Pravda*, 17th February 1956). These figures include a number—declining from 2,300 at the end of 1950 to 1,800 at the end of 1955—in non-agricultural activities (fishing, etc.).

[2] *Pravda*, 8th, 9th, 15th, 16th, 22nd March 1957 (number of soviets elected). Number of towns of higher than district subordination from *Narodnoe Hozjajstvo SSSR*, p. 23 (for beginning of 1956), corrected by notices in *Vedomosti Verhovnogo Soveta*. This latter source gives one fewer district and three fewer districts in towns than *Pravda*, possibly because of delays in gazetting changes. The figure for 'settlements' is 95 less than that in *Pravda*. It refers, however, only to 'workers' settlements' or 'settlements of urban type', whereas the *Pravda* figure includes all having settlement soviets. There is a small category of 'settlement soviets with the rights of village soviets'.

system. The category of towns overlaps widely in this respect with that of workers' settlements. Of the 1,543 towns in January 1955, 497 had less than 10,000 inhabitants, while one workers' settlement had some 60,000. However, the proportion of workers' settlements with under 10,000 inhabitants was much higher than for towns. There were 2,113 out of 2,441, and their average population was 4,346 as against 5,432 for towns in the same size-category. Towns with over 50,000 inhabitants numbered 261, and of these twenty-one had over 500,000.[1] As an index of population for the other units it seems that we have only the scale of representation in the Supreme Soviet (one member to 300,000 of population), though this can be no more than approximate. Thus Belgorod and Cherkassy regions each have five members and so presumably some 1,500,000 population, and most of the others created about this time have four. But not all regions approximate to this standard. The two outlying regions of Kamchatka and Magadan each have only one member in the Supreme Soviet and so presumably a population of less than 600,000, though Magadan, with an area of some 425 square miles, is the second largest in extent in the R.S.F.S.R. At the other extreme, Moscow region, excluding the capital itself, has nineteen members; Voronezh region (R.S.F.S.R.), even after the creation of a number of new regions mainly at its expense, still has eight members, and Stalino region (Ukraine) has thirteen—two for its largest town.

The progressive urbanisation of the country is strikingly expressed in the advancements, announced at a rate of two or three a week, of villages or previously dependent rural settlements and inhabited points to the status of 'workers' settlements' or 'settlements of urban type', and thence to town status, and the progress of towns from subordination to the district to subordination to the region (or republic). Absorption by a town to which the settlement was subordinate or merging with another settlement or town may spoil this progression, however, and downgrading is as easy as promotion, though less frequent. What change a village or equivalent unit experiences on advancement to the status of a workers' settlement, apart from acquiring new prospects of further advancement, is not clear, for its subordination is not usually changed. Advancement to the lowest category of towns also brings no change of subordination, but does change the list of administrative departments to be formed. Latterly there has been mention in the press of opinions favouring the abolition of the districts within medium-sized towns, but as yet the reductions made in the total number of such districts have been by amalgamation rather than by abolition.

For the present Mr. Khrushchov's schemes for the deconcentra-

[1] *Narodnoe Hozjajstvo SSSR*, p. 27.

tion of the management of economic affairs seem unlikely to cause any substantial change in the administrative map. His 'economic-administrative districts' proved, for the R.S.F.S R. by law of the republican Supreme Soviet in May 1957, to be all the six territories, all the fourteen autonomous republics, all the administrative regions except three, which for this purpose are merged with their neighbours, but not autonomous regions, and the city of Moscow—seventy in all, reduced by two by abolitions of regions in October. In the Ukraine, by decision of a plenary session of the republican party Central Committee in April 1957, the five most important of the twenty-six regions became economic districts in themselves, the rest were grouped into six districts. Three more districts were created in mid 1960. Kazahstan formed nine; Uzbekistan had four until July 1960, when like the eleven other union republics it became one. The development may ultimately extinguish the other regions, but for the present these are promised additional enterprises to run, while the council of the economic district looks after the most important.

It is hard to see why the village soviets should be rehabilitated, as the recent low-pressure campaign in the Soviet press in connection with the preparation of new regulations on their powers suggests.[1] Even now the average number of collective farms to such a soviet is a little under one and three-quarters. The farm members are already represented in the management of the farm, and the other inhabitants of the village can hardly amount to more than a school-teacher, the medical assistant, the few people who work in the village shop, if there is one, and the officials of the village soviet itself. There is probably not much that could economically be done in such a unit, whatever its legal powers. The services on the village budget, apart from the soviet's own maintenance, are said to include building and upkeep of village roads, maintenance and good order of collective-farm markets, playgrounds and kindergartens, schools up to the seventh year, except for payment of teachers' salaries, which are on the district budget, children's work out of school, libraries, reading huts—though the district culture department appoints the staff—clubs, dressing stations, etc. The cultural facilities are often mentioned among those which the farm provides for itself, and probably little road maintenance is done unless an industrial enterprise or farm is able to do it for itself. Few market facilities can be required where all are producers of the only commodities which may be produced by private enterprise. Village soviets' work in education, health, social care, posts and telegraphs and communications is mainly a matter of considering business for final decision by district

[1] Beginning apparently with an article in *Izvestia* of 17th June 1953.

soviet or its executive committee,[1] while to establish a new seven-year school one must go as high as the regional executive committee. The farm chairman is supposed to account for his activities both to the village soviet and to the assembly of his farm, but it seems that neither, nor even the district soviet organs, now has much influence over him. The need to repeat in new legislation the previous provision allowing a village soviet to direct productive enterprises has been questioned as 'in most regions of the R.S.F.S.R. the village soviets have no enterprises whether of industrial or communal-service nature'.[2] Things done in the name of the village soviet include the recording and authentification of small transfers of property and other legal documents, and assistance to the district tax agent—they lost their own tax-gathering powers in 1935. A few village soviets were, in 1954, still said to be exercising powers of 1927 to make searches and seizures, though this was properly for the 'organs of the Ministry of Internal Affairs'—that is, the police. It was stated that this 'leads to misunderstanding and dissatisfaction on the part of the population' and that the power should therefore be abolished.[3] They can make rules, but rarely do, for local good order and impose up to ten roubles fine or five days (in the R.S.F.S.R.) corrective labour for breach of them. An edict of January 1955 empowered village-soviet executive committees to impose prescribed fines and exact damages for harm done by animals and poultry straying in the collective-farm or state-farm fields. A joint commission of the executive committee and the management of the farm was to assess the extent of the damage. Most of these functions are work for officials and do not seem to require an elected body but for the demands of the revolutionary tradition.

Collective Administration

The revolutionary regime, we have seen, early abandoned its objections to a government of the traditional type, and the people's commissars and their officials soon settled into the ministerial tradition as it was known in Russia. In the first days there was a tendency for local soviets also to develop their own councils of people's commissars, but this was early discouraged. The place for the ministry was its traditional one—

[1] V. F. Kotok et al. in *S.G. i P.*, No. 8 of 1953, p. 42.

[2] Nemtsev in *S.G. i P.*, No. 8 of 1954, p. 53. Other Soviet writers, however, propose affirmation of the village's power to keep watch on enterprises under the management of the district, as, they suggest, it has in fact been doing.

[3] Ibid., p. 54. H. Dinerstein (*Communism and the Russian Peasant* (1955), p. 127) suggests, on the basis of interviews with former Soviet subjects, that the chairman of the village soviet is commonly regarded by the peasants as local representative of the coercive machinery of the state and in general more likely to be hostile than the chairman of the collective farm.

at the top. The new regime departed from the traditional pattern principally in a new emphasis on collective administration, or as the official terminology has it 'collegiality' (*kolegialjnostj*).

The Praesidium of the Central Executive Committee—a smaller inner group not constitutionally recognised until 1923, but certainly in being before then—seems to have been intended to keep a watch over the inherited administrative structure in the intervals between the sessions of the Central Executive Committee, though it early lost the power to exercise any effective influence over it. But it was also entrusted with the powers traditionally belonging to a head of state—dissolving and calling the legislature, instituting and conferring honours and awards, sending and receiving diplomatic missions, etc. Soviet sources commonly refer to its successor, the Praesidium of the Supreme Soviet, as the 'collective president' of the U.S.S.R. The new state of soviets was the negation of an autocracy and demonstrated this in not giving itself an individual head. But there are certain of the conventional functions of the head of state which cannot conveniently be regularly performed by more than one man—such as the receiving of foreign diplomatic representatives, the signing of legislation, and the presenting of decorations. Such functions were entrusted to the chairman of the Praesidium. Respectability and long standing in the party rather than brilliance or influence have been the characteristics of the men who have filled this office. Even Marshal Voroshilov, who probably had stood nearer to the centre of power than his predecessors, seemed a spent force before taking office. Mr. Brezhnev. succeeding in 1960, was not quite in this tradition.

A similar principle of collective headship was from the early days applied in the people's commissariats themselves. The commissar was not to be left with unchecked authority. Instead he was to be assisted and limited by a ministry 'collegium' composed of his deputy commissars and other principal officials appointed by the Council of People's Commissars. These might appeal against his decisions to the latter body, or, as was originally provided, to the Praesidium of the Central Executive Committee. As in most other matters, there has been some fluctuation of policy on this point. In March 1934, by resolution of the Seventeenth Party Congress, the collegium, in the commissariat or elsewhere, was abolished 'for the purpose of strengthening personal responsibility'. The commissar was to have not more than two deputies, and was to be assisted by an advisory council of forty to seventy members, half of them or more representatives of organisations and enterprises under the commissariat. In March 1936 the collegium was revived as indispensable, though without a constitutional right of appeal against ministerial decisions and without abolishing the councils. As yet their articulation into the administrative system as in practice it is required to work is imperfect.[1] A plenary session of the party Central Committee in July 1955 demanded improvement in the work of the ministry collegia, though it stressed that responsibility was to remain personal. This same duality between personal responsibility and the necessity for collective discussion applies, in Soviet writings, throughout the system of government, down to the local soviet.

In the early days of the new regime collective action was the rule in industrial management also, with managerial boards formed as to two-thirds of representatives of workers, and as to one-third of representatives of the technical staff approved by the workers' trade union. Lenin, however, soon saw the need to make one person responsible, and in industry as elsewhere the principle of 'one-man headship' (*edinonachalie*) came to be, and has remained, stressed in Soviet writing, with 'collegiality' retained principally as a belief in the necessity of good relations, of carrying people along with the official policy rather than overriding them. In the early days, however, competent managers, like competent military commanders, were not to be found among those in whom the regime placed full confidence, and their personal responsibility was checked by placing almost equal responsibility upon the secretary of the factory party committee and the head of the trade-union branch. In the autumn of 1929, however, this 'triangle' system was also condemned by the party, and in principle sole authority was placed in the manager's hands; the relations of the factory party committee to the manager have never since been precisely defined, but its power is still considerable. The trade unions became a very weak force, partly by reason of Stalin's mistrust of their leaders. In agriculture, general participation in management has survived better, at least in form, since reliance early came to be placed mainly on the collective farm (*kolhoz*) in which the cultivators are in form co-operative owners, not employed persons, and control the farm through their general assembly and a management board elected by it. But the difference is more apparent than real, and the collective farm has long been managed by its appointed chairman.

At the centre also the management of nationalised industry was from 1920 to January 1932 entrusted to a collective body, the Supreme Council of the Economy, though commissariats remained for such economic matters as transport, food, labour and posts and telegraphs, and they proved stronger. Since the Supreme Council's abolition only planning has remained nominally collective. Management was individualised and bureaucratised in the People's Commissariats—now ministries.

In the schemes of 1957 for the management of the economy, collective

[1] See p. 135.

action was again in favour. Most of the industrial ministries gave place to councils of the economy (*sovnarhoz*)—a name sanctified by revolutionary tradition—in the economic-administrative districts, co-ordinated since July 1960 by republican council of like title. The Supreme Council is not restored; central control is by the State Planning Committee, with other state committees. In the councils of the economy the extent of 'collegiality' seems limited; the chairman is very like a minister. In the factory general consultation is urged.

The Function of Soviet Constitutionalism

A constitution is a body of conventional relations and practices, departure from which in political action is apt to cause offence and friction. In this sense every political association has a constitution; there are some limits beyond which the organisers of the association's affairs would be ill-advised to go, though the limits may be very wide and it may be difficult to say in advance of the event where they lie. A written constitution is an attempt to formulate a significant part of this working constitution for the guidance of the participants in political action, usually upon association into a new state or as a condition of the continuance of obedience to an established ruler or system of rule which the subjects find it in their power to challenge. The idea of limitation is always present, and to be a useful guide to those whose conduct it purports to regulate the written constitution must indicate with reasonable clarity where the limitations lie, what sorts of action will be held to constitute a breach of it, and how wrong action will be proceeded against. A constitution which gives no such guidance, or which suggests that action will be taken which, in fact, nobody is in a position to take, is a bad constitution, such as littered the ground of Europe in the 1850s, or that of South America to the present day. For a genuine federation, as we have described it—that is to say, a federation in the American tradition—a written constitution is almost indispensable. The associating parties must know what they are surrendering, and will wish to indicate clearly the point up to which co-operation can be counted upon and beyond which there will be trouble. A written constitution may have other functions, and in course of time any satisfactory constitution acquires them. In particular it becomes a symbol of the state itself, venerated, even if unread. But this is no role for a new constitution.

The Soviet Union does not have the most obvious motives for adopting a written constitution. It is not a true federation, and by its official creed it can accept no limitation upon the will of those conventionally accepted as standing for the working people. It is true—as we have suggested that it is true for any state—that in practice some limitation must be accepted, if only at the point where further action in a given direction would provoke physical resistance on a large scale. This means that the leaders or those working under their orders must not offend too many influential people at the same time. But these are limitations such as cannot be conveniently defined in documentary form for permanent application; they are matters for tact.

Three constitutions have been made in Moscow for the whole of its dominions since the revolution: that of 1918, setting up the R.S.F.S.R.; that of 1923–4, recognising the establishment of the U.S.S.R.; and that of the 3rd December 1936, formerly known as the Stalin constitution, which is still in force. Under the last two of these the union republics and the autonomous republics have each made their own constitutions. The occasions of the two earlier constitutions are readily apparent. In 1918 there was the wish to fill the gap left by the dissolution of the Constituent Assembly and formally to declare the outcome of the revolution settled. In 1923–4 the formation of the federation itself is an adequate explanation. In 1936 the motivation was less obvious. Stalin himself provided an explanation at the extraordinary Eighth Congress of Soviets to which it was introduced on the 26th November 1936. He contended that the basic condition of the state had changed, and as a Marxist he stated this in economic terms. The New Economic Policy, which had been at its height in 1924, had left few traces by 1936. The *kulak* problem had been solved. The basis of society had been changed with the extinction of hostile class interest and its replacement by a friendly association of transformed classes. The working class could no longer be called a proletariat, and its dictatorship had entered into a second stage, which Stalin confusingly described also as the first stage of communism. This intermediate period he designated socialism, and for this the new constitution was to provide. It was an order in which 'all citizens have equal rights' and yet not equal positions, since 'personal labour... determines the position of every citizen in society'. The discrimination of the earlier stage was no longer needed, but essentials were unchanged. Stalin declared that 'the draft of the new constitution preserves the regime of the dictatorship of the working class, just as it also preserves unchanged the present leading position of the Communist Party of the U.S.S.R.'. For the reason why a change of incidentals needed to be made with such ceremony we must look outside Stalin's speech to the circumstances of the time. The rise of Hitler to power in Germany, and the explosive international situation of which the dangers were belatedly beginning to dawn on Stalin and his associates, gave them cause to seek to give assurances of reliability to potential allies abroad. A period of extensive purges in the party in the interest of the Stalin connection, with the wider and more violent action of the succeeding years in the making, called for similar assurances at home. Probably most Russian Marxists envisage, and many hope to see, a day when each man's duty, the nature of which is not for them in question, will be clear to him and he will perform it without the supervision and coercion needed while ends are still in dispute. They knew in 1936 that this stage had not yet come, but they needed the good opinion which it alone could bring them. They had to realise at once on their prospective inheritance.

The manner of the making of the 1936 constitution suggests this intent. On the 1st February 1935 the plenary session of the Central Committee of the party instructed Molotov to lay proposals before the Seventh Congress of Soviets, then already meeting, and gave him specific directions on the content of these. The Congress of Soviets unanimously approved the proposals, and its Central Executive Committee designated a drafting commission under Stalin to prepare the text. This was again submitted to the party Central Committee on the 1st June 1936 and approved. After that, by an entirely new departure, it was released for general public discussion in which, it was alleged, some 36,500,000 people participated. But though, it is said, 154,000 amendments were suggested by the public, only forty-three were accepted, and only one of these, the substitution of direct for indirect election to the Soviet of Nationalities, was of more than verbal significance. It may be inferred that the leaders desired the appearance, and probably the reality, of wide public support, but not if it would prevent them from getting their own way in all material respects. The concluding stage of enactment followed at the last of the Congresses of Soviets.

Contents of the Constitution

The 1936 constitution consists of thirteen chapters, designated respectively as: The Social Structure (Chapter I), The State Structure (Chapter II), The Higher Organs of State Authority in the U.S.S.R. (Chapter III), The Higher Organs of State Authority in the Union Republics (Chapter IV), The Organs of State Administration of the U.S.S.R. (Chapter V), The Organs of State Administration of Union Republics (Chapter VI), The Higher Organs of State Authority in the Autonomous Soviet Socialist Republics (Chapter VII), The Local Organs of State Authority (Chapter VIII), The Courts and the Procurator Service (Chapter IX), Fundamental Rights and Duties of Citizens (Chapter X), The Electoral System (Chapter XI), Arms, Flag and Capital

City (Chapter XII), Procedure for Constitutional Amendment (Chapter XII). The distinction between state authority and state administration is that between organs constituted in principle by elections and those constituted by appointment, the former including both the soviets and Supreme Soviets and their Praesidia and Executive Committees, the latter including the ministers and the Council of Ministers as a whole. This distinction is indicative of a way of looking at politics quite distinct from the early Marxists ideas, according to which the people would be actively involved in administration. It seems also to be at variance with the system as in fact it operates, but in a different sense, in that the principle of appointment extends to offices nominally in the elective line. The term 'local' as contained in the designation of Chapter VIII covers all levels of the system from the region down to the village—that is to say, all levels at which the soviet is not designated 'supreme'.

Chapters I and X are both declarations of faith rather than statement of verifiable facts or prescriptions which can be enforced against any person or public body by a court of law. There is no provision for, or evidence of, their ever being so pleaded. The rights stated are sometimes meaningless. Thus Article 7 (in Chapter I) states that 'every household in a collective farm . . . has for its personal use a small plot of household land as its personal property . . . a dwelling-house, livestock, poultry and minor agriculture implements . . .', and Article 125 (in Chapter X), guaranteeing the citizen's basic freedoms, states that 'these civil rights are ensured by placing at the disposal of the toilers and their organisations printing presses, stocks of paper, public buildings and streets, means of communication and other material conditions for the exercise of these rights'. Yet neither poultry nor printing paper is provided free; the state's role is the purely negative one of seeing that the peasant does not have enough of the former to be independent of the collective farm and rationing the latter to the very limited number of organisations permitted to engage in printing on a scale just sufficient for the circulation which it is thought that they should have. Other rights, though of ascertainable meaning, are in no way secured against circumvention. Thus Article 127 provides that 'citizens of the U.S.S.R. are guaranteed inviolability of the person. No person may be placed under arrest except by decision of a court or with the sanction of a procurator'. Yet there is evidence of arrests being made on the basis of blank warrants provided in advance by the procurators, or even without them, and there seems to be nothing to prevent this. We now appear to have the highest authority for believing that Stalin personally issued orders for the arrest of individuals.[1] It is probable that his subordinates did the like. It is

[1] Khrushchov, closed-session speech Twentieth Congress, *D. of S.*, p. 17.

questionable whether constitution-makers in the Soviet Union or elsewhere are wise to guarantee rights of which they lack either the means or the will to ensure the protection. The solemn affirmation of rights may help to build up respect for them, but repeated violation is apt to destroy respect for the law itself. One article in Chapter X, however, is important. Article 126, which guarantees the rights of Soviet citizens to unite in trade unions, co-operative societies, sports clubs, and so on, adds that 'the most active and politically conscious citizens in the ranks of the working class, working peasants and working intelligentsia voluntarily unite in the Communist Party of the Soviet Union, which is the vanguard of the toilers in their struggle to build communist society and is the guiding nucleus of all organisations of the toilers both social and state'. This is the first mention of the party in a Russian constitution. It appears in humble company, but it is unique of its kind, and, unlike the other forms of organisation mentioned in the same article, it is not declared to be open to all Soviet citizens. The constitution does not say who is to distinguish the degree of activity and political consciousness of aspirants.

Chapter II states at some length the rights of the federated units: to have their own constitutions, which take 'account of the specific features of the republic', and are 'drawn up in full conformity with the constitution of the U.S.S.R.' (Article 16); to secede from the U.S.S.R. (17); not to have their territory altered without their consent (18); to maintain direct relations with foreign states even to the extent of concluding agreements and exchanging diplomatic and consular representatives (18a); to have their own military formations (18b); and to retain full sovereignty except as defined in the constitution (15). The federal powers, however, by which the republican powers are limited, are defined in Article 14 in very comprehensive terms, including, as we have seen, determination of basic principles in a number of spheres for which the federation is not departmentally responsible. It is hard to think of any power which is left exclusively to the federating units, but if there is one it could readily be removed if its existence were found inconvenient; the item which vests in the federal authorities the 'determination of the principles of legislation concerning marriage and the family' was added in 1947. Recent changes reverse the trend, replacing exclusive by shared jurisdiction. Some powers granted were never intended to be operative; Article 17 has been explicitly so declared, and Article 18 seems to present no difficulty in practice. Articles 18a and 18b have not been applied, for though the union republics maintain ministries of foreign affairs, offers from foreign powers to establish direct relations have been refused, and they do not maintain defence ministries or, apparently, forces at all. Ministries are moved at will from the all-union to the union-republican category when it is desired to establish a branch in one republic or more. The order of the Praesidium of the federal Supreme Soviet making the change usually also 'recognises the necessity' that a corresponding ministry should be established at republican level. When it is no longer desired to act through a branch at republican level the ministry is as lightly returned to all-union status.

On political structure and machinery the constitution is too detailed for convenience. The specification in Chapter II of the territorial division of the several union republics down to regional level, deleted in February 1957 when these matters were transferred to the republics' own competence, used to require amendment at almost every session of the Supreme Soviet, and the articles in Chapter V which set out the designations of the all-union and union-republican ministries at federal level may well still do so. The increase in the early 'fifties in the number of republics divided into regions required the insertion of additional articles at the end of Chapter II, which were deleted on the abolition of those regions in 1953. Most changes have consisted in deletions and insertions in the existing articles. Shortly after the session —twenty days after that of May 1957—further changes of ministries or other institutions are made by edict, and they continue to appear at similar intervals until the next session comes along to confirm them, if by then they have not already been reversed.

The machinery provided in Chapters III–VIII and XI of the constitution forms the subject of our Chapter III, and Chapter IX comes into our Chapter V.

Here we need only note that in the field of legislation there is what appears to be a superfluity of means. Thus Article 32 states that 'the legislative power of the U.S.S.R. is exercised exclusively by the Supreme Soviet of the U.S.S.R.'. But Article 49 states that the Praesidium of the Supreme Soviet 'issues edicts' (*ukaz*), and it does not say about what. Article 66 states that 'the Council of Ministers of the U.S.S.R. issues decrees (*postanovlenie*) and dispositions (*rasporjazhenie*) on the basis and in pursuance of the laws in operation and verifies their execution', and a similar power is given to ministers individually to make such orders in their own fields (Article 73). Even so, the constitution does not indicate the full extent of the duplication, since it makes no mention of the machinery of the party or the measures which it enacts either alone or conjointly with one or more of the organs of the state.

Thus Article 32 suggests that the previous rejection of the separation of powers has been abandoned. But in fact the 'legislative power' (*zakonodateljnaja vlastj*) is only power to make the 'lex' (*zakon*), formal law so designated. In fact comparatively few of the rules which Soviet citizens have to obey are made in this form. As under the Tsars, most of the rule-making is done by ministers, either individually or collectively, in the Council of Ministers. The other means are for the more solemn regulations. There is no distinct executive power, but only a 'highest executive and administrative organ of the state authority', the Council of Ministers (Article 64), which is 'responsible and accountable' (Article 65) to the Supreme Soviet as 'highest organ of state authority' (Article 30), or between its sessions to the Praesidium (Article 65). The acts by which the Supreme Soviet makes ministerial and other appointments are spoken of by Russian theorists as 'acts of supreme administration'. For the other traditional division of state power, the judicial, there is the apparently more positive provision of Article 112, that 'judges are independent and subject only to the law', but this article has no ascertainable meaning; we will return to it in Chapter V.

Amendment of the constitution is in fact by the ordinary procedure for legislation—a vote in each house of the Supreme Soviet separately. Article 146 requires 'a majority of not less than two-thirds of the vote in each of its chambers', but as in practice no law (and no other proposal of however little importance) has ever failed to get a unanimous vote this provision is inoperative. Amendment after the event is a common practice. Thus, apart from the incessant changes of areas and ministries, school fees for higher education were imposed in 1940, contrary to Article 121, which as then worded guaranteed free education to all; foreign affairs and defence were added to the powers of union republics in February 1944; family legislation was added to the federal powers in July 1944; the age of eligibility to the Supreme Soviet was raised in October 1945—and all these changes were reconciled with the constitution by its amendment only in February 1947. In normal times the delay is shorter. No provision is made for the interpretation of the constitution other than that of sub-paragraph c of Article 49, which lists the interpretation of laws of the U.S.S.R. in general as one of the functions of the Praesidium of the Supreme Soviet; that is to say, a body formally an offshoot of the legislature itself. No mention is made of the possibility of declaring any act unconstitutional. It is hard to see that with so little binding force over other legislation the constitution can properly be described, as it is in its title, as a 'fundamental law'.

As we have seen, the rights of the union republics as guaranteed in the federal constitution include a constitution of their own 'which takes account of the specific features of the republics'. In practice these specific features seem to be very few. The official Soviet law textbooks cite as examples of such differences the provision in some constitutions for the existence within them of autonomous republics and regions, and differences in the number of republican ministries. In fact there is not very much else to point to, and these differences themselves are not very considerable; the republics are bound by federal recommendations as to the union-republican ministries to be set up, and republican ministries are very few. Otherwise the constitution follows the same model almost word for word. Such constitutions are made by the Supreme Soviet of the republic subject to confirmation by the Supreme Soviet of the U.S.S.R. The constitutions of autonomous republics within the R.S.F.S.R. are completely uniform. They are made by the Supreme Soviet of the autonomous republic, subject to confirmation by the Supreme Soviet of the R.S.F.S.R. The procedure in other union republics is presumably similar. The charters of autonomous regions, which correspond to constitutions and represent their principal distinction from ordinary regions administered under general legislation, are similarly confirmed by higher authority, and similarly seem to be uniform.

Utility of the Constitution

Stalin presented the constitution in 1936 as record rather than as precept. Thus he said to the Congress of Soviets: 'The draft of this new constitution is a summary of the path that has been traversed, a summary of the gains already achieved. In other words, it is a registration and legislative embodiment of what has already been achieved and won in actual fact.' The implication of this is that if the constitution and practice differ it may be the constitution which should be changed, in that it has ceased to be a registration and legislative embodiment of the latest achievement. In this lies the theoretical case for the *ex post facto* amendments. Such a record may be useful, nevertheless; but by reason of its inaccuracy, imprecision, incompleteness and impermanence it is unlikely that the Soviet constitution is much consulted by practical administrators, or by those who have to deal with them, for the purpose of finding out what the present organisation of the system of government is. Its false emphasis, as for example on the relations of elected bodies to their inner bodies, is likely to make it a poor guide for this purpose. The constitution has a large distribution within the Soviet Union, but it is likely that this is for educational rather than for practical purposes.

To obtain information on how the system works, one must look to the general legislation as well as to the constitution, and rather to the former than to the latter. Even this source is defective. The formal legislation published in the gazette of acts of the Supreme Soviet is, as we have suggested, little and uninformative, and the acts of the Council of Ministers are no longer published. It must be difficult even for the practising officials to know what the law is at the moment. Occasional digests of the law on particular issues are published by the several ministries for the agencies subordinate to them. Presumably also the official has the internal instructions of the public service to guide him, of which probably a higher proportion than in other countries are of a confidential nature. Some officials may be supposed to have the party directives, open or restricted, on which these are based. But the difficulty of maintaining uniformity of practice in such circumstances is probably still such as to constitute a major force of friction within the Soviet system. It must be particularly hard for the public, which cannot know how it stands with regard to the authorities on many particular issues, and must therefore make a large number of unnecessary applications and enquiries, though private contacts may obviate the need always to put these through official channels. We who stand outside the system are similarly in the dark. We may supplement the information of the written constitution by the same published sources, by the party charter, and other party measures, but the real constitution is obviously unwritten and consists in understandings as between persons.

But constitutions can have other functions: they are also ideology. Only in so far as they are intended for propaganda abroad can the constitutional documents of the Soviet Union perhaps be discounted as political institutions; that is to say, as means to facilitate the attainment of agreement among individuals. Their internal propaganda value, if they have any, makes for good government; that is to say, for the acceptance of the restraints of government without a sense of frustration of will. It is probable that they have some such value; to Soviet citizens, repeatedly told that their constitution is the most enlightened in the world, it probably seems so. To the federated and autonomous units their own constitutions are probably of some value as symbols of statehood.

CHAPTER III

Conventional State Machinery

The Representative Bodies—What They Are
The Supreme Soviet of the U.S.S.R. consists of two houses: the Soviet of the Union, popularly elected on the basis of one deputy for every 300,000 of the population (Article 34 of the 1936 constitution); and the Soviet of Nationalities, similarly elected on the basis of twenty-five deputies for each union republic, eleven deputies for each autonomous republic, five for each autonomous region, and one for each national area. The relation of representation to population in the Soviet of the Union cannot be precise, since in the formation of constituencies regions, though usually subdivided, are never grouped together. Any region of less than 600,000 population, therefore, presumably has one deputy, and above that a rise of less than 300,000 brings no increase. In the elections to the Soviet of Nationalities the inhabitants of autonomous or national units have votes for the representatives of the union republics within which those units are contained, as well as for the representatives of the units themselves. In addition to the members elected to the two houses in these distinctive manners, there are sixteen members elected for special constituencies for the armed forces stationed abroad. All are elected in the same fashion, but eight sit in each house. The Soviet of the Union had 708 members as elected in 1954, and 738 in 1958, and the Soviet of Nationalities 639 and 640. The two Houses in the Supreme Soviet of 1937, the first to be elected under the new constitution, and the only one before the war, were almost equal in membership, with 569 and 574 members respectively. The difference which has since developed between them is likely to increase, as the rising population of the U.S.S.R. is reflected in the membership of the Soviet of the Union. The Soviet of Nationalities has already declined in membership from a peak of 657, at the 1946 election, to which it was raised by war-time territorial acquisitions; the abolition of some of the autonomous units brought it down to its 1954 figure; the rehabilitation of some offset the reduction resulting from the diminution of the Karelo-Finnish autonomous republic. For much of their business the

two Houses work in joint session of all 1,378 deputies. The two Houses are elected at the same time for the period of four years. All four post-war elections have been held in February or March. Casual vacancies are filled by by-elections as they occur.

The fifteen union republics have each a Supreme Soviet of some 400–500 members, which is unicameral even in those republics which contain autonomous republics. The autonomous republics have somewhat smaller unicameral Supreme Soviets. In both classes representation is related to population. In the R.S.F.S.R. there is one deputy to 150,000 inhabitants; in the Ukraine one to 100,000; in Belorussia and Kazahstan one to 20,000; in Uzbekistan, Georgia and Lithuania one to 15,000; in Azerbaidjan, Moldavia, Latvia and Esthonia one to 10,000; in Kirgizia, Tadjikistan, Armenia and Turkmenia one to 5,000. In the Tatar and Bashkir autonomous republics there is one to 15,000; in the Mordovian and Chuvash one to 12,000; in Udmurt one to 7,500; in the Dagestan, Burjat-Mongol and Mari republics one to 6,000; in Karelia one to 5,000; in Komi and the North Ossetian republic one to 4,000; in Kabarda one to 3,500; in the Yakut republic one to 3,000;[1] others are unknown. They also are elected for periods of four years, but not simultaneously with the Union Supreme Soviet. The first republican Supreme Soviet elections under the current constitution were held in 1938, and since the war they have been held in the years following the election to the Union Supreme Soviet—in 1947, 1951, 1955 and 1959, in each case in February.

The various levels of the administrative structure—territories and regions, areas, districts, 'villages', towns and settlements—have their own soviets. There were 59,097 at the 1957 elections, including autonomous regions and national areas, with a total membership of 1,549,760, though a number of people seem to serve simultaneously on soviets at more than one level. The number of soviets was down by about 450 since the 1955 elections, but the number of members was about 13,000 up. The size of the soviets is fixed by republican legislation within limits set by the republican constitution except in the Baltic republics and Moldavia. For the largest cities membership is specifically prescribed; otherwise the constitution relates it to population. They vary widely in the proportions provided for the largest units (regions or large cities), but not very much in the range of size which they produce. A region or territory has a soviet with a minimum membership of sixty (Kirgiz con-

---

[1] Figures for union republics from constitutions as published in 1956. Figures for Karelia from constitution of Karelo-Finnish union republic as published in 1951. Figures for the other autonomous republics in R.S.F.S.R. from constitutions as published in 1955.

stitution, 1951) or seventy (Ukrainian constitution of same year). Maxima are not specified, but the regional soviet of Moscow, the area of which does not include the capital city, had after the 1953 elections a membership of 148. That of Kiev region in 1947 had 204. Soviets of areas (national or administrative) seem to have a membership of between forty and sixty-five. District soviets were uniformly prescribed to be of twenty-five to sixty members, on a basis of one to 1,000, until the R.S.F.S.R. constitutional amendment of March 1955 changed the minimum to thirty-five. Village and settlement soviets in the R.S.F.S.R. and probably elsewhere have since 1955 been of fifteen to thirty-five members on a scale, between these limits, of one to 100 inhabitants. The minimum was previously nine and before the 1953 election the maximum was twenty-five. Town soviets necessarily vary considerably in view of the difference in size and status of the towns. The constitution of the R.S.F.S.R. as amended in March 1955 provides for a minimum membership of thirty-five where the town has a population of less than 12,000; previously the minimum was twenty-five and there was a maximum, apart from a few stated exceptions, of 700. The soviets of the largest cities have diminished in membership as the populations which they represent have increased; that of Moscow elected in 1955 had 813 members as against 1,500 in its predecessor of 1953, and over 2,100 before the 1939 elections, but in 1957 it again rose to 853, and in 1959 to 860. Districts within towns have from thirty-five members (to, in Moscow, some 250). Local soviets are unicameral, elected for two-year terms (Article 95 of federal constitution); elections were held in 1939, in December 1947–January 1948, in December 1950 January 1951, February 1953, and in March of 1955, 1957 and 1959.

With the adoption of direct elections to the central legislatures the local soviets have ceased to be in any material sense 'the political foundation of the U.S.S.R.' (Article 2 of the federal constitution). In so far as they genuinely function they are 'local authorities', though involved in the general business of the state in a manner characteristic of the local-government bodies of continental Europe rather than of Britain. The Supreme Soviets, similarly, are now 'parliaments', despite the objections of Lenin, theoretically continued by his successors, to parliamentarianism. They may differ from the similar institutions of other countries in the quality of their performance but not in the nature of the task purported to be assigned to them. The state of soviets, if it was ever to be found in the Soviet Union, is there no longer.

The councils of the economy of the new economic-administrative districts are not elected bodies. They are appointed by Councils of Ministers of the republics, and are answerable only to them.

How They are Formed

Before 1936 only the village and town soviets were directly elected, the higher levels having congresses of soviets elected up by the soviets or congresses of soviets at the level below, right up to federal level. The franchise for the popular election at the lowest levels was not an equal one. Lenin and his successors habitually emphasised the distinction between their form of state, or 'proletarian democracy', and 'bourgeois democracy' in that the former frankly recognised its class basis, whereas the latter sought to conceal it. Certain classes of people were therefore excluded from the franchise: persons engaging in commerce or employing hired labour for profit, persons living on unearned income, priests and monks, members of the Imperial Family and holders of certain pre-revolutionary offices, such as the procurators and police officers. Aliens resident in the Soviet Union, however, enjoyed the franchise on equal terms with Soviet citizens and any discrimination on a basis of race, religion or sex was forbidden. Above the level of elections, in the congresses of soviets, advantage was given to the urban proletariat by providing a higher proportion of representation for the town than for the village soviets. Thus in the district congresses of soviets in the R.S.F.S.R. and the Ukraine there was one deputy for each 300 inhabitants in the villages and one for every sixty voters in the towns, or in plants or factories outside them. At the federal level these figures were 125,000 inhabitants and 25,000 voters respectively. The method of voting was open, and much was made of the fact that the election took place not in territorial units but in the factories wherever possible.

By the constitution of 1936 all this was changed. The vote was given to 'all citizens of the U.S.S.R. who have reached the age of eighteen, irrespective of race or nationality, sex, religion, education, domicile, social origin, property status or past activities'. The insane and criminals whose sentence explicitly included deprivation of electoral rights were alone denied the vote (Article 135), though a decree of the federal Central Executive Committee of the 16th October 1937, apparently extending the latter deprivation to all persons in custody, has been quoted by a post-war source as being still in force.[1] Thus the enfranchised alien and the excluded classes disappeared from the system together. The age of eligibility was similarly placed at eighteen, but by an edict of the Praesidium of the Supreme Soviet of the 10th October 1945 this was raised to twenty-three for election to the federal Supreme Soviet, and by a similar edict of a year later it was made twenty-one for election to the Supreme Soviets of the union republics. The

[1] Askerov et al., op. cit., p. 332.

age of voting remains unchanged. Election to soviets and Supreme Soviets at all levels became direct, and the method prescribed was the secret ballot. In contrast to the system provided in Great Britain, however, the voter is required not to mark the name of the candidate for whom he wishes to vote but to cross out the name of the candidate for whom he does not wish to vote. Though still in the electoral regulations, this requirement ceased to be printed on the ballot paper in 1946 as a belated recognition of the fact that there had never been more than one candidate for any place at issue in any election, central or local.

All elections are held in single-member constituencies, so that for the bicameral federal Supreme Soviet the voter casts his vote in two constituencies of different sizes at the same time, or, if he lives in an autonomous or national unit, in three. The same polling stations are used and the votes are distinguished by the use of ballot papers of different colours. Elections of any one category—federal, republican or local—in any one republic are held on the same day—always a Sunday—though in republican or local elections different groups of republics may poll on different days, a week or sometimes more apart. Voters absent from their places of residence on polling day may obtain certificates entitling them to vote in the places where they happen to be for the candidates there standing, even, it seems, in local elections.

The conduct of the elections to a Supreme Soviet is entrusted to a Central Electoral Commission appointed by order of the Praesidium of that Supreme Soviet. Election commissions for elections to the Soviet of Nationalities are appointed by the Praesidia of Supreme Soviets and executive committees of soviets of the several autonomous and national units. Those for constituencies are appointed by the similar organs at regional level, or republic where there is no region, and those for polling stations by the executive committees of district or town soviets. The members are to be appointed from among members of the party, trade unions, youth organisations and various cultural societies, and upon their suggestion. Their political reliability is consequently unimpeachable.

The onus of registration lies not upon the voter but upon the lowest organs in the soviet system—the village-soviet executive committee, or the soviet itself if there is no executive committee, and executive committees of settlements, districts within towns where the towns are so divided, and the towns themselves where they are not. The issue of certificates to their registered voters who will be absent on polling day rests with the same authorities. Appeals against non-inclusion or other faults in the electoral lists lie to the district people's court, the lowest unit of the soviet judicial system, and its decision is final. To secure election the candidate is required to obtain an absolute majority of the vote cast provided that not less than half of those entitled to vote have in fact done so.

Article 141 of the constitution secures the rights to nominate candidates to public organisations and societies of the working people, Communist Party organisations, trade unions and co-operatives, youth organisations and cultural societies. Electoral regulations extend the exercise of the right also to assemblies of workers and other employees at their places of work, collective-farm members on their farms, and members of the armed forces in their units—and it is in fact by such bodies that the nominations are ostensibly at least always made. A Russian university textbook explains that 'in the U.S.S.R. it would be inappropriate to give the right of proposing candidates directly to individual persons. Firstly, citizens of the U.S.S.R. have every possibility of proposing this or that candidate at the general assemblies of collectives of toilers, or through the organs of social organisations. Secondly, the proposing of candidates by collectives and organisations of toilers corresponds to the high level of development of organised social consciousness in the Soviet state'.[1]

The nominations then made are finally sorted out and placed on the ballot paper by 'pre-election constituency conferences of representatives of the various collectives', which, it is agreed, always produce one single satisfactory candidature,[2] but there seems to be satisfactory evidence that the conference in fact has no sorting out to do. The lists put up by the nominating meetings may, in fact, contain several names, but that is because, particularly in the small constituencies used for local elections, any one factory may contain voters from several constituencies. When, in fact, the lists proposed by the various meetings are put side by side it is found always that they contain just sufficient real candidates to provide one for each constituency. There have generally been also some unreal candidates; it was the custom for Stalin himself and each of the leading figures of his entourage to have himself nominated in a number of constituencies, from all of which he would subsequently withdraw except in the one constituency where he was the only candidate. Khrushchov, though latterly similarly acclaimed, seems at present to withdraw earlier and more discreetly. Where such a bogus plurality of candidates was presented to the constituency conference, it did not attempt to cut it down but confirmed both candidatures.[3] The candidate is registered with the constituency election

[1] Askerov et al., op. cit., p. 324.
[2] Ibid., p. 325.
[3] T. H. R. Rigby in *Political Quarterly*, July–September 1953, p. 315 (central elections), and in *Australian Outlook*, March 1954, pp. 20–1 (local elections).

commission. The ballot paper contains the candidate's name, the name of the organisation nominating him and the fact that he is a party member if he is. Party membership, however, plays no part in the campaign; all candidates are placed before the electorate as 'the bloc of communists and partyless people', and in the lists of candidates as published in the press party membership is not indicated.

The fact that the ballot paper is valid without marking has an important consequence for the conduct of the election, for the voter's only reason for using the screened voting booths for which all polling stations are required to be provided is to vote against the candidate. Official propaganda has done nothing to discourage open voting, but has rather favoured it as an act of civic courage. The press frequently publishes accounts of irregularities in the conduct of elections, such as the failure to provide voting booths or the failure (in the case of a by-election upon the amalgamation of two village soviets) to give any notice to the electors before polling day, but failure to insist on voters' going through the forms of secret election is never mentioned, and there is no suggestion of improper influence on the selection of candidates. Where these things happen—and they evidently do—it is by design.

The absence of alternative candidates does not mean that the outcome is everywhere certain before polling takes place. At the local elections of 1939 and in all local elections since then a number of candidates have failed on the grounds that they had not secured the necessary absolute majority. Presumably this is due to the local occurrence of a very low poll, though some of the voters may have crossed the name out or else spoilt their ballot papers. In such a case the election is invalidated and has to be held again. But such cases are very few; there were only 125 in 1939 out of some 1,400,000 places at issue, and the proportion does not seem to have risen materially since. The same procedure is presumably followed for any subsequent election until a candidate does secure the necessary majority. In general, declared participation in elections is good beyond all belief. By 1937 it was already 96.8 per cent of the electorate, and in 1950 and 1954 it was 99.98 per cent. In 1957 the local election poll was equally good—reaching 100 per cent for regions and districts in Tadjikistan and 99.9 for all soviets in Georgia. Towns in Esthonia were well below standard with a 99.32 per cent poll. The proportion of those voting in 1954 who voted for the candidate was 99.79 per cent for the Soviet of the Union and 99.84 for that of the Nationalities. In 1957 it varied between 98.91 per cent (R.S.F.S.R. villages and settlements) and 99.96 (Turkmenian villages). It is therefore surprising that any candidates at all fail to get the votes required. Possibly such incidents are arranged to give the appearance of democracy, but they could be genuine; it is likely that there is some local variation and that a degree of secretiveness which would be unsafe in one place may be indulged in in another.

Elections can have other purposes than the selection of representatives. They can be used as an index of the control of the regime over its subjects, and the percentage of participation is still apparently taken seriously in the Soviet Union's communist neighbour states, where a low poll in a locality is presumptive evidence of the inefficiency of the local organisation. But with polls approaching as nearly to perfection as do those of the Soviet Union, even this function of elections is losing its point. The high proportion of voters participating is still regularly quoted but possibly mainly as a demonstration of solidarity aimed chiefly at the outside world. The provision of a special occasion for party workers and helpers to practise their skill as agitators is probably a more real consideration. In the 1950 local elections 3,750,000 people were said to have been engaged in the work of the electoral commissions in the R.S.F.S.R. alone, and several million more as agitators and in similar capacities in the constituencies. It was claimed that in the 1955 local elections fourteen to fifteen million people were employed as agitators.

Elections are also demonstrations. Conducted as they are in a holiday atmosphere of music and flags and portraits of the leaders, they are a stimulating experience. This is comprehensible in the circumstances of the Soviet peoples, with their lack of any extensive previous experience of elections and their habituation over a long period to other purely symbolical demonstrations, such as May Day celebrations and meetings in support of the various campaigns of the authorities on issues of national or international affairs. Also the approach of election day is used, as are May Day and the anniversary of the revolution and formerly Stalin's birthday, as an occasion for a production drive and the demand of an extra display of energy to complete other tasks.

The analyses of membership presented to the opening sessions of the soviets by their mandates commissions are the principal official indications of the nature of the product of this process. Membership of one or other of the officially recognised social classes, party membership or candidate status, age, sex, education and possession of honours or decorations, are the categories employed. Thus in the Supreme Soviet elected in 1954 63.1 per cent of the members of the Soviet of Nationalities and 57.3 per cent of those of the Soviet of the Union—or 60.1 per cent of the whole—were shown as belonging to the intelligentsia, the rest being divided between workers and peasants, with a slight advantage to the former. Party members and candidate-members formed 75.9 per cent (639 members) of the Soviet of Nationalities and 79.8 per cent

(708 members) of the Soviet of the Union—77.9 per cent of the whole. The proportion of members of the intelligentsia had risen sharply from one election to the next; the proportion of party members represented a decline from the level of previous post-war elections—81 per cent in 1946, 83.5 per cent in 1950—though their absolute number rose from 1950 to 1954 and even the proportion was still above the level of 1937 (76.1 per cent). Among the local soviets the social composition seems to vary considerably; the proportion of party membership declines steeply as one goes down the scale from the federation towards the village, and it also varies markedly from one republic to another. Thus in the 1947 election the proportion of party members in the local soviets in Armenia was stated to be 52.57 per cent, and in the newly acquired republics of Moldavia and Lithuania only 13.41 per cent and 11 per cent respectively.[1] In 1957, however, their proportions, while still among the lowest, had risen to 39.2 and 32.14 per cent respectively. Esthonia had 33.7. Armenia still had the highest proportion, with 59.6, followed by Kazahstan, with 49.99 per cent. The R.S.F.S.R. had 45.5.[2] But these official classifications are in some sense misleading. That by membership of the party is no doubt genuine, but not very important. By the rules of the party members are specifically charged to concert their actions on the basis of the party line, in soviets as in any other type of body. There is no body similarly able to act against them. The other members are non-party, not anti-party, and there is every reason to suppose that the party has had the decisive voice in their selection. The classification by social status is particularly unsatisfactory. Before the late 'thirties members of public bodies were apparently reluctant to classify themselves as belonging to the intelligentsia, and would if they could claim working class or peasant status, if only on the basis of a previous occupation which they had abandoned, or, it seems, often on the basis of family origin. Since the establishment of a new Soviet intelligentsia it has apparently been less usual to assume disguise in this respect, but there is still some evidence of a random element in the classification. Always a number of those classified as workers or peasants are found to be holding posts which by the authorities' own standards put them in the intelligentsia; it has been calculated that if occupation be taken as the standard of classification— and this produces a result more meaningful from the point of view of the

---

[1] John Hazard, *Law and Social Change in the U.S.S.R.* (1953), pp. 75-6; and same author, 'Political, Administrative and Judicial Structure in the U.S.S.R. Since the War', *The Annals of the American Academy of Political and Social Science*, May 1949, p. 10.

[2] *Pravda*, 8th, 9th, 15th, 16th March 1957.

non-Soviet observer—the figures for the 1954 Supreme Soviet are 83.3 per cent intelligentsia, 10.5 per cent workers and 6.2 per cent peasants.[1]

Another such analysis of the membership shows 554 persons employed in full-time state administration, as ministers, chairmen of soviet executive committees, etc., or full-time party office as secretaries or leading workers of party committees, or in similar positions in trade unions and the youth organisations, all of which form a single service with transferability of individuals. A further twenty-four members are employed in the machinery of coercion, police, procurators and ministers of justice, who form an almost completely separate service from the rest of the state apparatus. The armed forces had seventy-three members, all of them of high officer rank; 218 were employed in industry (ninety-eight of them as workers, forty-seven as foremen and brigade leaders, and the rest in higher capacities), 298 in agriculture (including sixty-three ordinary collective-farm members), and 201 in various forms of intellectual work, including teachers, artists and doctors. There were nine others of miscellaneous occupations.[2] Such classifications are necessarily arbitrary, since apart from the police and the soldiers, who keep very largely to their own specialities, there is a fairly high mobility of individuals between these classes. But they are of interest in that they tend to show that the general pattern of composition of the Supreme Soviet remains similar from one election to another. In 1950 the figures were: state-party administration 578, coercion 39, forces 43, industry 142, agriculture 214 and intellectuals 196; there were seventy-eight ordinary workers and seventeen collective-farm members. This is probably a result largely of deliberate composition, for in the individual memberships there is a rapid turnover. About two-thirds of those elected in 1950 had never served in the Supreme Soviet before, and only eighteen of the members of the Soviet of the Union and twenty-two of the members of the Soviet of Nationalities elected in 1946 had served in the previous one elected in 1937; the turnover in 1954 seems also to have been high, especially among the leading party workers. At the lower levels there seems to be a similar rapid turnover; the Supreme Soviet of Latvia, for example, elected in 1955, had 112 new members among its total membership of 200, and only four of the members elected in 1948 to the Leningrad regional soviet were re-elected to it in 1950. Of the thirty-five members elected to the village soviet of Suharevo (Moscow region) in 1953, eighteen were new, and

[1] Boris Meissner in *Osteuropa*, No. 3 of 1954, p. 216.
[2] N. Gradoboev, 'Sostav Verhovnogo Soveta SSSR 1954', *Vestnik Instituta po izucheniju istorii i kultury SSSR* (Munich), No. 4 of 1954, p. 59.

among the 1,500 elected to Moscow city soviet at the same elections there were 672 new members.

The Soviet constitution allows the electorate to recall its representatives in any directly elected body at any time. This right seems very rarely to have been exercised, but in late December 1956 one Latvian constituency was reported to have recalled its deputy to the republican Supreme Soviet for untrustworthiness and failure to carry out constituents' instructions.

What They Do

Article 46 of the constitution states that the Supreme Soviet of the U.S.S.R. is convened by its Praesidium[1] twice a year, and that in addition the Praesidium may call an extraordinary session at its own discretion or on the demand of one of the union republics. According to Article 41 sessions of the two Houses begin and end simultaneously. Except in the war years, when only a few brief extraordinary sessions were held, the Supreme Soviet seems to have kept, on average, though not literally, to the legal requirements, but the meetings are very short, seldom lasting longer than a fortnight in the year. Thus the fourth Supreme Soviet, elected in 1954, convened from the 20th to the 27th April of that year, from the 3rd to the 9th February, the 4th to the 5th August. and the 26th to the 29th December 1955, the 11th to the 16th July 1956, the 5th to the 9th February, the 7th to the 10th May, the 6th November and the 19th to the 21st December 1957. This is held a virtue in that 'One of the most important peculiarities of the Supreme Soviet of the U.S.S.R. . . . lies in the fact that it is a working institution, called not only to accept the laws but also to ensure their carrying into effect. This is the basis of the sessional order of its work. The Supreme Soviet of the U.S.S.R. does not, like bourgeois parliaments, sit almost without intermission, but is called for short sessions. Such a manner of operation permits the deputies, who after their election remain workers in the national economy, in science and culture, the state machinery and so on, not to be cut off from their basic work and to keep check in real life on the carrying out of the laws and actively to promote their realisation.'[2]

The frequency of meetings of Supreme Soviets of union republics and autonomous republics is prescribed in their own constitutions, but all agree on the same minimum of two sessions a year. The frequency of sessions of local soviets is also covered by the republican constitutions;

[1] See p. 111.
[2] M. P. Kareva and G. I. Fedjkin, *Osnovy Sovetskogo Gosudarstva i Prava* (1953), p. 223.

that of the R.S.F.S.R. prescribes four meetings a year for soviets of regions, territories and towns divided into districts, and six for all others. Until March 1957 a monthly meeting was required of town and village soviets. Other republics agreed except Kazakhstan which required only four meetings a year at district level and three at higher levels. A case for the reform in so far as it concerns the villages was made in 1954 in one of the more authoritative central organs: 'The necessity has developed to restrict the number of sessions held by village soviets in order to free the chairman for immediate organisational work in the villages. It is enough, in our opinion, if sessions of village soviets are held once in two months.'[1] In part, however, it was perhaps just a recognition of the futility of insistence on more meetings. Thus it was reported in 1956 that 'Not infrequently . . . sessions of Supreme Soviets, in spite of the demands of the constitution, are held only once a year',[2] and local soviets, at the higher levels in particular, made, apparently, an even worse showing. In 1955 the soviets of two of the six territories and four of the fifty-four regions in the R.S.F.S.R. had held no sessions at all, while all the towns of republican subordination in the same republic, 66.6 per cent of area soviets, 40.3 per cent of settlement soviets and 36.5 per cent of those of villages had fallen short of the requirements of the law. The constant complaints on the subject in the press do not give the other levels a better record. For example, it was reported in 1952 that in a number of districts in Voronezh region only four sessions had been held in the past year instead of six, and in at least two, only three; one district soviet had held only one session in the first four months of the year. A district soviet in Tjan-Shan region and one of its village soviets had met only once in nine months of 1953, and two more villages only twice.

All soviets and the two Houses of the federal Supreme Soviet verify their own mandates after the usual fashion of the elected bodies of continental Europe; that is to say, they would themselves hear disputes concerning the credentials of members if there were any. In fact such disputes do not occur. The first business on the agenda of the two Houses of a newly elected Supreme Soviet, meeting separately, is to appoint their mandates commissions of seventeen members each, which

[1] V. A. Nemtsev in *S.G.iP.*, No. 8 of 1954, p. 54. *S.G.iP.*, No. 3 of 1956, p. 8, agrees on the ground that only thus can village soviets reasonably give instructions to their executive committees—as to assert their authority over them they should—as to the subject on which they are to report at the next session, but, strangely, as late as 24th February 1957, and in *Pravda*, K. M. Ozolins, Chairman of the Praesidium of the Latvian Supreme Soviet, ridicules this argument.

[2] *S.G.iP.*, No. 3 of 1956, p. 6.

report back at a later stage of the proceedings, but while they do their work the rest of the Supreme Soviet's business is not suspended. Thus the Houses of the present Supreme Soviet appointed their mandates commissions at their first session on the 20th April 1954, and heard their reports on the 23rd, having in the meantime elected their other commissions, confirmed the Council of Ministers in office, and carried the budget through its first stages. The commission remains in being for the whole term of election of the House, and similarly reports on the credentials of any members elected in by-elections.

Each body of Supreme Soviet status has its own chairman and a number of deputy chairmen, who are elected by it at its first session before the adoption of agenda, and remain in office for its whole term of election unless released. Thus the federal Supreme Soviet has a chairman and four deputies for each House, the unicameral Supreme Soviet of the R.S.F.S.R. has a chairman and eight deputies, four republics prescribe four deputy chairmen, one three and the others two. When the two Houses of the federal Supreme Soviet meet in joint session, as they do for a large part of their business, the chairmen of the two Houses preside alternately. Between sessions the posts of the chairmen involve them in certain duties such as the signing of messages to foreign parliaments and perhaps some organisational work as well; they are not, however, full-time posts. Mr. V. T. Lacis (to March 1958) and Mr. Ja. V. Peive (since then) of the Soviet of Nationalities were also chairmen of the Council of Ministries of Latvia; Mr. P. P. Lobanov of the Soviet of the Union is chairman of the Academy of Agricultural Sciences. Mr. A. P. Volkov, who was chairman of the Soviet of the Union until July 1956, was at the same time chairman of the executive committee of Moscow regional soviet. He was released from his house chairmanship, however, on appointment to federal ministerial office, which suggests that the two are regarded as incompatible, though by the reforms of May 1957 Mr. Lacis was included in the federal Council of Ministers by virtue of his republican office. Local soviets elect a chairman from among their members for each meeting.

Also chosen by the Houses of a newly elected Supreme Soviet are the standing commissions. Those of each House of the present federal Supreme Soviet are: a commission on legislative bills of nineteen members, a budget commission of twenty-six and a commission on foreign affairs of eleven. At its session of February 1957 the Soviet of Nationalities, in the spirit of the current emphasis on decentralisation of management and the rights of the nationalities, formed an economic commission of a chairman—one of the secretaries of the Central Committee of the Ukrainian party—and thirty members—two from each union republic. The activities of the commissions are now more publicised than formerly. It seems that those on bills and the budget at least meet a few weeks before the Supreme Soviet—often in joint session of the commissions of the two Houses—and prepare their business largely in sub-committee having power to call officials. If they are effective bodies they must have done their work and concerted a policy before the Houses meet. When, after hearing the report of the Minister of Finance at a joint session, the two Houses withdraw into separate session to hear the co-reports from the chairmen of their budget commissions they are invariably presented with identical recommendations for increases over the Minister's figure of expenditure and—always a larger increase—revenue. The assignments of the former to the several republics and of the latter to particular taxes is always identical, though the exposition may vary.

The standing commissions of local soviets have, at least in origin, rather different functions. They are the heirs to the 'sections' or groups of soviet deputies and 'activists'—interested citizens from outside the membership—formed by the lowest-level soviets for their several classes of business. The sections were one of the many attempts in the Soviet system to create a fluid outer layer of public support, and vigilance, around the organs of authority. By 1936 they had 3,639,061 members. They had their own inner bodies—or 'bureaux'—of three to five, including the head of the appropriate administrative department, but as the section itself had no executive powers the bureau's function was vague. In the reforms on the making of the new constitution the sections came to be replaced by the standing commissions, which differ from them principally in being established in local soviets of all levels, and not merely the lowest, in having no inner bureau, though they have a chairman and secretary, and if large enough a vice-chairman, and in that the activists now have no vote. It is not clear how the activists are disadvantaged thereby, since the votes can apparently only pass resolutions for the soviet's executive committee to endorse, or not. The largest soviets (regions and cities) are recorded as having up to fifteen of these bodies, and every village soviet should have three to five of them. The most common types are for the budget, for agriculture and for various social services, such as education and health; they are also formed for the various classes of industry. They may inspect, or depute members or activists to do so, though their power to inspect enterprises subordinate to higher authorities than their own soviets, or to pay expenses of inspection, has been questioned. They may attach a co-report to the departmental report to the soviet. The executive committee should invite them when measures or other matters concerning them are under consideration. It seems that in practice the executive committee often invites only their chairmen, or even fails to consult them at all, and ignores any co-reports submitted. If in their inspections the commissions detect criminal fault they are to report it direct to the procurator. It is evident that apart from this sending of 'signals' to higher authority they are valued for their utility in keeping the public aware of official aims and running campaigns, such as road repairs by voluntary communal labour. It is in this sense that *Izvestia* can report[1] that 'millions of working people are recruited for the commissions' work'. There are about 2,000,000 regular activists.[2] Members of executive committees are not supposed to serve on standing commissions—though when the village soviets were smaller it was apparently common for them to do so—and in the biggest towns others in leading positions are exempt. All other soviet deputies are supposed to serve, though they are not apparently always eager.

The two chambers of the Supreme Soviet of the U.S.S.R. are required to vote in separate session upon all laws formally so designated, among them the budget which takes up a large share of the time. Other legislation is inconsiderable. For other business—largely appointments and the hearing of reports—the two Houses meet and vote together. Voting, as in all soviets, is by show of hands. A novelty at the sessions of February and May was the interpellation of the government by groups of deputies. This business, taken in joint sittings, produced assurances of official concern for cultural contacts abroad and the cessation of hydrogen-bomb tests. Until December 1958 the Great Hall of the Kremlin, used also for meetings of the R.S.F.S.R. Supreme Soviet, party congresses and the larger conferences was the sole meeting hall. When the two Houses were sitting separately one normally had the hall for the morning and the other for the afternoon, the allocation alternating from day to day. If a joint session had to be fitted in one of the Houses might have to meet in the early evening. Now one House can sit in the new Kremlin theatre. Meetings may be taken entirely in joint session, such as the second one of 1955 which was devoted entirely to the report of Mr. Bulganin on the conference of Heads of Governments in Geneva. By the constitution of the U.S.S.R. (Article 38) the two Houses of the Supreme Soviet are given equal powers to initiate legislation. Measures for the confirmation of edicts of the Praesidium, which apart from the budget form the greater part of the business, are introduced by the secretary of the Praesidium. Original legislation is generally introduced by a minister. Participation in debate is relatively poor, and the speeches never give any indication of difference of opinion.

[1] *Izvestia*, 3rd July 1953.   [2] Nemtsev, op. cit.

A representative selection of members from different parts of the Union declares support for the measure, and in the debate on the budget suggest reasons why more provision should be made for particular purposes of interest to their own republics or regions, but never any manner in which this increase might be provided for to the detriment of other areas. In the local soviets the theme seems to be rather the claims of allegedly neglected services within the excessive range for which officials there, as elsewhere in the system, are held responsible, or cases of inefficiency or malpractice by individuals. It is evident that there also debate is lacking and speeches far from spontaneous. The practice of having all speeches prepared and approved by the chairman of the executive committee in advance has been officially condemned, though in consequence of the attitude of some chairmen members often seem still find it safer. Advance notice to members to speak is approved.

Many important matters do not come before the Supreme Soviet for decision, notably the five-year (since 1958 seven-year) plan. However, measures to give effect to it do. The budget under the last five-year plan was passed before acceptance of the plan by the party congress.

According to Soviet official sources there are three categories of Supreme Soviet business: Laws (*zakon*), defined as 'Acts of Supreme Legislation'; Decrees (*postanovlenie*), defined as 'Acts of Supreme Administration'; and a third category described as 'Acts of Supreme Supervision'.[1] The second category consists of acts making or confirming appointments; the third of resolutions—which in practice are usually also called Decrees—for the approval of reports from organisations subordinate to the Supreme Soviet. The distinction between the first and second categories corresponds to the procedural distinction between business to be voted upon in joint session and that which can only be voted in separate session. The two Houses individually may make 'decrees', but only for such internal matters as the appointment of their own commissions. In addition, the Supreme Soviet may, and frequently does, pass resolutions giving expression to its views on foreign relations and similar matters.

The Supreme Soviet of 1954 at its session of that year passed five laws: one for the budget of that year, one for the transfer of the Crimean region from the R.S.F.S.R. to the Ukraine, one to confirm an edict of the Praesidium amending the law on military service, one confirming an edict of the Praesidium repealing one of 1947 which had forbidden marriages of Russians with foreign subjects, one making the usual amendments of the constitution. It made three decrees: one for the appointment of its own Praesidium and two in connection with the

[1] A. M. Vasiliev in *S.G. i P.*, No. 8 of 1953, p. 25.

re-appointment of the government. The second session, in 1955, again passed a budget law and a law changing the status of certain ministries and making the necessary amendments to the constitution. Three other laws were passed amending the penalty for certain offences and one to exempt government housing property from tax. Ten decrees were passed concerning the filling of posts in the Council of Ministers and the Supreme Court, including the release of Mr. Malenkov from the post of Chairman of the Council of Ministers, and one declaration on foreign policy. The third session passed only one decree, approving Mr. Bulganin's report on the Geneva Conference. The fourth session again passed a budget law and a law on the usual amendments to the constitution in respect of administrative areas and the composition of the Council of Ministers, and an additional law amending the constitution in respect of the composition of Councils of Ministers of the union republics. Other laws confirmed edicts of the Praesidium which had amended the law on the disposal of certain state property, reduced the competence of the people's courts, reduced the scope of the criminal law prohibiting abortions, and amended the regulations concerning the supervisory function of the procurators. It passed thirteen decrees concerning the appointment of ministers and members of the Supreme Court and approving the exchange of parliamentary delegations with other countries and the results of the travels of Mr. Bulganin and Mr. Khrushchov in India, Burma and Afghanistan.

The fifth session, of July 1956, was particularly active. It passed laws to make more generous the state pensions to employed persons on retirement and to approve the change of status of the Karelo-Finnish republic and its reception into the R.S.F.S.R. The other three items of original law-making were all constitutional amendments: one making the usual changes of areas and ministries, one making the changes necessitated by the Karelo-Finnish development and one rewording an article on citizens' rights to take account of the establishment of seven-year compulsory schooling throughout the Union and the abolition of school fees. Laws in confirmation of edicts of the Praesidium numbered seven: two on changes in the frontiers of the Kazah republic, four amending the conditions of labour, and one providing for the compulsory insurance of collective-farm animals. There was a declaration in support of a proposal of the Japanese parliament for the prohibition of nuclear weapons and the cessation of their testing, and an appeal to all parliaments of the world for disarmament. One original decree of the Supreme Soviet was passed validating until the next elections the position of the members of the Soviet of Nationalities for the former Karelo-Finnish republic, and there were five more decrees confirming edicts of the Praesidium on appointments to ministerial office. An original decree, issued unsigned—perhaps because purely declaratory—approved the policy and actions of the government on disarmament and nuclear weapons. The ministerial changes required each house to make two decrees to change its officers.

The sixth session, in February 1957, passed a brief, and unusual, law, approving the annual plan, the budget law and five other original laws: increasing union republics' powers in judicial matters, granting them power to form territories and regions, amending the federal powers on transport as defined in the constitution, approving the new instrument governing the Supreme Court (and amending the constitution on this) and abolishing transport courts. Seven laws confirmed Praesidium edicts: one extending the powers of regional courts and abolishing local organs of the Ministry of Justice, two on tax relaxations, two on points in labour law, one on labour disputes procedure, one rehabilitating certain dissolved autonomous units. Three original decrees on appointments were passed—two to change the secretary of the Praesidium and one to appoint the Supreme Court bench—and eight decrees confirming Praesidium edicts on appointments. One original decree approved the government's foreign policy. A decree of each House accepted formal mandates commission reports on by-election returns. The Soviet of Nationalities passed two more to set up its economic commission.

The seventh session, in May, passed two original laws: for the new economic-administrative structure and for the attendant constitutional changes. Two confirmatory laws concerned tax reliefs and revised regulations on military crimes. Four confirmatory decrees approved appointments. One original decree, stated to arise from an interpellation, endorsed government policy on the cessation of hydrogen-bomb tests. An address to the American and British legislatures on this topic was approved, and greetings to the Hungarian parliament. Each House passed decrees accepting by-election returns.

For the business of a local soviet we may take as an example the account given of the six meetings of a district soviet in Leningrad region during 1952.[1] At its first, on the 8th February, it heard a report on the work of the executive committee during 1951. At its second, on the 9th March, it heard two reports—one on the readiness of collective farms and machine-tractor stations for the spring sowing, and the second on the work of the soviet's standing finance and budget commission, presumably on the preparation of the budget, though reports suggest that in fact the standing commissions are not always kept very

[1] G. I. Petrov in *S.G. i P.*, No. 6 of 1953, p. 58.

well informed by the officials on this subject. At the third, on the 9th May, it heard a report on the fulfilment of the district budget for 1951, and confirmed the budget for 1952. At the fourth, on the 20th June, it discussed the progress of rural and collective-farm improvements in the district. At its fifth, on the 5th August, it discussed the carrying-out of the state plan for raising output from animal husbandry; and at its sixth, on the 28th November, it heard two reports: one on living conditions and medical facilities for the population and the other on the work of the executive committee's commercial department. This seems to be almost the model of a soviet's work; the only criticism made in the journal which reported it was directed against the excessive concentration of meetings in the first half-year. On the work of the lowest levels of the system it was reported in December 1947 that 'the questions discussed at sessions of local soviets are often narrow and monotonous. Take, for example, the sessions of village soviets. On their agenda there are usually only questions on the preparation and carrying out of the current agricultural campaigns. Meanwhile such matters as observing the collective-farm statute, the organisation of labour in the collective farm, the development of public stock-breeding, the work of institutions of culture and enlightenment and schools and co-operatives, and the proper upkeep of villages are only discussed in rare cases'.[1] Village soviets may perhaps have taken the advice to some extent, but such reports as we get of their more recent business does not suggest any fundamental improvement in the quality of their work. In town soviets, too, proceedings seem often to be tedious for the ordinary deputy, since the organisers attempt to crowd the business into too little time, and the period for discussion is fully occupied by 'a small group of deputies and numerous guests, the representatives of the authorities'.[2] It is complained that they are told of the business to be transacted only two or three days before the session, and that on the budget, in particular, they have a mass of figures hurled at them without previous preparation, so that 'nothing remains but to raise a hand quite mechanically'. The same complaint is made of the work of republican Supreme Soviets. In Kazakhstan, it was reported in 1956, it had been the practice to commission speeches long in advance. Deputies assigned the task wrote out their speeches and read them at the session. There and in other republics the work of the Supreme Soviet had the character of a 'parade'.[3]

Criticism of the administration has always been a purpose of the local soviets. The local leaders have to be kept up to the mark, men with ideas

[1] *Partijnaja Zhizn*, No. 12 of 1947, p. 8.
[2] Letters from deputies of Voronezh town soviet, *Izvestia*, 18th May 1956.
[3] *S.G. i P.*, No. 3 of 1956, p. 7.

for getting results advertised and restrictive local alliances split open. The soviet provides one of the means by which this may be done and through which higher levels can get matters aired and keep themselves informed. Attempts to suppress such criticism are frequently denounced in the press. Nevertheless in one form or another they are probably the rule rather than the exception. Leningrad region, for example, does not come up to the standard of its district quoted above; its executive committee, in common with those of Moscow—of which a present member of the Council of Ministers was latterly chairman—Khabarovsk, Krasnojarsk and Novgorod, had, according to a report of 1956, not reported to its soviet for nine years. Only two regional executive committees in the whole of the R.S.F.S.R. had done so in the last year, together with 23.3 per cent of the district executive committees (as against 48 per cent in 1954), 46.6 per cent of those of towns (as against 70.5 per cent) and 24.6 per cent of the districts within towns (as against 64.7 per cent). The performance lower down was presumably better, since the allover percentage was 67.5 (against 81.6).[1] Despite the approval of it in principle, to voice criticism is probably always a perilous activity, not to be undertaken without previous clearance from higher levels. Of the higher soviets, including probably all the Supreme Soviets, it can hardly be a real purpose; the leaders are too august, and their disgrace, if it comes, comes through other channels, unless authority wishes to reassure public discontent or teach some lesson.

Soviet deputies have some opportunity to make up for their passivity in the sessions by their intercession with the authorities on behalf of their constituents. A Supreme Soviet deputy reports that since election (that is, in some sixteen months) he had received about a thousand appeals for help, most of which could be settled locally or through the appropriate ministry.[2] But even local soviet members do not find it easy. 'Your constituents ask, let us say, for the lighting of a street or the opening of a food stall. You go to the town executive committee office, and there they announce that "There is no provision for it in the budget". Deputies must often blush and admit their impotence to carry out the commissions of their constituents.'[3] Moreover, there are no residence rules for Soviet political representatives. In the local soviets— around the larger towns at least—it seems not uncommon for the deputy to live outside the area of the soviet's authority altogether. Such limitations on local interest—which are not peculiar to the Soviet Union—

---

[1] *S.G. i P.*, No. 3 of 1956, p. 9.
[2] V. Kositski in *Izvestia*, 23rd July 1955.
[3] Letters from deputies of Voronezh town soviet, *Izvestia*, 18th May 1956. The citizens may have recourse to other lines of approach; see p. 241 below.

probably apply with even more force at the centre. The rigidities of plan and budget are probably more difficult to circumvent in Moscow than in the provinces, and it seems improbable that the generals and police chiefs and party functionaries, who make up a large part of the Supreme Soviet, have any deep roots in their constituencies. These factors, with the deputy's extreme impermanence, the infrequency of his residence in the capital on Supreme Soviet business, and the fact that votes are committed in advance and so not available for trading, make it almost certain that they do not have a postbag of American congressional proportions. They are men of influence in a country where influence counts—the high proportion of Georgians and Armenians who have held leading posts under the regime is probably consequent, directly or indirectly, upon the presence of Stalin, Beria, Mikojan and others of their compatriots at the centre of power—but it is in their permanent professional capacities rather than in their transient character of deputies that it can best be exercised.

The soviets are also briefing conferences for their members in their capacity, which official writings emphasise, as organisers of popular effort. Membership of a soviet is an honour, a mark of favour from the government which alone in the Soviet Union can confer prestige, and which grants it only on obligation of service in the furtherance of its own purposes. The deputies are the leaders and instructors of the activists, charged to explain thoroughly to them, personally as well as by their ritual actions in the sessions, the nature and importance of the decisions of the soviet, its executive committee and higher authority, and to guide them in such purposes as carrying into effect the latest ideas on the permanent problem of agriculture or local building work, by voluntary effort or otherwise. It is the practice for the soviets themselves to hold occasional meetings of their activists, and there has been some indication that confusion has developed in the minds of members and of the public as to the distinction between such meetings and the full sessions.

Service in the soviets is also regarded as a school of government, and this has been offered in explanation of the rapid turnover of members. It seems probable that this is largely humbug; at least in the Supreme Soviets the members are already too highly placed in the service of the system to benefit much from the distant view of government work which is there offered to them. The Supreme Soviet, however, is a highly artificial creation, and we cannot judge the whole system by it. It may be that there is some truth in the claim as applied to the lower levels. Service in a local soviet may offer experience of minor leadership in the local community which may lead to higher things, and the chance for the local leaders and promising new recruits to observe one another at work.

We do not have to seek for reasons why people attend the Supreme Soviet. Its membership comprises a selection of the most highly placed persons in the system. They probably find their activities there tedious, but they are no more likely to think them wrong than are the participants in the annual general meeting of a completely controlled subsidiary company—as is the Soviet State to the Communist Party—and they may well regard an occasional few days of boredom as a reasonable obligation of their station. For the more obscure minority the session is a chance to mix with the great, a chance to see and be seen; it is an outing with free transport to the capital, and at least as much excitement as attends party rallies and similar occasions in other countries. To the peasant there may be sufficient attractions of this sort even in service in a republican Supreme Soviet. In any case, the deputies have probably not much choice. Service in the Supreme Soviet or in a local soviet is an assigned duty like any other. To refuse it is to reject an important opportunity of securing a place in the establishment.

The Inner Bodies—How They are Formed

Since their earliest days the soviets have shown a persistent tendency to the formation of inner bodies, often at two or three removes from the directly elected bodies. These are commonly designated executive committees, praesidia and bureaux, usually in that order of remoteness from the elector. The last two take their names from the German and French terms respectively for the bench of chairman, vice-chairmen, secretaries and others appointed by deliberative bodies to direct their proceedings, though in fact in the Soviet system they do not perform these functions. Neither praesidium nor executive committee presides at Supreme or local soviet meetings—that is the function of the permanent or temporary chairman already mentioned.

The largest towns at least have more than one inner body. The terminology seems to be fluid; thus Moscow in 1937, when its soviet numbered over 2,000 members and its executive committee about seventy, had a praesidium of the executive committee of fifteen and a bureau of the praesidium of the executive committee of five. In the 1950s Moscow's executive committee was reduced to a chairman, a secretary, eight vice-chairmen and fifteen members; the first ten formed a praesidium (as also reported at Leningrad); in 1955, however, we hear that 'in the executive committees of the local soviets of toilers' deputies of Moscow and Leningrad, which are distinguished by the magnitude of their work, there have been established narrowly "collegial" organs, the bureau of the executive committee, consisting of the chairman of the executive committee, his vice-chairmen and the secretary. Without replacing the executive committee as a whole the bureau settles urgent questions.'[1] A decision of Moscow city executive committee of 24th March 1959 appointing its inner body of eight (chairman, two first vice-chairmen, four vice-chairmen and secretary) again called it a praesidium.

The inner body of a Supreme Soviet is designated praesidium, presumably because before 1936 the federal and republican representative bodies were themselves designated executive committees. It is chosen by the newly elected Supreme Soviet at its first meeting and holds office until a successor is appointed after the next general election. It consists of a chairman, a number of vice-chairmen, a secretary and members all selected by the Supreme Soviet entirely from among its own members and with obvious regard rather to representational considerations than to personal eminence. The chairman of the Praesidium of the federal Supreme Soviet in particular, in view of the functions of headship of state which, we have seen, fall more upon him than on his colleagues, must be selected with such considerations in mind. The office has been held successively by the revolution's show peasant who had the merit of having been also a worker, by a leader of the trade unions, and now by a soldier enjoying the widest popular respect and closely associated with the leaders ever since the revolution. The number of vice-chairmen increased to sixteen with the number of union republics, and was reduced to fifteen on re-election in March 1958 in consequence of the abolition of the Karelo-Finnish union republic. All are also chairmen of the praesidia of their republican Supreme Soviets. It is never suggested in Soviet sources that the one office is held *ex officio* in virtue of holding the other, and since election to the two offices rests with two different bodies it would probably be impossible to provide formally for this. But with party direction of all appointments this presents no difficulty in practice. There is a secretary of the Praesidium who counts as a member of it, and usually introduces its decrees to the Supreme Soviet for confirmation. He is a sufficiently powerful figure for it to be thought worth while at the death of Stalin to change the holder of the office and to transfer it to a secretary of the party Central Committee. The office of assistant secretary, to which the previous secretary, Mr. A. F. Gorkin, was demoted, was a new one as far as official mention reveals and of indefinite status; it was no longer listed in 1954. Mr. Gorkin, however, continued in public life, regained the secretaryship in September 1956, and went on in February 1957 to be chairman of the federal Supreme Court, being succeeded at the Praesidium by the second secretary of the Communist Party of Georgia. Besides

[1] V. D. Sorokin and Ju. E. Smelev in *S.G. i P.*, No. 6 of 1955, p. 11.

these officers, the Praesidium had until 1946 twenty-four members, a number then reduced to fifteen and increased to sixteen in 1958. These members always include a few of the leading figures in the party, in 1954–8 Mr. Khrushchov, the first secretary; Mr. Kirichenko, first secretary of the Ukraine Communist Party; and Mr. N. M. Shvernik—all members of the Praesidium of the federal party Central Committee. Mr. Shvernik, chairman of the Supreme Soviet Praesidium until Stalin's death, may have been elected to it in 1954 in virtue of his office at the time of chairman of the Central Council of Trade Unions, as was his predecessor in that office, rather than because of his party rank. Another member was Mr. P. K. Ponomarenko, then ambassador to Poland, and formerly first secretary of the Kazah republican Communist Party, and in that capacity a 'candidate' member of the Praesidium of the Central Committee. Other members were of lesser personal significance, some notably so, and they appear to have been selected primarily so as to represent sections and interests in the state. They included at the time of election six first secretaries of regional party organisations (Moscow, Leningrad, one in the R.S.F.S.R. and three autonomous republics), the Minister of Health of the Burjat-Mongol A.S.S.R. (also presumably representing the autonomous units, as well as the state, as distinct from the party), Marshal Budjonni as permanent representative of the army, a doctor and a professor of history. The last died in May 1957, but the vacancy was not immediately filled. The pattern does not vary much from one Supreme Soviet to another, although sometimes the youth and women's organisations have their representatives. Members are never appointed specifically in any of these capacities, but only as Supreme Soviet deputies.

In the union and autonomous republics the number of vice-chairmen and members differs. The R.S.F.S.R. has fourteen vice-chairmen, one for each of its autonomous republics; Georgia has two, who are specifically stated to represent its two autonomous republics; and Azerbaidjan one each for both its autonomous republic and its autonomous region. Uzbekistan, with only one autonomous republic, and Kazakhstan, with none, have three vice-chairmen. Other republics, without autonomous republics, have two. Members vary from fifteen in the Ukraine, Belorussia and the Kazah republic to five in Esthonia. The R.S.F.S.R. has thirteen. All autonomous republics have two vice-chairmen (except the North Ossetian, which has only one) and from seven to twelve members.

Below the republican level, and so the level of Supreme Soviets, the corresponding organs are designated executive committees. According to Article 99 of the federal constitution they consist of a chairman, vice-chairmen, a secretary and members. Usually they seem to have some seven to fifteen members in all. The constitution also provides in Article 100 that for the smallest of the village soviets no executive committee need be appointed; the executive and administrative functions of the soviet are there performed by a chairman, vice-chairman and secretary elected by the soviet. It is not clear how this differed from an executive committee except in the absence of the obligation to appoint members other than the three designated office holders; Soviet writers suggest that in many such cases these 'in reality form an unofficial executive committee of the soviet'[1] with all its powers, and declare incorrect the view that in such cases all business must be taken in full soviet. In some places, however, 'the absence of executive committees had a negative effect on organisation and mass work. Sometimes the collegiate principle of deciding questions was supplanted by personal direction from the chairman'.[2] The consolidation of the village soviets in recent years has consequently been accompanied by a campaign for the introduction of executive committees at village level. Whereas, the same source stated, 600 of the 882 village soviets in Tula region had formerly been without executive committees, all village soviets in the region had lately elected executive committees of two to four members apart from the three office holders. In some places where for geographical or other reasons the village soviets had not been consolidated there were still reported in August 1955 to be some without executive committees, but by May 1956 it could be stated categorically that 'As a result of the enlargement of village soviets there are no soviets left such as might not elect executive committees'.[3]

The chairman of the executive committee is appointed to office by the party committee at the immediately superior level (e.g. the region for a district chairmanship). He seems to be fairly free to choose, and dismiss, the other members, though he evidently needs the confirmation of the next higher authorities in both the party and the soviet executive committee hierarchies, which if he is in good standing should cause him no trouble. The vice-chairman and secretary, appointed by the party committee at the soviet's own level, are members, and the first secretary of the local party committee seems always to be included. For the rest of the members the chairman looks mainly to his departmental heads. The more important of these, who are most likely to be included in the executive committee, are also appointed to office by the corresponding party committee; the executive committee is left to fill the minor posts. Formally the election of the executive committee, including the designa-

[1] G. I. Petrov in *S.G. i P.*, No. 8 of 1955, p. 32.
[2] *Izvestia*, 29th July 1954.
[3] *S.G. i P.*, No. 3 of 1956, p. 8.

tion of its chairman, vice-chairman and secretary, requires a vote of the soviet, and the appointment to office of departmental heads requires that of the executive committee, with confirmation by the head of the corresponding branch of the next higher level (the minister for regional appointments). A recent detailed study finds no evidence of a soviet's ever objecting to the list of executive committee members proposed to it, though a departmental head failed to secure re-election,[1] and a case has been reported where the members of a new consolidated village soviet rejected the candidate proposed as chairman by the district executive committee chairman in preference to the chairman of one of the two merged soviets; the district chairman, who was allegedly motivated by personal spite, refused to allow the members to speak, and it does not seem that they were allowed to succeed on the vote.[2] So submissive are the soviets that it seems not to be uncommon for them to allow their executive offices to be given to persons not among their own membership, which is not only improbably generous but also plainly illegal. At the beginning of 1956, it seems, 534 persons were serving as chairmen of the executive committees of local soviets in the R.S.F.S.R. of which they had not been elected deputies, and a further 1,491 were similarly serving as vice-chairmen or secretaries. In 1954 1,411 of the 13,311 chairmen of executive committees in the Ukraine and 1,643 of the equal number of secretaries were not qualified for their office by membership of the soviets.[3] It is not clear why the party did not have them elected to the soviet; lack of time is a possible explanation in view of the accounts which we get of the frequency of transfer of such officials, as of other managerial personnel. Another factor may be indifference to forms such as is expressed in the apparently common failure to hold by-elections to fill vacancies in local soviets.[4]

The indications are, then, that the chairman's control over his colleagues is far-reaching. Certainly according to the principle of one-man headship it is he who must take the blame for whatever goes wrong; but again, according to the equally emphasised principle of collegiality, he will lay himself open to censure if he does not consult his colleagues in the executive committee on all matters except those of the greatest urgency. It is probable that, in general, the executive committee is an effective deliberative body, as the soviet which elects it is not. But it is not a parliament; it is a cabinet composed predominantly, though not

---

[1] T. H. R. Rigby, *The Selection of Leading Personnel in the Soviet State and Communist Party* (London University Ph.D. Thesis, 1954), pp. 388–9, 390. (Work quoted in further references as Rigby, Thesis.)
[2] *Izvestia*, 18th December 1954.
[3] *S.G. i P.*, No. 3 of 1956, p. 9. [4] Ibid., p. 5.

entirely, of departmental ministers engaged in full-time public service. They are not politicians but officials, of whom probably most look to make their way in the same branch of state service at higher levels; departure into such activities as the management of a collective farm may, however, diversify, and if successful probably materially advance any career, and full-time party office opens the way to the big prizes.

The union and republican praesidia were from the first deprived of departmental responsibilities by the creation of the Councils of People's Commissars, now the Councils of Ministers, and these latter are the true counterpart at these levels of the executive committees. Article 71 of the federal constitution and Russian legal writers refer to the federal Council of Ministers as the Government (*praviteljstvo*) of the U.S.S.R., though such analogies as this suggests with other systems are largely misleading. By Article 70 the Council of Ministers is composed of a chairman, an unspecified number of first vice-chairmen and vice-chairmen, ministers—of whom fifteen (1960) hold ministries designated as such in the constitution and others may by law of May 1957 be personally appointed from among the vice-chairmen and heads of department of the state planning committee—the fifteen chairmen of the councils of ministers of union republics, added by constitutional amendment of the same date, and eighteen agency heads not bearing the title of minister but similar in function. Appointment is by edict of the Praesidium, with later confirmation by the Supreme Soviet, or occasionally directly by decree of that body, if it happens to be sitting. In July 1960 there were two first vice-chairmen, four vice-chairmen and twelve personally nominated ministers. With two men doubling two posts this gives a Council of sixty-seven (fourteen presumably working outside Moscow) —too large for policy-making. Others may attend, with or without votes.[1]

Departmental ministries are highly impermanent and their ministers of small personal standing. Most seem to be career specialists, changing their designations from time to time, but not straying far from the range of business in which they have made their careers. The late Mr. I. A. Lihachov, for twenty-four years director of the country's largest motor vehicle factory before becoming in 1953 federal Minister of Motor Transport and Highways, removed to the similarly named

[1] M. A. Gurvich (*Sovetskoe Finansovoe Pravo* (1954), p. 155), mentions that at the discussion of the budget in the Council of Ministers 'leaders of ministries, central institutions and authorities of the Union and representatives of the union republics can report on their differences with the Ministry of Finance of the U.S.S.R. . . .' An edict of the 31st August 1956 conferred a decoration on Mr. Ju. I. Dudin, 'permanent representative of the Council of Ministers of the Ukrainian S.S.R. attached to the Council of Ministers of the U.S.S.R.'.

post in the government of the R.S.F.S.R. on the abolition of the federal ministry in May 1957. Mr. S. A. Shashkov, Minister of the River Fleet, did likewise at the same time, and Mr. N. K. Baibakov and Mr. I. A. Benediktov, victims of amalgamation in planning and agriculture, respectively, followed a year later. The last had filled leading posts in his speciality for twenty or more years—with a very brief excursion as ambassador to India. Mr. A. S. Pavlenko, Minister of Power Stations—an all-union ministry offering no such republican retreats—became first deputy minister when Mr. Malenkov moved in from the chairmanship of the Council of Ministers, and resumed the ministerial chair when he left for Kazahstan in July 1957. The late Mr. I. I. Nosenko, who made his career, crowned with ministerial office, in Shipbuilding, made two extensions into wider fields as Minister of Transport Machine Building and of Transport and Heavy Machine Building during periods of ministerial amalgamation. Mr. N. S. Ryzhov moved round a narrow circle of ministries—textiles, consumer goods and (twice) light industry—before being sent as ambassador to Turkey in February 1957. There have been some who were more versatile, particularly those of the revolutionary generation or with considerable experience as party officials, and so particularly the most eminent. The late Mr. A. P. Zavenjagin diversified a career in ferrous metallurgy with a period in Internal Affairs, though apparently mainly on its industrial side, and ended with responsibility for atomic energy as Minister of Medium Machine Building. Mr. L. M. Kaganovich, disgraced in June–July 1957, held ministerial office in transport—which was thought to be his speciality—heavy industry, the fuel industry, foreign trade and the building materials industry. Mr. L. G. Meljnikov, having been dismissed from the first secretaryship of the Ukrainian party, was briefly ambassador to Rumania before becoming Minister for the Coal Industry—a post abolished in May 1957. Mr. N. A. Mihailov, formerly head of the youth organisation and then ambassador to Poland, became Minister of Culture, and Mr. P. K. Ponomarenko, a former holder of that office, replaced him in Warsaw, having been a republican party secretary in between. The Ministry of Foreign Affairs has been exceptional in requiring an intimate of the leaders rather than a technical specialist, though with the appointment of Mr. A. A. Gromyko in February 1957, it has come nearer to the general pattern. Since 1953 the leading figures have not usually taken ministries but, if they appeared in the Council of Ministers at all, served without departmental responsibility as first vice-chairmen and vice-chairmen. The obvious distinction between their status and that of their normally more transient administrative colleagues adds to the improbability that much deliberation on policy takes place in the full Council of Ministers.

Of the members of the Council of Ministers who are not called by the ministerial title one is the chairman of the management board of the State Bank, which in April 1954 was separated from the Ministry of Finance. Another, added in May 1957, as part of the drive for greater business efficiency, is the head of the Central Statistical Administration. The others are all chairmen of committees, and have in general been rather more considerable figures than the ministers. Two are vice-chairmen of the Council of Ministers: Mr. V. N. Novikov, chairman of the State Planning Committee of the Council of Ministers, and Mr. A. F. Zasjadko, chairman of the State Scientific-Economic Council of the Council of Ministers. Mr. Novikov's predecessors since the May 1957 reform—which made them chief co-ordinators of economic management—have been a first vice-chairman (Mr. Kuzjmin, 1957-9) and a vice-chairman (Mr. Kosygin, 1959-60). Mr. Kaganovich, Mr. M. G. Pervuhin and Mr. M. Z. Saburov had at times combined committee chairmanship with first vice-chairmanship of the Council, which they lost early in July 1957, and the late Mr. V. A. Malyshev and Mr. V. A. Kucherenko similarly combined it with vice-chairmanship. The last is apparently still chairman of the State Committee of the Council of Ministers on Building Questions, but lost his vice-chairmanship of the Council in a reorganisation in December 1956.

Other State Committees of the Council of Ministers are (in July 1960): on Grain Products, on Aviation Technology, on Automation and Machine-Building, on Radio and Electronics, on Professional and Technical Education, on External Economic Relations, on Defence Technology, on Shipbuilding, on Chemistry, on the Use of Atomic Energy, on Labour and Pay Questions, and on Cultural Relations with Foreign Countries, as well as the State Scientific-Technical Committee, the Committee of Soviet Control and the Committee on State Security attached to the Council of Ministers. Apart from the last two, these seem to be rather planning and research than management bodies like the old industrial ministries, though the chairmen of the first four were formerly ministers of ministries of closely similar names, and the rest seem to have risen by practical work in relevant sections of the economy. One vice-chairman (of the State Scientific-Economic Council) was created minister in June 1960 (without specific legal authority). Others rank with deputy ministers, and are appointed by the Council of Ministers itself. Committee members seem to rank with heads of departments.

In the rush of joint decisions of the party Central Committee, Council of Ministers and Praesidium of the Supreme Soviet upon Stalin's death there was one 'to recognise the necessity of having within the Council of Ministers, in place of two organs, the Praesidium and the bureau of the Praesidium, one organ, the Praesidium of the Council of Ministers of the U.S.S.R.'.[1] There had been both an inner cabinet and an inner-inner cabinet, both undisclosed; only the former was to remain. The membership of this was defined as consisting of the chairman of the Council of Ministers and the first vice-chairmen. At the time Mr. Malenkov filled the former office and there were four of the latter—the late Mr. L. P. Beria, Mr. Molotov, Mr. N. A. Bulganin and Mr. Kaganovich. There were then no vice-chairmen not designated as 'first', though when the Supreme Soviet met a few days later Mr. Mikojan was so appointed, presumably without membership of this Praesidium. Mr. Malenkov was a vice-chairman from February 1955 to July 1957. Mr. N. A. Bulganin was appointed chairman on the 8th February 1955 and removed on the 27th March 1958 (both by decree of the Supreme Soviet) in favour of Mr. N. S. Khrushchov, who added the post to his cares as first secretary of the party. The first vice-chairmen are Mr. Mikojan, appointed by edict of the Praesidium of the Supreme Soviet of the 28th February 1955 (with Mr. Pervuhin and Mr. Saburov) and Mr. Kosygin, appointed vice-chairmen in December 1954 (also with Mr. Pervuhin and Mr. Saburov), relieved in December 1956 on transfer to the new contrivance for current economic co-ordination, the State Economic Commission of the Council of Ministers (abolished five months later on establishment of the present system), and re-appointed on the 6th July 1957 when the death of one vice-chairman and the dismissal of the other had left the category extinct; he was promoted in May 1960 (all by edict). These three survivors should constitute the Praesidium of the Council of Ministers, if for practical purposes it still exists. The vice-chairmen are Mr. D. F. Ustinov, former Minister of Defence Industry, appointed to his present post in December 1957 on abolition of the ministry, Mr. A. F. Zasjadko, appointed in April 1958, Mr. N. G. Ignatov, member of the leading body (Praesidium) of the party, and Mr. Novikov, both appointed in May 1960.

The members of the federal government are not invariably members of the Supreme Soviet. Thirty of the ministers and five other Council members in 1954 were not members of the present Houses, elected in that year. The representation was much the same in the 1946 Supreme Soviet, worse in 1937 and much worse in 1950. It does not

[1] Published 7th March 1953 in *Pravda* and elsewhere.

matter much. As is the practice in other countries of continental Europe, ministers who are not members are allowed to speak in either House in connection, though not always very close connection, with legislation or aspects of the budget concerning their ministries. Thus at the session of December 1955 the Ministers for the Oil Industry and for Higher Education, neither of whom was a member, reported generally on the activities of their ministries in the budget discussion in the Soviet of the Union and the Soviet of Nationalities respectively. Since before the 1957 sessions the power under Article 71 of the constitution to put questions to ministers or to the government as a whole for oral or written answer was not exercised, general ministerial attendance was unnecessary. The one contrived interpellation at each of the two sessions of February and May 1957 suggests no change of substance. Nor, since the Supreme Soviet has no part in the making or breaking of ministers, is it necessary that members should have a close acquaintance with them. Ministers of the U.S.S.R. are officials rather than politicians, as also are local executive committee members.

Governments of union republics and autonomous republics are similarly composed. In May 1957 the R.S.F.S.R. provided for three boards with chairmen in the Council: the State Planning Commission, the Committee of State Security and the State Scientific-Technical Committee.[1] Power is taken to confer the status of minister not only on vice-chairmen and heads of department of the planning commission, but also on chairmen of councils of the economy. As in the R.S.F.S.R. there are sixty-eight of these the potential size of the Council is considerable.[2] Presumably the chairmen of the republican councils of the economy set up in July 1960 in republics with more than one local council have also become members.

A republican council of ministers seems to have its inner body—though perhaps called 'bureau' rather than 'praesidium' (as, e.g., in *Izvestia* of 18th November 1955 on Tadjikistan)—probably of the chairman and all his deputies—some four or more persons.

What They Do

Apart from the acts of their several members, Councils of Ministers at all levels are, like the Tsars' Committee of Ministers, empowered to issue decrees (*postanovlenie*) and dispositions (*rasporjazhenie*) in their

[1] *Izvestia*, 30th May 1957. The federal constitution, as revised shortly before, provided, instead of the last of these bodies, for a committee on building and architecture in union republics. The R.S.F.S.R., however, which had one, abolished it.

[2] Previously the usual membership had been about thirty. See, e.g., particulars for the Central Asian republics given by B. Hayit, *Osteuropa*, No. 2 of 1956.

corporate capacities. The former category, issued over the signatures of the chairman and the head of the office, 'are, as a rule, normative acts'[1] —though they seem to include at least the more important official appointments—the latter, signed by a vice-chairman, deal apparently with particular cases. In principle such measures can only be in amplification of a law (*zakon*), but in fact the laws are few and vague, and, as we have suggested, the Council of Ministers is the principal source of Soviet legislation. Soviet writers insist on the inferiority of such acts in standing to laws, but 'The decrees and dispositions of the Council of Ministers are not subject to oversight in respect of their legality by any organs except superior organs of state authority. Acts of the government are obligatory for unconditional application by all, including the courts'.[2] Only the Supreme Soviet and its Praesidium can disallow, so that in practice such acts are equal in authority to laws. The Council is also responsible for approving the instruments (*polozhenie*) defining the organisations of the several ministries and for giving them general directions. Thus we find the Latvian Council of Ministers in June 1953 directing the Ministry of Housing and Civil Building to undertake important constructional work in one of the districts, and subsequently being called to account for failing to insist on progress reports from it. Councils are empowered[3] to disallow orders and instructions of the several ministers. The Praesidium of the Council of Ministers has not legislated in its own name; it has been concerned with policy, much as are cabinets in other political systems.

The legislation made by means of the Praesidium of the Supreme Soviet is less in volume than that of the Council of Ministers, but it is substantial, and much of it is important. Not all its measures need confirmation by the Supreme Soviet, only its appointments of ministers and 'those decrees which the Praesidium of the Supreme Soviet of the U.S.S.R. has made in the interval between sessions in the process of partial fulfilment of the obligations of the Supreme Soviet of the U.S.S.R.'.[4] Such decrees may extend to the creation of new criminal offences, important changes in civil law and the establishment or abolition of government departments. Interpretation of laws, which the constitution leaves to the Praesidium, is a negligible part of its work. The granting of honours and awards and the movement of diplomatic staff form a large part of its published acts. Its ministerial appointments

---

[1] Ts. A. Jampolskaja, *Organy sovetskogo gosudarstvennogo upravlenija v sovremenny period* (1954), p. 169.
[2] V. F. Kotok in Askerov et al., op. cit., pp. 295–6.
[3] Article 69 of the federal constitution.
[4] A. M. Vasiliev in *S.G. i P.*, No. 8 of 1953.

are made declaredly on the proposal of the chairman of the Council of Ministers, and it is likely that the proposals for its other acts come to it from the same quarter.

We have what purport to be accounts of proceedings at meetings of the federal Council of Ministers, and presumably such bodies do sometimes meet in full session to settle inter-departmental problems in relation to legislation and otherwise, though perhaps not very often. It is less certain that the Praesidium of the federal Supreme Soviet ever meets. Its functions and its members, we have seen, are not departmental, and the requirements that for representative purposes its members should be selected from posts geographically widely dispersed itself unfits it for regular work as a deliberative body. Its decrees are signed only by the chairman and the secretary; the only recent exception to this was the conferment of a decoration upon the chairman himself, which was signed by a vice-chairman in his place. In the smaller republics the institution may perhaps work to better effect. The Armenian praesidium is said to be holding regular sessions and hearing reports, from the chairman of the Council of Ministers among others, on the carrying out of suggestions made by members of the Supreme Soviet, and to have attached to it an organisational department, with instructors, for the improvement of administrative methods in the republic at large. Even the Praesidium of the Council of Ministers, which looks like an effective cabinet, has not been a negotiation of diverse political forces, despite the presence of conflicts of personality. It was a co-optive team, and largely a form of action for persons with a real standing derived from their position and connections in the highest organs of the party. It is difficult and not very meaningful to determine whether at any given moment they were acting in their party or their state capacity.

These inner bodies play a constitutionally declared part in the Soviet system of multiple supervision. Under Article 69 of the federal constitution the Council of Ministers has the power to suspend decisions and orders of the Councils of Ministers of the union republics 'in respect of those branches of administration and economy which come within the jurisdiction of the U.S.S.R.', which in practice means any in which it is disposed to interest itself. Thereafter action would presumably be taken under Article 49, by which the Praesidium of the Supreme Soviet may annul decisions and orders of both the federal and the union republican Councils of Ministers if they do not conform to law. No details of any such cases of disallowance have been published; if there have been any they can only have been disallowances of republican, not of federal, measures. The Praesidium of the Supreme Soviet is obviously a weaker body than the Praesidium of the Council of Ministers, and probably than the Council of Ministers as a whole in respect of the importance of its members. Below, the government of a union republic, it seems, has as one of its major tasks systematic consideration of reports from the corresponding organs at the next lower level, Councils of Ministers of autonomous republics and executive committees of territories or regions—or districts if the republic is not divided into regions—on their work, usually accompanied by 'co-reports of persons who upon the instructions of the Council of Ministers have previously examined the activity of the executive committee concerned'.[1] The same happens at these lower levels. The republican Council of Ministers may disallow acts of a ministry, or council of the economy of an economic administrative district, or local executive committee. It may suspend those of a local soviet.

The work of local soviet executive committees is complex, and of the same markedly economic bias as is found in the higher levels. Russian writings deny the existence in the Soviet Union of any distinction between central and local government. The executive committee is the agent of the soviet at its own level and of the whole system of the state and is accountable to the latter, through the executive committee at the next higher level, as well as to the former. A district executive committee in Leningrad region was stated to have on its work plan for the fourth quarter of 1952 thirty-one items, of which seventeen were economic and financial, ten cultural and four organisational. The first category included the state of completion of field work in two collective farms, the readiness of collective farms generally for the winter maintenance of cattle, the fulfilment of the district budgets for the first nine months of the year and the results of the fulfilment of the plan for the development of the economy in the same period. By 'organisational' were meant matters such as the distribution of personnel, organisation of a check on the performance of decisions taken, and organisation of work with, and by, the masses. District soviets generally were taken to task for their lack of attention to cultural and organisational matters, and to complaints and reports from the working people.[2] In a later article by the same author the regional executive committee of the Leningrad region was criticised for issuing instructions on the repair of tractors and agricultural machinery in identical terms to all machine-tractor stations without examining the special circumstances of each.[3]

Another class of business mentioned as belonging to the soviets is the carrying out of the military call-up and the maintenance of records of

---

[1] Jampolskaja, op. cit., p. 208.
[2] G. I. Petrov in *S.G. i P.*, No. 6 of 1953, p. 60.
[3] *S.G. i P.*, No. 8 of 1953, p. 23.

defence obligations in respect of liability to provide horses and transport, as well as the certification and administration of the privileges and benefits belonging to the dependants of service men.

In the town the character of the work has been somewhat different, with most of industry under the direct control of higher levels, leaving, unlike agriculture, little scope for local intervention. Already in 1931 there were noted 'views that there is nothing for the town soviets to do, since all the most important measures pass them by'. They were reminded that there was scope for them in public works and the organisation of the food supply, and that 'the restaurant is a workshop of the factory'.[1] To the present day it is probably true to say that the activity of the town soviet and executive committee is probably nearer to that of West European local authorities than that of other soviets and executive committees, though the difference is one of degree only; economic affairs still remain prominent, at least in the form of a concern for the supply and marketing of consumer goods, and even social affairs are wider in scope than in other countries by reason of the very limited field left in the Soviet Union to private initiative of any sort. There we find executive committees heavily burdened with business on such matters as housing, the recognition of entitlement to accommodation and to various forms of social-service benefits, adoption orders and transfer of personal property. It has been complained that under present legislation they are obliged to waste time considering claims to benefit which on the basis of the facts as determined and reported to them by their officials they are not empowered to reject.

Executive committees are required to agitate with the appropriate ministry concerning any neglect of local interest, and slackness on the part of the ministry is not an excuse which will save them from denunciation in the press if nothing is done. As with higher soviet organs they issue formal acts of two classes: 'decisions' (*reshenie*) issued on the basis of collective deliberation, and 'dispositions' (*rasporjazhenie*) issued by individuals—at present, it seems, only the chairman, though it has recently been suggested that this should be extended to his deputies for the departments entrusted to them—though in the name of the executive committee as a whole. In 1953 the Leningrad town soviet gave 3,100 decisions and 1,736 dispositions; in 1954 the figures were down to 2,025 and 1,458 respectively as a result of one of the periodic offensives against bureaucracy. As in any other administrative system, there must be much business done in the name of the executive committee which it does not need to discuss, and, as we have suggested of village

[1] Leading article in *S.G. i R.P.*, No. 1 of 1931, p. 3.

soviets,[1] this routine office work may well be seen by the authorities as the main practical justification for the soviets and their inner bodies. In eight months of 1954 the town executive committee of Millerovo (Kamensk region, R.S.F.S.R.) issued to citizens 6,000 certificates of various kinds and certified 4,000 entitlement books for state assistance, more than 3,000 forms for obtaining internal passports[2] and 3,000 fuel books for railway personnel. It was suggested (by the secretary) that the number of such documents could be reduced by a half or two-thirds.[3]

District and town executive committees generally, it seems, meet two or three times a month, and those of villages somewhat less frequently. This is held to be sufficient for matters requiring collective consideration and, Soviet writers say, the distraction of a large number of meetings is detrimental to the day-to-day guiding work of the executive committee. Much of the detailed business, it is suggested, might be transacted out of the session by the chairman, secretary and others directly concerned, though this might require minor amendment of the law. Cases of meetings being held up to eight times a month are reported, and some are inordinately long. *Izvestia* reported in 1950 a meeting of Voronezh regional executive committee, which took twelve hours and covered seventy-five questions. The executive committees meet in private and do not publish minutes, but there are indications in the form of criticisms in the press to suggest that debate, though freer than in the soviet, is not free or always effective. In the usual fashion of soviet administration the chairman is liable to rebuke from higher quarters if he does not give due attention to his colleagues, but is held personally responsible, at peril of his own career, if plans are not fulfilled in good measure and time. The executive committee as a whole is often rebuked for failure to engage the members of the soviet or standing commissions in the conduct of its work; it 'severs itself from the masses and works in a rut'.[4]

The supervision exercised over an executive committee is not intended to be dependent solely on the zeal of its immediate superior. If the latter does not take action it is the duty of its own superior to do so. Regional executive committees are commended in the press for supervising carefully the direction of villages by districts.

---

[1] See p. 78.
[2] See p. 194.
[3] *Izvestia*, 6th October 1954.
[4] *Partijnaja Zhizn* (No. 12 of 1947) complains that many members of executive committees consider that only the instruction department is concerned to see that all soviet deputies are involved in the work of the soviet, whereas it should be the concern of all.

Yet, in general, supervision remains inadequate. An *Izvestia* article of September 1955 complained that this had meant that the procurator's office had had to enter objections against 161 decisions and dispositions of local soviet executive committees in 1954 and 124 in 1955. The regional and territorial executive committees, it was complained, rarely took the trouble to check up on what their counterparts at district and village level were doing. Some higher executive committees merely added to the burdens upon their subordinates by insisting that the latter discuss at their meetings the higher level's latest decisions.[1] This is perhaps a residue of recent illiteracy, where the written word does not mean much unless read out and illustrated.

The praesidia and executive committees provide means by which the strictly managerial quality of the Russian political system may be reconciled with the myth of the supremacy of the soviets which is fundamental to the ideology. They are at best no more dependent on election than are most boards of directors in the British economy, and are selected for much the same tasks on the basis of much the same qualities, but it is in the name of the elected bodies that they act. This is exemplified in the gazette of Acts of the Supreme Soviet, which is filled almost entirely with decisions of its Praesidium. The myth is less strictly kept up at the local level, where the whole staff and organisation are ascribed to the executive committee and not to the soviet. Russian sources speak in general terms of the soviet structure, meaning the state as distinct from the party chain of command, but they always refer to the departments, or the officials, of the regional executive committee, rather than to the regional soviet.

An act of a council of the economy is called *reshenie* or *rasporjazhenie*, as is that of a local soviet or its executive committee, and presumably with the same distinction between the two. It is admitted by Soviet writers that these bodies are under single, not dual, subordination, that they are 'organs of the centre in the localities' which 'cannot be fully subordinate to the local organs of authority'.[2] They are in fact provincially located ministries and several have former federal ministers as their chairmen.

[1] G. I. Petrov in *S.G. i P.*, No. 8 of 1955, p. 25. The same writer (in *S.G. i P.*, No. 6 of 1953, p. 62) stated that executive committees of district soviets rightly 'give guiding instructions' on the preparation and conduct of village-soviet sessions, 'but they must not themselves plan the conduct of the sessions', since this is constitutionally a responsibility of the village chairman. Such fine distinctions between educative guidance and manipulation must make life very difficult for the soviet official.

[2] V. F. Kotok, A. V. Luzhin and M. I. Piskotin in *S.G. i P.*, No. 5 of 1957, p. 16.

The Ministries and Departments

The Supreme Soviet meeting of May 1957 brought the number of federal ministries down to twenty-five, as in the brief experiment on Stalin's death, and with one fewer in the All-Union category:

All-Union[1]:
  Aviation Industry
  External Trade
  Maritime Fleet (i.e. merchant shipping)
  Defence Industry
  Ways of Communication (which runs the railways)
  Radio Engineering Industry
  Medium Machine Building
  Shipbuilding Industry
  Transport Construction
  Chemical Industry
  Power Stations

Union-Republican[2]
  Internal Affairs
  Higher Education
  Geology and Maintenance of Mineral Resources
  State Control
  Health Protection
  Foreign Affairs
  Culture (concerned with forms of intellectual influence other than formal education)
  Defence
  Communications
  Agriculture
  State Farms[3]
  Commerce
  Finance
  Grain Products

This represented already a considerable departure from the established practice in which the Council of Ministers was a meeting of the chief directors of the several industries. The previous list, passed by the Supreme Soviet in July 1956, included additionally:

[1] Article 77 of the constitution (in the Russian alphabetical order).
[2] Article 78.
[3] This translation is accepted as being conventional. The literal translation is 'soviet farms'.

All-Union:
  Automobile Industry
  Machine Building
  General Machine Building
  Instrument(*Pribor*)-making and Automation Devices
  Machine Tool and Appliance (*Instrument*) Industry
  Constructional and Road Machine Building
  Building of Enterprises for the Oil Industry
  Building of Power Stations
  Tractor and Agricultural Machine Building
  Transport Machine Building
  Heavy Machine Building
  Electrical Engineering Industry

Union-Republican:
  Paper and Wood Products Industry
  Urban and Rural Building
  Light Industry
  Lumber Industry
  Oil Industry
  Industry of Meat and Dairy Products
  Food Products Industry
  Constructional Materials Industry
  Fish Industry
  Building
  Building of Enterprises for the Metallurgical and Chemical Industries
  Building of Enterprises for the Coal Industry
  Coal Industry
  Non-ferrous Metallurgy
  Ferrous Metallurgy

Within three weeks there were changes in the new list. In three years Aviation Industry, Defence Industry, Radio Engineering Industry, Shipbuilding Industry, Chemical Industry, State Control, Commerce and Grain Products had gone, yielding their functions to lower administrative levels, to the State Planning Committee, or to state committees of the Council of Ministers. Power Stations had become Building of Power Stations, Higher Education had inserted 'and Middle Technical' into its title, and State Farms had merged in Agriculture.

The all-union list had been reduced even before 1956, and in May

1956 the all-union Ministry of the River Fleet and the union-republican Ministries of Motor Transport and Highways and of Justice were abolished at federal level. The last two left behind vestigial agencies, the Chief Administration for the Building of Motor Roads and the Juridical Commission (for legal drafting and codification), both attached directly to the Council of Ministers.[1] There were already a number of such agencies differing from ministries in having no individual representative in the Council.[2] The Central Statistical Administration arose from among them to full Council of Ministers status in May 1957, and the State Committee on Cultural Relations with Foreign Countries and the Chief Administration on the Use of Atomic Energy in May 1960.

The ministries at the level of the union republics also fall into two categories: the union-republican and the republican. The former, by an inconvenience of terminology which exists in Russian as well as in English, means, as we have seen, not a ministry existing at the level of a union republic, but one which exists both at that level and at federal level. The republican ministries are those which have no direct superior at federal level. Since ministries may be, and have been, created in the union-republican list, or transferred to it from the all-union list, upon the creation of a branch in a single union republic, not all the ministries on that list at federal level are to be found in any given union republic. The R.S.F.S.R., which may be taken as reasonably representative, has, according to Article 54 of its constitution as amended in May 1957, all the union-republican ministries on the federal list except those for Higher Education, Geology and the Maintenance of Mineral Resources, and State Farms. On the last it anticipated federal abolition by one day. The other two seem still to be peculiar to the Ukraine and the Kazah republic respectively, for the sake of which they were transferred to the union-republican list in 1955 and 1956. The republican ministries, although at the discretion of the republics, have never differed much from one to another. In the R.S.F.S.R. they now are:

Motor Transport and Highways
Paper and Wood Products Industry
Municipal Economy (local public works)
Lumber Industry
Popular Instruction (basic education)
River Fleet

[1] The edicts abolishing the ministries also declared the intention of establishing these independent agencies.
[2] On the Central Statistical Administration see p. 118. An extensive list of such agencies, past and present, is given in Boris Meissner, 'Die gesetzgeberische Tätigkeit des obersten Sowjets . . .', *Europa Archiv* (1953), pp. 5698–5701.

Social Security
Building
Justice.[1]

The second and fourth in this list had previously been union-republican; the Ministry of Building was a new creation in May 1957, although the republic had previously had one for Urban and Rural Building. This and six other union-republican ministries were dissolved at the same time, as were republican ministries for water economy, local industry and fuel industry.

It is debatable, but unimportant, whether the councils for the economy are ministries of this type, since their chairmen, if designated ministers, will have no direct superior as such, or whether they are union-republican, as coming under the republic's State Planning Commission—as it is stated that industries which have no ministries of their own will do—and so under the federal State Planning Committee. In any case they, and all ministries of either type, will continue to form part of a Union-wide system.

The ministries of autonomous republics are not similarly divided into categories; all have been subordinate to some ministry at the level of the union republic, which might itself be either republican or union-republican in structure. Thus the constitution of the R.S.F.S.R. as revised at the meeting of the Supreme Soviet of that republic in January 1956 and not subsequently amended, provided for the following ministries in all autonomous republics within the R.S.F.S.R.:

Internal Affairs
Health Protection
Municipal Economy
Culture
Local Industry
Food Products Industry
Elementary Education
Agriculture
Social Security
Commerce
Finance
Justice.[2]

In those autonomous republics where the nature of the economy justifies

[1] Article 55 of the republican constitution.
[2] Article 69.

it there may also be established, with the permission of the Supreme Soviet of the R.S.F.S.R. in each case, ministries of light industry and the lumber industry. In addition to the ministries, there are also at autonomous republican level administrations; that is to say, agencies of lesser standing than full ministries but answerable, like them, direct to ministries at the level of the union republic and, like them, represented by their heads in the Council of Ministers of the autonomous republics. Such administrations in the autonomous republics of the R.S.F.S.R. are for

> Motor Transport and Highways
> Building and Architecture
> Constructional Materials Industry, and
> Fuel Industry.[1]

Territorial and regional soviets in the R.S.F.S.R. are required to form the following departments and administrations under their executive committees, each being subordinate to the appropriate ministry:

Departments for
> Health Protection
> Municipal Economy
> Popular Instruction
> General Affairs
> Building and Architecture
> Social Security, and
> Finance.

Administrations for
> Motor Transport and Highways
> Internal Affairs
> Culture
> Local Industry
> Building Materials Industry
> Agriculture
> Fuel Industry, and
> Commerce.

With the approval of the republican Council of Ministers they may have other departments or administrations appropriate to the conditions of the local economy. In addition they all have a planning

[1] Article 69.

commission and 'cadres' (personnel) sector under the direction of the chairman of the executive committee.[1]

For towns and districts no 'administrations' are constitutionally required to be formed, but a list of 'departments'—in Soviet terminology usually smaller units—is prescribed,[2] which includes most of the same branches of action, and in suitable circumstances the regional soviet may authorise departments or administrations for municipal economy, local industry, commerce or agriculture. There should be a 'militia' (i.e. general police) administration or department in place of the internal affairs administration. Both of these are innovations of December 1956. Previously there had been administrations of the ministry attached to the executive committee, but not even nominally under its control. The Ministry of Justice lost a similar power of attachment in August 1956. All-union ministries still retain it.

As with ministries, the higher-level unit of any branch, apart from supervising, may itself direct the more important enterprises or institutions. Thus the district departments for popular instruction direct and inspect schools of general education under the supervision of the regional department, while the region itself runs directly teachers' training institutions and children's homes. District agricultural administrations were to be abolished by a ruling of the Council of Ministers,[3] following a plenary session of the party Central Committee in September 1953 which gave the machine-tractor station an increased role as an organ for the control of agriculture, and to the district party organisation an increasingly direct responsibility for direction through the M.T.S. When in 1958 this phase passed with the M.T.S. the district agricultural administration came back; close party control remained. Throughout, the M.T.S. was to prepare its plans on the basis of the general state plan as worked out in local detail by the executive committee, and to submit it to the executive committee for approval. Certainly the chairman of the district executive committee is still, among others, held responsible for the state of agriculture in his district; and though Mr. Khrushchov in his speech to the September 1953 plenary session declared that 'it is enough to have within the district executive committee a few workers for planning and account keeping',[4] the need for well-qualified staff for this work has since been more, rather than less, emphasised. The need has apparently been recognised to have at district level departments for building in collective

[1] Article 92 of the republican constitution.
[2] Articles 96 and 99.
[3] E. V. Shorina in *S.G. i P.*, No. 8 of 1955.
[4] *Pravda*, 15th September 1953.

farms, but there does not seem to be any record of whether they have in fact been instituted. The party is often mentioned, though not with approval, as duplicating the work of other departments of the district executive committees, and so do other organs outside the soviet structure. An article by a soviet official in September 1954 mentioned the case of his own district where the commerce department had as its only official a director 'who actually has nothing to do. All trade in the district is handled by the board of the district union of consumers' co-operatives'.[1] The soviet executive committee commonly by-passed its own department in dealing with such matters. It is possible that such departments will go the same way as the agriculture administration.

The internal structure of the ministries was latterly supposed to be based on the branches of production for which they were responsible, or sometimes divisions of these by area. Out of the direct managerial line there might be administrations and departments for particular kinds of services, such as the auxiliary engineering services required by non-engineering industries, and always for finance and for personnel and organisation, as well as various inspectorates to keep a watch on enterprises and activities not under the ministry's direct management.

The surviving ministries, and the planning bodies in their capacity of ministries for everything else are in the new managerial structure supposed to confine themselves to inspection, planning and co-ordination, stopping short of the direct management of enterprises. Drastic reductions in the numbers of offices and officials directing industry from outside the factory have been reported over the last two years or more. The latest changes cannot help much here. The federal State Planning Commission had in July 1957 twenty-three specialised departments for the several branches of industry, as well as nine for such fields of concern as long-term plans, current plans, prices and costs of production, labour and wages, and foreign economic relations, and also a technical and economic council. Moscow city council of the economy had early in 1958 fourteen industry-branch departments and a staff of 2,500. Other councils had as few as 700.

The organisation for the time being permitted is defined in an instrument (*polozhenie*) approved by the Council of Ministers for each ministry. The minister may have a number of deputy ministers, now apparently unlimited except by the *polozhenie*, to look after the several main divisions of the ministry. Commonly there seem to be six or seven. Like the minister himself, these are specialist officials rather than politicians, although some of them appear in the Supreme Soviet. The structure was always more closely comparable to the head office of a

[1] *Izvestia*, 28th September 1954.

large firm than to a ministry as known in most non-socialist countries. In general it, and its principal administrations and equivalent divisions, were all located in the capital city, federal or republican. Lately, however, authority has manifested the intent to move suitable ministries to the centres of the areas where their industry is practised, and in 1955 the Ukrainian Ministry of the Coal Industry was stated to have moved already from Kiev to Stalino. The administrations, departments and minor offices of the ministries include some located with, and under the principle of dual subordination belonging to, the local soviets.

The two classes of acts issued by ministers, as distinct from, and subordinate to, those of the Councils of Ministers, are called instructions (*instruktsia*) and orders (*prikaz*). They differ in that the former are, in principle, normative—binding upon all—while the latter are addressed to a particular quarter. The titles quoted in Soviet sources do not suggest much real difference, except that the order is perhaps more limited in its scope of application—in time or in space, and that appointments and dismissals of individuals always fall into that class. A major purpose of ministerial instructions seems to be to prescribe rules for the economical use of scarce materials and the adoption of new practices. In ministries of the union-republican type the act of the federal minister may take effect not only in the ministry at republican level but also in organs subordinate to it. Thus we find an order of the federal Minister of Agriculture in August 1954 dismissing the director of a machine-tractor station in Azerbaidjan as well as denouncing as unsatisfactory plans made by the corresponding ministry in that republic, and inflicting a reprimand on the minister and a severe reprimand on his deputy. In another case reported the federal minister for the Meat and Dairy Products Industry issued one order to the minister in Kazahstan to administer a severe reprimand to a director of a meat works, and another a week later administering the reprimand himself. Though far-reaching, however, the authority of the ministry seems to have been, and probably still to be, strangely limited in content. In 1953, in connection with the drastic and very temporary amalgamation of ministries upon the death of Stalin, it was announced that the powers of the ministries, and of the ministers personally, were to be greatly increased, specifically in respect of power to vary the purposes to which the financial and material resources assigned to their ministries were to be applied and control over enterprises subordinate to them. By May 1955, however, part at least of this design did not seem to have progressed very far. An edict of the Praesidium of the Supreme Soviet still had 'to commission the Council of Ministers of the U.S.S.R. to establish a procedure for the re-allocation and realisation of surplus equipment and materials not in use, having regard to substantially increasing the rights of ministries of the U.S.S.R. and directors of enterprises in the utilisation of the said equipment and materials'.

Within the ministry, we have suggested, the minister is not now substantially limited by his collegium, and the responsibility for whatever is done or omitted is his. The collegium, however, is conceived to have an important part to play in the perpetually difficult task of keeping watch on what is going on at lower levels, checking on performance by the ministry's own departments and by republican ministries and other subordinate organs—and like the Councils of Ministers sending out their own teams to gather material for a co-report by which the report of the subordinate body may be checked. It also participates in the drafting of the more important instructions and orders, and in the selection of personnel, and considers and agrees to official criticism of the ministry. It considers ways of promoting new processes and 'socialist emulation' —the officially sponsored competitive bidding-up by enterprises and organisations of production targets and commitments generally—and, like other deliberative bodies, is expected to draw into its work a wide circle of activists—specialists, directors of enterprises and learned institutions and inventors of new techniques. Like all such, it is expected to be a show, an inspiration, a conscience and a watchful eye; unlike some, it is probably the scene of real, though often limited, discussion. It seems normally to meet at least monthly, though attendances are apparently sometimes poor and discussion narrowly departmental and overburdened with petty detail. The collegium of the Ministry of Communal Economy of the Tadjik republic was taken to task in the press for discussing the repair of bathhouses in three district centres. It was observed that 'In a number of union and republican ministries the role of the collegium is reduced to frequent and prolonged meetings, to listening to extensive, often superficial reports and empty speeches and to adopting various measures of extremely little organisational importance'.[1] It was declared to be unwise to leave to individual deputy ministers or other officials the drafting of the findings. Like other directing bodies, they are apt to be slack in checking that anything is done about their instructions and to word these in such vague form as to make such checking very difficult.

Councils of the economy of economic-administrative districts, which have in themselves a close resemblance to a republican minister and his collegium, have attached to them advisory bodies called technical-economic councils. These are composed of experts, worker-innovators and others amounting in Moscow city to some five hundred persons.

[1] *Izvestia*, 13th August 1955.

CHAPTER IV

The Party

Structure

Within the multiplicity of machinery for the regulation of life in the U.S.S.R. a duality is particularly emphasised; it is that between the state (or soviet) structure and the party, charged equally and severally with responsibility for almost all tasks which the leaders impose. The soviet structure is the territorial network of more or less ineffective elected bodies and more effective inner bodies and professionally-staffed offices which we have been studying. The party structure closely resembles it at all levels from the district upwards and changes in conformity with its constantly changing organisation. There is, however, one significant difference of terminology: autonomous republics have party organisations designated not 'republican' but 'regional', just as do the regions, autonomous or administrative. The union republics have terminologically greater dignity. Their parties have their own names—e.g. the Communist Party of the Ukraine or the Communist Party of Georgia—and congresses and central committees, as at federal level, instead of the conferences and committees which exist lower down the line. Their position, however, does not in substance differ very greatly from that of the organisations in the autonomous republics or regions. The Eighth Congress of the party in March 1919 stated in its resolution that the recognition of separate soviet republics did not imply the reorganisation of the party on a federal basis. It added: 'The central committees of Ukrainian, Latvian and Lithuanian communists enjoy the rights of regional committees of the party and are wholly subordinate to the Central Committee of the Russian Communist Party.' Central decisions were to be unconditionally binding upon them. The present rules indicate no change in this policy; republican communist parties are throughout mentioned in the same paragraphs with the organisations of territories and regions, and no indication is given of any distinction from them except in point of terminology. Officials are posted as freely to republican communist party posts as they are to posts in the regions of the R.S.F.S.R., and some manage in the course of a career to serve in the party organisations of several different republics. The R.S.F.S.R. is unique in not having a party organisation of its own. The Twentieth Congress in February 1956 established for the first time a bureau of the Central Committee on party work in the R.S.F.S.R., but as a purely appointive and instrumental body in no way comparable with the structure existing in other republics. This is not, in fact, a discrimination against the R.S.F.S.R., but one in its favour. The Communist Party of the Soviet Union is, in fact, the Russian Communist Party, and the communist parties of the other republics are its branch organisations.

The party rules (*ustav*) have been amended several times since their adoption by the Eighth Party Congress in 1919, but these revisions—in 1922 (Twelfth Party Conference), 1925 (Fourteenth Congress), 1934 (Seventeenth Congress), 1939 (Eighteenth Congress), 1952 (Nineteenth Congress) and 1956 (Twentieth Congress)—have effected no such fundamental changes as have been made in the constitution of the state. In its own mythology the party has not changed or needed to compromise; being guided not by considerations of expediency but by knowledge of the universally applicable laws of history, it can allow no areas of autonomy. Hence its rules, unlike the constitution, do not purport to describe the sort of order known in the West as democratic, but an order based on democratic centralism, something distinct, unique and constant. The changes have been in inessentials, among them the party's name. The Bolshevik section of the Russian Social-Democratic Workers' Party took at its Seventh Congress in March 1918 the name of Russian Communist Party (Bolsheviks) by way of dissociation from the reformist Social Democracy of the West. Subsequently, upon the formation of the Soviet Union, it changed its name to All-Union Communist Party (Bolsheviks). In 1952 at the Nineteenth Party Congress it dropped the designation of 'Bolsheviks', long unnecessary for identification, and assumed its present name, The Communist Party of the Soviet Union. In the title of all rules from 1922 to 1939 inclusive it described itself as a 'Section of the Third International'.

The absence from the party's history of the formal constitutional break of 1936 is reflected in its structure of representative machinery. The system of multiple indirect election formerly underlying the congresses of soviets is there still in operation, and the double set of inner bodies which formerly existed in the All-Union Congresses of Soviets still exists in the party at all levels. As the party has not had to compromise with the demand for federalism there is no 'senate-type' second chamber at the top, and as it has not had to compromise with traditional methods of administration the excrescence of the Council of Ministers finds no counterpart in the party structure.

The primary organisations of the party, until the 1939 revision of the rules known as 'cells', are not based on territorial units as are the lowest organs of the soviet system, but on units of economic activity—the factory, the government office, the military or naval unit, the machine-tractor station and, increasingly nowadays, the collective farm and the state farm. Provision is made for the formation of territorial primary organisations where the economic organisations in any area are too small to form organisations of their own, but this is a last resort. Apart from the general assembly of their members, which is required to be held monthly, primary organisations having fifteen members or more form a bureau and all primary organisations, regardless of the membership, have a secretary. If the organisation has a hundred members or more he is a full-time paid official; otherwise he combines his duties with other employment. In factories where there are over fifty party members or candidate members the primary party organisations may, with district or town permission, be formed in the several divisions, sections or workshops instead of the factory as a whole. In smaller factories party groups, under the direction of the single party organisation, may be established in the several working brigades. Where the factory has over 300 members and candidates, and the regional or equivalent party authorities approve, there may be, apart from the party organisations in the several sections, a higher party committee for the whole factory. Originally the party cells were financed locally by the soviet executive committees, but from early in 1920 the practice was adopted of financing them from the centre, in order to make them independent of any local control and amenable to central discipline. Party Groups (Chapter XI) are combinations of three or more members in soviet, trade-union or other organisations to maximise their influence in the party's interest by concerting in advance their action on the basis of its policy. Their formation is obligatory wherever the conditions for them exist.

From the district to the region the outermost of the three rings of the party organisation is known as the conference; in the union republic it follows for its greater dignity the terminology used at the centre, and is called a congress, but with no difference in substance. At all levels the rules empower it to elect its next inner ring, the committee, and also the checking ('revision') commission, which is supposed to keep some watch on its behalf over the financial probity and working methods of the committee, and to hear reports from both these bodies and other organisations at its level. It also elects its own delegates to the conference or congress at the next higher level, and the regional conferences (republican congresses, etc.) are specifically empowered to discuss 'questions of party, soviet, economic and trade-union work' in their areas. Such bodies are required to meet upon the demand of a third of the members in their areas. If there is no such special occasion for a meeting they are to assemble once a year at district level and in towns which are not themselves divided into districts, and once in two years in territories, regions or areas and in the towns which are divided into districts. Congresses of republican parties in republics which are not divided into regions are also required to meet once every two years, but by an amendment to the rules adopted at the Twentieth Congress of the party in February 1956 republics which are so divided need have a congress only once in four years. Before the same congress the interval at regional (etc.) and area levels was eighteen months and there was no distinction in favour of the towns containing districts. It seems that, as at all-union level, conformity to rules in this respect has been imperfect. Neither the rules nor so much information as we have about the practice give much support for the declaration in the former that the conferences and congresses are 'the supreme directing organ of each party organisation'.

The committees, or at republican level central committees, hold office from one conference or congress to the next, and during that time 'conduct all current business'. Specifically they are charged with maintaining control over all party undertakings in their areas, securing the prompt performance of party instructions, appointing the editors of party newspapers at their levels and directing them, promoting Marxist-Leninist education and intolerance of shortcomings, managing party financial and other resources and rendering account to the next higher committee of their activities. The district committees, apart from being responsible for oversight of the primary organisations, are charged with directing the activities of soviet and social organisations by means of the party groups within them. The rules make no provision concerning the size of the committees, but those elected in some of the larger towns or districts within them seem to have been fairly uniformly of forty-five to fifty; possibly in rural districts they would be rather smaller. They are required to meet at district level not less than once monthly, at area level not less than once in three months, and at regional, territorial and union republican level once in four months. These intervals were in the case of the last two levels doubled by the Twentieth Party Congress. This does not suggest that they are very important bodies. Their main function is to elect a further and, as far as we know, ultimate inner body, the bureau.

Bureaux at district and town level are required to consist of seven to nine members. At area level the number is nine, and at regional, territorial and republican level eleven. These bodies all include the secretaries of the party organisations at those levels. As worded before the Nineteenth Congress (1952), the rules suggested that the secretaries were additional to the bureau, though they were always regarded as being of it; they were then included within it and limited to three in number at all levels. At the Twentieth Congress (1956) the limitation on numbers were removed, partly, it seems, in consequence of the general fluidity of organisation which obtains in the party as in the state, and partly by reason of the appointment of additional secretaries to work permanently in the field in connection with the responsibility lately assumed by the party for the direct management of agriculture. At all levels the appointment of secretaries needs confirmation by the next higher level of the party. The post of first secretary is probably the most powerful single office at any given level throughout the Soviet state, and at regional level he is the heir to the full authority of the pre-revolutionary governor. There is also a second secretary responsible particularly for the internal organisation and sometimes for the propaganda-agitation departments of the party machine, though the junior secretaries often include a propaganda specialist. Special agricultural secretaries at district seem not to have lasted long.

Congresses of the Communist Party of the Soviet Union are now required to meet once every four years. This requirement was placed in the rules in 1952, and the Twentieth Party Congress in 1956 met within the time prescribed. It was the first time that the party had complied with its own rules in that respect since 1925. As the rules then stood, All-Union Congresses were required to be held annually, and until then had been so held since the revolution; thereafter they became less frequent, meeting at intervals of two, three, four, five and finally thirteen years (1939-52). The Seventeenth Party Congress, meeting in 1934 when annual sessions were long a thing of the past, changed the requirement to once in three years, and so it remained, though unobserved, until 1952. It may be that the party's reformation in this respect will prove to be permanent, but it is hardly to be expected that congresses will be effective in making party policy. Their size—in 1956, 1,355 delegates with voting rights representing the members on a scale of 1 to 5,000, and eighty-one delegates without voting rights representing the candidate members on the same scale—is too large, though smaller than before the war, when the scale of representation was different. They are even now too infrequent, and the tradition of the party is against their effective predominance. The rules of the party define the functions of the congress as consisting in hearing and confirming the reports of the Central Committee of the party and the Central Checking Commission, both of which it also elects, and other central organisations of the party, reviewing and amending the programme and rules of the party, and determining the practical line of the party on the main questions of current policy. In practice they are used almost entirely for the announcement by the leaders of important new developments of the party line, and there is no effective discussion. With the rise of Stalin and his elimination of Trotski, which, we have already seen, was completed by the time of the Fifteenth Congress in December 1927, debate vanished from the party congresses. Previously an occasional vote had gone against the official leadership, but thereafter all decisions have been unanimous and in the desired direction. The congresses are numbered in series from the first in Minsk in 1898. The next four were all held abroad, the sixth was held in Petrograd in July–August 1917, between the revolutions, the seventh in the same place in March 1918, and all subsequent congresses in Moscow. Until 1934 and from 1939 to 1952 there was provision in the rules for the calling of conferences also at federal level. These differed from congresses in that the delegates to them were supposed to represent the party organisations rather than their members. Certainly they were smaller bodies, although subject to the same laws of expansion as most deliberative bodies in the Soviet Union; before their abolition they had already come to have about a thousand participants. They became increasingly rare after 1926, being held only in 1929, 1932 and 1941. Unlike the congresses, they had no authority to decide issues of policy, but were merely advisory to the party Central Committee. The business which they transacted was nevertheless very similar in kind to that of the congresses, and the 1922 revision of the party rules was in fact made by a conference, the Twelfth.

The inner body of the congress of the party as a whole is, as in the union republics, designated the Central Committee. At both levels the Central Committee is in theory the supreme authority when the congress is not in session, but it seems to have followed the usual course of increasing numbers and declining powers. Unlike most bodies, in fact, the Central Committee seems never to have experienced any reversal of the tendency to expansion. From a membership of fifteen, together with eight 'candidates' or probationary members—all full members of the party—at its first post-revolutionary election in March 1918, it had, as elected at the Nineteenth Congress in 1952, grown to 125 and 111 full members and candidates respectively, and at the Twentieth Congress in 1956 to 133 and 122 respectively. The full members included all the members and candidates of the Central Committee's inner body, or Praesidium (which we will shortly examine), and all the secretaries, as had always been the rule. They included the chairman and all the first vice-chairmen of the Council of Ministers, who were also all members of this party Praesidium, and all the vice-chairmen of the same body, of whom one, Mr. Malenkov, was, by reason of his former office, also a member of the party Praesidium. They included two of the other three members of the Council of Ministers not designated by the title of minister, and twelve ministers. Twenty-four ministers were candidate members of the Central Committee. Mr. Popov, chairman of the Bank, and seventeen ministers so designated were neither members nor candidates of the Central Committee. Party secretaries were, as usual, the strongest single contingent. All fifteen republican first secretaries, the Ukrainian second secretary, thirty-eight first secretaries of regional committees (including three from autonomous republics) and town committees of similar standing, the first secretary of one town of regional subordination and the second secretaries of Moscow and Leningrad regions and Moscow city were all full members. Two other secretaries of the Ukrainian party, the second secretaries of the Uzbek and Kazah parties, twenty-five first secretaries of regional or equivalent committees (including three from autonomous republics and three from towns) and one from a district within the city of Moscow were among the candidates, as also were five officials of the Central Committee administrative staff. Ten full members and eleven candidates were members of republican councils of ministers—most of them chairmen. One chairman of the praesidium of a republican party was a full member and five were candidates. Holders of these last two categories of offices are members of the inner bodies of the central committees of their republican parties, but otherwise membership of such inner bodies does not of itself give a claim to a place in the central committee of the all-union party. The Ukraine has in the praesidium of its central committee four full members of the federal Central Committee, as well as three candidates among its own full members, two among its candidate members and one more among its secretaries not members or candidates of the praesidium. In their equivalent bodies the parties of Tadjikistan and Armenia have no member or candidate of the union central committee except their first secretaries. Among other interests represented in the federal Central Committee the armed forces were prominent, with six members (five Marshals of the Soviet Union and one political major-general) and thirteen candidates (including an admiral and a Marshal of Aviation). A variety of other interests were represented, including ambassadors, trade-union and *komsomol* officials and representatives of the literary unions and the principal party publications. Two candidates were factory managers, one manager of a mine, one chairman of a collective farm and one a factory worker.

Members and candidates of the Central Committee alike are entitled to attend meetings, though the candidates have no votes, so that it has already become a somewhat unwieldy body for the taking of decisions.

As with other bodies, plenary meetings early became infrequent. They were originally required to be held twice monthly, and then from 1921 once in two months, from 1934 once in four months, and from 1952 once in six months. To this last requirement they at present seem to conform, though this, it seems, has not always been so. Mr. Khrushchov is reported to have said that in the last fifteen years of Stalin's life plenary sessions were hardly ever called, and that during the war there was none at all.[1] The published record bears him out only in part; one such session is supposed to have been held in 1939 and two in 1940, and the decisions in January 1944 to adopt a new national anthem in place of the Internationale and to allow union republics to maintain armed forces and establish direct foreign relations were announced as having been taken at a recent plenary session;[2] but certainly only one is clearly recorded between the end of the war and Stalin's death (held in February 1947). Such sessions are used mainly to publicise declarations of policy, as are the congresses, and also progress reports, for which their greater frequency renders them more suitable. They have been the scene of many of Mr. Khrushchov's pronouncements on problems of the economy—especially agriculture—and how to solve them. Other speakers have been largely non-members brought in for the occasion. The party's principal decisions are promulgated in the name of the Central Committee, and the whole immensely important central staff of the party is deemed to be in its service. Its members are probably the principal advisers of the top leadership, but the Central Committee itself seems to have little life of its own independent of that leadership, and, according to the common pattern, its powers have passed to an inner body elected by it, though in 1958 Mr. Khrushchov seems to have mobilised it against a hostile majority in that body.

The federal Central Committee and that of the Ukraine have for most of their history differed from other party committees in having two bureaux, for policy and organisation, known as the politburo and orgburo. Immediately before the October revolution a body by the name of politburo was instituted with seven members, of whom Lenin was chairman, with the task of preparing for action, but it does not seem to have functioned effectively, principally because the ease with which the revolution was achieved obviated the necessity. The two-bureaux structure came into being by a resolution of the Eighth Congress of the party in March 1919. A politburo of five members was set up to decide

---

[1] Khrushchov, closed-session speech, Twentieth Party Congress, *D. of S.* p. 10.
[2] *KPSS v Rezoljutsijah i reshenijah s'ezdov konferentsi i plenumov Ts. K 1898–1953* (Moscow 1953), II, 1018 (work quoted in further references as *KPSS v Rez.*); *Pravda*, 28th January 1944.

on questions which did not admit of delay and to report fortnightly to the regular plenary sessions of the Central Committee. The orgburo, also of five, was similarly to report fortnightly on 'organisational work'. In respect of influence the politburo early drew ahead for obvious reasons. Lenin at the Ninth Congress explained that any question at all could be considered one of policy upon the request of a single member of the Central Committee. The politburo could and did expand its competence to cover the whole territory of organisation belonging in principle to the orgburo, leaving the latter body only to fill in the details of its decisions.[1] The politburo was independent of any organ in party or state, although much doubt was expressed by foreign observers in Stalin's lifetime whether even its members had any effective influence with Stalin on matters of policy. Mr. Khrushchov has since confirmed, if we may trust the accuracy of the record and discount the desire of the speaker to dissociate himself from the past, that on many matters of substance they were not only not consulted but not even informed.[2] Of Stalin's six fellow-members of the politburo at the time of the death of Lenin only one survived the purges of the period of his rise to full power, and that one, Bubnov, soon lost his influence and, apparently, his liberty. Those who took their places were of Stalin's choosing, and themselves had an insecure tenure both of office and of life, and no certainty of being consulted on any particular issue that might arise. Mr. Khrushchov has apparently explained how the greater part of the work of the Praesidium was in fact performed by various small working parties chosen from among its members by Stalin, and how Mr. Voroshilov at least was interdicted from attendance at full sessions unless with Stalin's specific permission for each occasion.[3]

At the Nineteenth Party Congress in 1952 the politburo was abolished and replaced by a new body called the Praesidium of the Central Committee, with a greatly enlarged membership. Instead of eleven members and one candidate there were now twenty-five members and eleven candidates. This was generally interpreted at the time, probably rightly, as an attempt by Stalin to apply at the highest level of the party the technique of weakening by swamping which he had applied to other organs and to the party as a whole. One full member of the old politburo, A. N. Kosygin, was reduced to candidate membership of the new body; another, A. A. Andreev, who had already had to take the blame for faults in agricultural policy, was dropped altogether, being reduced to candidate membership of the Central Committee; the rest, including Shvernik,

---

[1] See instructions of Lenin quoted in Khrushchov, closed-session speech, Twentieth Party Congress, *D. of S.*, p. 7.
[2] Ibid., pp. 9, 32.   [3] Ibid., pp. 31–2

became full members of the Praesidium. The additional members brought into the Praesidium were mostly younger men of the generation which Stalin himself had trained, ministers, first secretaries of party regional committees, ideologists and others. Immediately upon Stalin's death, however, in March of the following year the position was in fact reversed without the formality of calling another party congress. The name of 'praesidium' was kept, but the membership was reduced to the proportions of the old politburo, with ten members and four candidates. The members in the order in which they were named in the announcement of appointment, which since it is neither alphabetical nor in order of seniority of appointment was presumably one of precedence, were: G. M. Malenkov, L. P. Beria, V. M. Molotov, K. E. Voroshilov, N. S. Khrushchov, N. A. Bulganin, L. M. Kaganovich, A. I. Mikojan, M. Z. Saburov, M. G. Pervuhin, of whom the last two—both of them vice-chairmen of the federal Council of Ministers—were among the new men brought in in the previous year and the others were all the members of the politburo less the deceased (Stalin) and the already demoted (Kosygin and Andreev). The candidate members were: N. Shvernik, P. K. Ponomarenko, L. G. Meljnikov and M. D. Bagirov. Three of these had been full members of the larger Praesidium of 1952: Mr. Shvernik, who at the same time was removed from his post as chairman of the Praesidium of the Supreme Soviet and returned to trade-union work; Mr. Ponomarenko, until then a central committee secretary and Minister of Agricultural Procurements, now relieved of those offices on appointment as Minister of Culture; and Mr. Meljnikov, then first secretary of the Ukrainian party. Mr. Bagirov, first secretary of the Azerbaidjan party and a member of the Praesidium of the Supreme Soviet, had not been either member or candidate in 1952. Mr. Beria was removed from office about the middle of the year, and on the 13th July 1955 two new full members, Mr. A. I. Kirichenko and Mr. M. A. Suslov, were added. The former, who had become first secretary in the Ukraine upon the dismissal of Mr. Meljnikov in June 1953, had apparently been made candidate member of the Praesidium before the end of 1954; the latter, who had made his career in the party officialdom and had since 1947 been head of the Central Committee's propaganda and agitation department, can have achieved candidate membership of the Praesidium only in the early part of 1955. The Praesidium of eleven members thus composed was re-elected in its entirety at the 1956 congress. In accordance with the collective-leadership fashion of the time its members were then listed in alphabetical order. The candidate membership, however, was entirely changed except for the perpetual Mr. Shvernik; Mr. Ponomarenko had been appointed first secretary of the Kazahstan Communist Party in March 1954, and ambassador to Poland a year later; Mr. Meljnikov had been disgraced for mishandling the Ukraine, though not irretrievably; Mr. Bagirov was involved in the fall of Beria, disgraced and killed, though his fate was not revealed until May 1956. There were now six candidates, listed, unlike the full members, in apparent order of precedence: G. K. Zhukov, Marshal of the Soviet Union and Minister of Defence; L. I. Brezhnev, then first secretary in Kazahstan (as formerly in Moldavia) and briefly before Stalin's death a Central Committee secretary; N. A. Muhitdinov, first secretary in Uzbekistan; D. T. Shepilov, a central party official then serving as chief editor of *Pravda* and by recent appointment a Central Committee secretary; E. A. Furtseva, first secretary in the city of Moscow and the first woman candidate member of the Praesidium or politburo, and Mr. Shvernik.

The next change was the appointment, made at the plenary session of the Central Committee in February 1957, of Mr. F. R. Kozlov, first secretary of Leningrad region, as a candidate member. A further plenary session at the end of June made more drastic changes as part of Mr. Khrushchov's settlement of accounts with his rivals. Mr. Molotov, Mr. Kaganovich and Mr. Malenkov were deprived of their places in both the Praesidium and the Central Committee; Mr. Saburov ceased to be a member of the Praesidium, though no mention was made of his expulsion from the Central Committee; Mr. Pervuhin was reduced to candidate membership of the Praesidium; Mr. Shepilov lost that status and his membership of the Central Committee. The total membership, including candidates, was raised to twenty-four, seven over the maximum for politburo or Praesidium at any time except the last months of Stalin's life. Mr. A. B. Aristov, Mr. N. I. Beljaev, Mr. N. G. Ignatov and Mr. O. V. Kuusinen were raised directly to full membership of the Praesidium without previous service as candidates. The first and last of these had been full members of the enlarged Praesidium of Stalin's last months, and the third a candidate; the first and third had been Central Committee secretaries under Stalin, and the first and second had been so serving since July 1955, the second being as such responsible for the implementation of Mr. Khrushchov's agricultural ideas; the first three had much experience as regional first secretaries, and the fourth, Finnish by birth, and a party member since 1905, had been a leading official of the Comintern and of the Karelo-Finnish republic. Mr. Brezhnev, Marshal Zhukov, Mr. Kozlov, Mr. Shvernik and Mrs. Furtseva were more orthodoxly promoted. Mr. Ja. E. Kalnberzins, Mr. A. P. Kirilenko, Mr. V. P. Mzhavanadze, first secretaries in Latvia, Sverdlovsk region (R.S.F.S.R.) and Georgia respectively, Mr. K. T. Mazurov, chairman of the Council of Ministers of Belorussia, and Mr. P. N. Pospelov, a Central Committee secretary, became candidates for the first time; Mr. Kosygin and Mr. D. S. Korotchenko, chairman of the Ukrainian Supreme Soviet Praesidium and a member of the 1952 party Praesidium, returned. In late October Marshal Zhukov lost his places in Praesidium and Central Committee. In December Mr. Muhitdinov was made full member. Mr. N. V. Podgorny, first secretary, Ukraine, and Mr. D. S. Poljanski, R.S.F.S.R. Council of Ministers chairman, were made candidates in June 1958 and, with Mr. Kosygin, full members in May 1960. Mr. Beljaev and Mr. Kirichenko were dismissed then; Mr. Bulganin had gone in September 1958. Mr. Voroshilov retired in July 1960. This left fourteen full members and seven candidate members.

The Ukrainian party still follows federal practice, having a praesidium; all of the other parties have a bureau as before. Such bodies, however called, copy the federal Praesidium; when the latter had eleven full members, ten republican bureaux had the same number, the rest having fewer and the Ukrainian Praesidium, with seven, least of all. Members include the chairman of the Supreme Soviet Praesidium and of the Council of Ministers. The chairman of the Committee of State Security and the General Officer Commanding troops there are commonly members, together with leading party workers. In all republics, except the Ukraine, they include the first, second and three other secretaries; in the Ukraine two secretaries appointed in 1956 were neither full nor candidate members. All republics but three had at that time some candidates.

The commitment of the party to operative management put great power in the hands of whoever could manipulate its internal administration. It was upon realisation of this, above all, that Stalin built his power. At the Ninth Congress, in 1920, the secretariat, instituted at the same time as the politburo and orgburo, was greatly strengthened by the appointment of three full-time secretaries and acquisition from the orgburo of all 'current questions of organisational and executive character', including the patronage for staffing the state system with reliable men. In April 1922 Stalin first achieved secretarial office, by decision of a newly elected Central Committee, and, unlike any previous holder, was given precedence over his fellows by the addition after his name of the words 'General Secretary'. In any case he could hardly have failed to dominate his companions, the recessive figures of Molotov, who alone of the three had been appointed a secretary already in the previous year, and Kuibyshev. It was probably not then intended to make this office one different in kind from its fellows. Stalin continued throughout his life to sign the party decisions as 'secretary' of the party and not as 'General Secretary'. Nevertheless the distinction was made and was justified. As far as his office was concerned the rapid changes of the previous years were at an end for the rest of his life. In contrast, the other secretaryships changed hands with fair frequency, though no longer as the result of faction conflict in the party; they came to be held by young and promising men whose claim to the office was evidently the favour of Stalin himself. The 'apparatus', or official staff, of the party continued to be ascribed officially to the Central Committee, but in practice it was directed by the secretary general and the secretariat, itself nominally an organ of the Central Committee. In the reorganisation of the top structure of the party in 1952 the orgburo was abolished at the federal level and in the Ukraine; the secretariat took over its functions.

The death of Stalin on the 5th March 1953 provided some test of the strength of the office. Malenkov, who among the secretaries of the party had seemed the most obviously intended by Stalin as his successor, especially since the death of Zhdanov in 1948, was relieved of his secretaryship on the 14th March and so was left with only the state office of Chairman of the Council of Ministers, which by Soviet tradition was the lesser post—one which until 1940 Stalin had left to one of his subordinates—and seems so to have remained. Khrushchov had a week earlier been relieved of his duties as first secretary of the Moscow party organisation to concentrate on his work in the Central Committee, and in the list of secretaries published on the occasion of Malenkov's resignation his name was placed first, followed by four others. On the following 12th September he was formally designated 'First Secretary', and under this changed title he seems to have continued to fill Stalin's role. Possession of the first place in the party administration had been shown not to give power of itself, but the position of Khrushchov suggests that it is a position which a strong man can use with great advantage. Like Stalin during the greater part of his career, Khrushchov held no state office other than membership of the unimportant Praesidium of the Supreme Soviet so long, apparently, as he felt he could safely leave detailed administration to men of lesser standing. In March 1958, however, intensified competition in the leadership induced him to assume the chairmanship of the Council of Ministers from Mr. Bulganin, who had held it since Malenkov's resignation in February 1955.

The junior secretaries continue to be comparatively transient. In the first changes after Stalin's death Mr. Ponomarenko and Mr. Ignatov were released to take ministerial posts (Ignatov in fact went to party posts in Leningrad and Orel) and Mr. Brezhnev on becoming head of the navy's political administration. They were replaced by Mr. S. D. Ignatiev, formerly Minister of State Security; Mr. P. N. Pospelov, ideologist and former editor of *Pravda*; and Mr. N. N. Shatalin, of the party's staffing department. These, together with Mr. Khrushchov and Mr. Suslov, surviving from the time of Stalin, made up the secretariat. Mr. Ignatiev lasted only until the beginning of the following month, being dismissed for his part in the 'doctors' plot' plan. Mr. Shatalin subsequently disappeared from the record. On the 13th July 1955 Mr. A. B. Aristov, who had already once been a Central Committee secretary in the Stalin period, Mr. N. Belaev and Mr. Shepilov were added, and at the 1956 Congress Mr. Brezhnev returned and Mrs. Furtseva was added. Mr. Shepilov ceased to be a secretary in December 1956, six months after taking ministerial office, was reinstated in February 1957 upon vacating that office, and broken at the end of June. In his place the new party Praesidium member Mr. O. V. Kuusinen was appointed. In December 1957 Mr. Muhitdinov, Mr. Kirichenko and, again, Mr. Ignatov, all party Praesidium full members (the first newly admitted), were appointed. Mr. Beljaev, then sent to Kazahstan as first secretary, fell out of the list. Mr. Kirichenko left in disgrace in May 1960, when Mrs. Furtseva and Mr. Ignatov were released to government appointments and Mr. Aristov and Mr. Pospelov to their work in the Central Committee bureau on the R.S.F.S.R.; Mr. Kozlov was appointed. In July Mr. Brezhnev was released to act as head of state. All five secretaries were then members of the Praesidium. Before June 1957, in contrast, the secretariat included two members, three candidates and three non-members. In republics, except the Ukraine, all secretaries were bureau members.

Party congresses elect another continuing body, the Central Checking Commission, charged by the rules to maintain a check on '(a) the expeditiousness and accuracy of the conduct of work in the central organs of the party and the efficiency of the apparatus of the secretariat of the Central Committee, (b) the treasury and enterprises of the Central Committee of the party'. It reports to the congresses on such matters as the collection of revenues and local, not central, efficiency in tasks of propaganda, party education, etc. Its membership has grown greatly with the passage of time from an original three to thirty-seven in 1952 and sixty-three in 1956. The party secretaries and the generals are prominent among its members, as in the Central Committee, but it is clearly a second team. Until the introduction of the chairmen of the republican Councils of Ministers into the federal Council of Ministers the latter had no members on the Commission; thereafter it contributed three. Of its forty-six new members in 1956 three had been members and six candidate members of the Central Committee.[1]

Another central organ for which provision has been made in the rules of the party since 1925 is the Committee of Party Control[2] now elected by the Central Committee. Before the passing of the rules of 1952 this was known as the Commission of Party Control, and before the rules of 1939 it was a body elected directly by the congresses. The change of terminology probably has no significance other than a belated recognition of its changed method of appointment. Its powers as defined in the rules are the maintenance of a check over members and candidates of the party for the avoidance of breaches of party or state discipline and departures from the programme and rules of the party, the hearing of appeals from decisions of the next subordinate level, the central committees of union-republican parties and territorial and regional committees, and the award of party punishments—expulsion or reprimand. Under the 1925 and 1939 rules attention was directed to the supervision of institutional rather than personal activities; the commission was charged with supervision of the fulfilment of party decisions by party organisations and soviet and economic organs and checking on the work of local party organisations. There is no reason to suppose that these functions have been dropped. The 1952 rules, as a departure from their predecessors, specifically provided for representatives of the commission at republican, territorial and regional levels, who should be independent of the local party organisations, but a resolution of the Twentieth Party Congress of February 1956 deleted this provision from the rules. This may indicate a realisation that the Soviet system of government in its state and party machinery together is grossly oversupervised. It seems that such independent emissaries of the party centre were in existence before 1939, and it is not necessarily to be assumed that their existence is now at an end. It is not even clear what this assumption, if correct, would amount to, for similar functions have throughout been performed by an organ, if not several organs, of the

---

[1] See particulars of members of the Central Committee and checking commission given in Appendix to Boris Meissner, *Sowjetrussland zwischen Revolution und Restauration* (1956).

[2] The Russian word *kontrolj*—in very frequent use in Soviet official discourse—has the sense of its French rather than its English near-homonym. No clear distinction of meaning can be made between it and the word *revizija* (adj. *revizionny*) used in the name of the checking commission just mentioned, though there is perhaps some difference of emphasis. *Revizija* seems particularly to suggest duplication—the establishment of one organ to keep general watch on another; *kontrolj* is particularly associated with the checking on the fulfilment of instructions, by individuals or collective organs in the state machine, and synonymous with 'verification of performance' (*proverka ispolnenija*)—another term in very frequent use. For example of a technical sense see pp. 205–6.

party staff coming under the general direction of the secretariat; such supervisors may look less impressive than those charged directly by the politburo or Praesidium, but probably the work goes on much as before.

Since early days there has been latent in the system the idea of a regular way of progress at the higher levels of the party: from candidate member of the Central Committee to full membership, thence through the orgburo, or a junior secretaryship, or both of them, to candidate membership of the politburo, and so to full membership of this higher body. The relative status of the central checking commission has always been rather indefinite; its members seem to rank with, but after, the candidates of the Central Committee, though a fall from the latter to the former status is by no means irredeemable. At times such as the years of relative stability between the end of the purges and the death of Stalin the pattern became fairly clear. But stability in the Soviet Union is never more than relative. The rigidly status-conscious party bureaucracy with its probationary layers of 'candidates' is something of a vision of the less troubled world which may be but is not yet—like the constitution, though more fully realised. The aims and character of Stalin made the selection process highly personal, and the rates of progress of different individuals have varied greatly; it seems that the manœuvrings among Stalin's principal successors and their retainers, to preserve a balance or establish a hegemony, have since operated to the same effect. Thus Mr. Shvernik, who was elected a candidate member of the politburo in 1939, remained in that position until October 1952 and from March 1953 to June 1957. Apparently he did not look very profitable to potential patrons. But Mr. Malenkov, who was appointed a candidate member in 1941, became a full member in 1946; Mr. Bulganin was appointed a candidate in 1946— and a member of the orgburo in the same year—and a full member two years later; Mr. Kosygin, appointed candidate in the same year, had to wait a year longer for full membership. Mr. Kirichenko, Mr. Suslov and Mr. Kozlov served only very short terms as candidates, presumably because they are clients of Mr. Khrushchov, and the four newest entrants to the Praesidium seem, for the same reason, to have escaped such service altogether. The situation at the lower level is quite as fluid. The 1956 Congress elected fifty-two new full members to the Central Committee; only twelve were taken from among the candidate members, and three from among members of the Central Checking Commission; the rest were completely new to the central elected bodies of the party. Seventy-five new candidate members were elected, four of them, including Mr. Meljnikov, had been demoted from the status of full members, five transferred from the Central Checking Commission, and the rest were completely new. The new full members who had never served as candidates included a vice-chairman of the Council of Ministers and four ministers—those of Internal Affairs, Agriculture, the Coal Industry, and Heavy Machine Building. It seems likely that the importance of their departments was held of itself to warrant their immediate advancement, and similar considerations seem to apply to such advancement among the local party secretaries. Of the direct appointments to full membership of the Central Committee five were republican party first secretaries, three first secretaries of territory committees, thirteen first secretaries of regions, all important, and the second secretaries of Moscow town and regional committees. The status distinctions are important because the desire for stability leads to their being felt to be important, but they are of little value as indices of presumptive rights of succession to higher offices. The candidate's distinction from the outsider in this respect is as vague as, in a system where votes count for little, is his formal distinction from the full member. The real distinction seems to be one of probability; in a quiet period the full member at any level is more likely than not to survive re-election, while the chances are against the candidate.

Staff

The party rules adopted in 1934 and those adopted in 1939 specified the departmental organisation of the party staff which should exist at the centre and at the various subordinate levels, but in the 1952 rules these provisions were dropped and we have no complete account of the present position. The organisational structure has in fact been subject to variation in response to the course of a debate of the party with itself, characteristic of many which may be observed in the Soviet system and evidenced, as usual, not by open differences between individuals but by repeated changes of the single official policy. The issue was whether the departments should be organised principally on the basis of the several fields of economic activity to the advancement of which the party (as almost everything else in the Soviet system of government) is directed, or according to the nature of the services—indoctrination, staffing, technical guidance and general supervision—which it provided for all alike. Thus the 1934 rules provided that the Central Committee staff should be organised into seven departments: for agriculture, for industry, for transport, for planning, finance and commerce, for the political and administrative machinery, for the leading party organs, and for culture and propaganda of Leninism, and also the Marx-Engels-Lenin Institute, having the status of a department, and two 'sectors' for office business and for special business (police). Republican parties and territorial and regional committees were to have the same functions divided out among four departments. In the 1939 rules, however, the divisions of the Central Committee organisation were given as the 'cadres' (i.e. staffing) administration (*upravlenie*), an administration of propaganda and agitation and departments (*otdel*) for organisation and instruction (i.e. for keeping a watch on lower party organisations and improving their methods), for agriculture and for schools; lower committees had departments for the first four functions and also military departments. The function of these last bodies was defined in the rules as 'giving help to military organs in connection with the maintenance of accounts of liability to military service, organisation of the call-up, mobilisation in the event of war, organisation of anti-aircraft defence, etc.' It was prescribed that there should be separate secretaries at regional, territorial and republican levels for propaganda and agitation. In 1948 the propaganda and agitation administration was demoted to the status of a department, and the separate departments within it for the press and other media of propaganda were renamed 'sectors'. Organisation by services rather than by the industries served seems to have been the favoured principle during Zhdanov's ascendancy, but since his death in August 1948 there has been a return to the 1934 pattern, with the abolition of the cadres administration and the transfer of its functions to departments responsible for the several industries, including agriculture, and the general administration. Since formation of the bureau on the R.S.F.S.R. the industrial departments (perhaps somewhat amalgamated for elimination of over-specialisation) and the department for party organs (organisational and instructional, probably also keeping watch on trade-union and youth organisation (*komsomol*) branches) have each been divided into two departments (one for the R.S.F.S.R. and one for all the other union republics. General propaganda and agitation still have a department of their own, divided into sectors for the various media, though there are departments for culture and science, and for schools which may now be separate from it. There is probably still a special section, for police, and a foreign department for relations with communist parties abroad and to watch over foreign affairs generally.

A part of the central organisation which has never been specified in the rules is the system of party schools under the control of the federal and republican central committees and the committees of territories and regions. By a decision of the Central Committee of the 2nd August 1946, designed to remedy the excess of small and inadequate training courses, schools were to be established at federal level and at the level of region, territory and republic, or in the first instance at a limited number of such centres. The federal school was to have two 'faculties' (*fakultet*), one to train leading party workers—secretaries and heads of departments of regional and territorial committees and republican central committees and secretaries of area committees and the town committees of the larger towns, and the other to train leading soviet workers—chairmen, vice-chairmen and heads of departments of regional and territorial executive committees, chairmen and vice-chairmen of Councils of Ministers of union and autonomous republics, and chairmen of executive committees of town soviets in the larger cities, as well as the corresponding officials of the youth organisation. There was also to be a separate department (*otdel*) to train editors and deputy editors of regional, territorial and republican newspapers. The school was to provide a three-year course —reduced to two years in 1956, when a correspondence course was also started—and a nine-month refresher course. At the regional level the schools were to have the same two faculties, though only a selected few of them were to have the department for newspaper editors. They were to train—since 1956 in a four-year course—officials of similar categories but at the level of districts, primary party organisations and village soviets. For all of them middle-school education was prescribed as a condition of entry, and there was to be an entrance examination. At the end of the course there was to be a further examination which in the federal school might lead to the conferment of the academic title of 'candidate', the Soviet equivalent of the master's degree, otherwise conferred only by universities and institutions of university status. In addition, there was established by the same decision an Academy of Social Sciences, which is also under party management, training ideologists for the party organisations, universities, learned institutions, and specialist journals in a three-year course, and this was given power in suitable cases to confer the doctor's degree. The decision required that within the next three to four years the 'basic leading cadres' at all levels of the party and soviet machines should be passed through the full or refresher course of such schools. Students could be recommended by their party organisation, but it was also open to them to make applications themselves.

Work in the Forces and with Youth

The rules make provision in general terms for the formation of party groups, each with its own secretary and with responsibility to the local district or town party organisation, to work in all congresses, consultations and elected bodies of soviets, trade-unions and other organisations where there are three or more members of the party for the purpose of maximising the party influence. In addition, provision is made for the special circumstances of work in ministries and in the armed forces. For the former it is provided that secretaries of primary party organisations in ministries are confirmed by the Central Committee of the party—not by a district committee as for a factory party organisation—and all communists working in the central organisation of a ministry belong to one party organisation for the whole ministry. The organisation of party work in the armed forces is rather more distinctive. Rules provide for Chief Political Administrations of the Soviet army and naval forces of the U.S.S.R. working in the capacity of departments of the Communist Party of the Soviet Union and under the special instructions of the Central Committee. Though independent of the local organisations, they are charged to work in close co-operation with them. Full-time officers of this service, holding military ranks but exempt from general military duties, are posted to all units down to company level, this lowest level being added only at the beginning of 1950. The origins of the office go back to the earliest days of the regime when technical military competence and political reliability were not to be found in the same hands and the military commanders were consequently held, like factory managers, to need watching. Political commissars, reliable party men not usually skilled in the military arts, were appointed with authority co-ordinate with that of the commanders and power of veto over their orders, as well as general concern for the state of loyalty and morale in the unit. The title of political commissar was felt to be inappropriate once the regime had built up its own military profession and the principles of one-man headship had been established there as in industry, leaving to the party officer mainly educational duties, and after some two years of hesitation and repeated reversal of policy connected with the varying fortunes of the Finnish and German wars the designation was abandoned in 1942, in favour of the present designation of 'deputy to the commanding officer for political matters' (*zampolit*). Many men of the old type remained, but with the changed character of the work it became the practice to recruit persons of superior educational standard from among serving officers and men. Latterly the policy seems to be to recruit among those who have been through the normal officers' training. This is a network which has no counterpart in civil life. Primary party organisations with their own party organisers (*partorg*), and party bureaux with their own secretaries, exist in the forces much as outside, at company, or sometimes platoon, and at battalion level respectively, but they are subordinate to the political administration network, and their full-time officials are a little lower in rank than the *zampolit* at the same level and form part of his staff. Until 1956 the rules of the party provided for a special organisation of the party bodies in the country's transport services corresponding to that in the armed forces and subject to political administrations in the ministries of ways of communication, the maritime fleet and the river fleet. The Twentieth Party Congress of 1956 abolished this special provision in respect of transport.

A special section of the rules provides for the work of the party among young people. The All-Union Lenin Communist League of Youth (the *Komsomol*) is described in an official publication as 'a mass non-party organisation uniting in its ranks the broad strata of progressive Soviet youth'. Despite the use of the term 'non-party', the same source adds that the organisation 'is connected with the party, and forms its reserve and its helper in the work of the communist education of the young generation',[1] and the party rules state that it 'carries out its work under the direction of the Communist Party of the Soviet Union'.[2] Its central committee is subordinate to the Central Committee of the party, and its local organisations are 'directed and checked' by the corresponding party organisations. The structure of the league consequently corresponds to that of the party at all levels from the primary organisation upwards to the All-Union Congress, which, like that of the party, meets once every four years. It is, however, appreciably less restrictive than the party in its admission policy, though it seems to have been more so than the junior organisation for children of the ages of nine to fifteen, the Pioneers. It presents itself as both a preparation and a test of fitness for admission to the party, and so helps to build up the prestige of the latter as an élite organisation. Apart from this eliminating process there also appears to be much voluntary abandonment of the race to show political worthiness. Despite the increased comprehensiveness of party membership of latter years this relation between the two organisations seems likely to continue, for according to the official figures the *Komsomol* also has grown vastly in membership with 9.3 million members at the time of its Eleventh Congress in 1949, which was already more than that of the party, and more than twice as many—18,825,000—at its Twelfth Congress of March 1954. According to the party rules members of the *Komsomol* are required to leave it upon joining the party 'unless they occupy directing posts in the *Komsomol* organisations'. This provides for the requirement made in the rules of the *Komsomol* that organisations of that movement shall each have a leader who is a member of the party, as the *Komsomol* itself provides leaders for the organisations of the Pioneers. The work of these organisations consists largely in political education and indoctrination, but the years of eligibility to the *Komsomol*

[1] *Spravochnik propagandista i agitatora* (1955), pp. 29–30.
[2] Rule 60.

(fifteen to twenty-six) cover a sufficient stretch of adult life to make the league a useful auxiliary to the party in practical tasks. *Komsomol* members form joint organisations with members of the party where the latter are few in number and take their share in the recurrent campaigns of political action among the masses and in such arduous and valuable manifestations of enthusiasm as the development of new towns or of the virgin lands of Kazakhstan, the building of factories, and drives for the improvement of production in town and country.

Membership

The rules provide (Rule 2) that 'any toiler who does not exploit the labour of any other, who is a citizen of the Soviet Union, accepts the programme and rules of the party, co-operates actively in their realisation, working in one of the organisations of the party and fulfilling all the decisions of the party, may be a member of the Communist Party of the Soviet Union'; but the suggestion of a more restrictive admittance policy which we see in the constitution is in fact supported by the persistent practice of the party. The rules of the party themselves provided (5b): 'The question of admittance of the party is considered and decided by the general assembly of the primary party organisation, the decision of which enters into force on confirmation by the district committee, or, in towns where there is no division into districts, by the town committee of the party.' This process has to be gone through twice. Recruits are first admitted as probationary members or, in the party's terminology, 'candidates', and only when they may be supposed to have acquainted themselves with the aims and methods of the party, as full members. Clearly this is something that one cannot just join by turning up at the meeting with an initial subscription in one's hands. A recent reiteration of the official doctrine on the point declares that 'the party does not chase after quantity of accessions, understanding that its strength consists not in the quantity of members but, above all, in their quality. . . . The party regulates the business of admission with regard to the tasks which lie before it at this or that stage of activity'.[1] The principles on which the selection is made have therefore varied considerably from time to time in the party's history.

Though appropriate in a period of conspiracy, the selective and severely disciplined party which Lenin created in the Bolshevik faction after the split of 1903 was less so in the period of revolution, when concealment was no longer in question and the concern was rather to secure at least the acquiescence of as many people as possible and,

[1] *Pravda*, 6th April 1956.

where occasion offered, to mobilise them for action. By the time of the first ('February') revolution of 1917 the Bolsheviks probably had not more than 40,000 members, which put them well behind the Constitutional Democrats (that is, the liberal party), the Menshevik wing of their own Social Democrat Party, and the Social Revolutionaries, who were dominant in the rural parts.[1] The rules adopted by their Sixth Congress in August 1917 prescribed the conditions of membership on much the same terms as Lenin had tried to have incorporated in 1903, but the specific requirements for admission were liberal. Any person might be admitted on a recommendation of two persons to the party organisation, subject to confirmation by the next general assembly of members of the organisation. Estimates of membership in the succeeding months vary widely, but by January 1918 it had risen to 115,000 members,[2] and for the first time the workers' party had acquired a solid mass of worker supporters. The peasants were still few.

The circumstances of the civil-war period intensified the motives for attaching to the party all who were not committed against it and also provided an opportunity of gaining a foothold in the rural areas and undermining the Social-Revolutionary influence there. An appeal at least to that class of peasant from which the committees of the poor were recruited was clearly both advantageous and possible. Thus by the beginning of 1921 the membership of the party had risen to substantially over half a million,[3] while the proportion of the members classified as workers had declined markedly since the immediately post-revolutionary period (January 1918) from 56.9 per cent to 41 per cent, and the proportion of peasants had risen from 18.5 per cent to 28.1 per cent. The office workers and others showed a smaller but still appreciable rise from 28.6 per cent to 30.8 per cent.[4] The Tenth Congress in March 1921, however, recorded concern at the combined effect of losses of worker members in the civil war and the removal of the majority of the survivors from work in the factories to organise the new society and the admission of 'lower-middle-class intellectual and semi-intellectual

---

[1] 'A. Uralov' (A. Avtorhanov), *The Reign of Stalin* (1953), p. 17. But by May, according to the present official data, the figure was 80,000 (*KPSS v Rez.*, I, 332). I. Deutscher (*Stalin, a Political Biography* (1949), p. 143) gives the February figure as '30,000 at the most', and quotes a Soviet source for a figure of about 76,000 for May.

[2] M. Fainsod, *How Russia is Ruled* (1953), p. 211, quoting 1930 edition of Large Soviet Encyclopaedia. *KPSS v Rez.* (I, 403) gives 'not less than 300,000' for March, though allowing that only 170,000 were represented at the party conference of that month.

[3] Fainsod (op. cit., p. 211) gives 576,000, *KPSS v Rez.* (I, 514) gives 732,521 for March 1921.

[4] Fainsod, op. cit., p. 213.

elements, petty-bourgeois and not yet worked over in the spirit of communism, whom the party has not yet digested'.[1] Such further intensive drives to get people into the party as did occur before the final consolidation of Stalinism in 1939 were associated, unlike that of the civil-war period, with attempts to alter its social composition in the direction of a more marked proletarian element. These latter movements were the so-called Lenin Draft of 1924, the successful attempt—ostensibly in honour of Lenin, who had just died—to recruit by an intensive three-month campaign the force of not less than 100,000 'workers from the workbench' which a party conference some ten days before had set as the target for the next year, a further less successful attempt in the following year and a similar drive in 1927 in honour of the tenth anniversary of the revolution. In reality these were all part of Stalin's drive to power, the attempt to swamp the membership of the party as it existed at the time of Lenin's death under a much greater volume of new recruits of a type who would be readily manipulable to his purposes. The worker could be used both against the intellectuals, whose influence in the party was still strong in Lenin's lifetime and whose theories diverged from those of Stalin in a manner inimical to his aspirations after monolithic solidarity, and against the peasants, whose loyalty was not to be relied upon in the period of mass forcible collectivisation.

These occasional drives to get people in were superimposed upon a more constant and increasingly severe policy for keeping people out, and periodically for weeding out those who were in. Already in March 1919 the Eighth Congress ordered a re-registration of the membership, with a special check on all who had joined since October 1917. In December 1919 the Eighth Conference of the party stiffened the rules concerning admissions. The two sponsors for each new recruit were now required to be of at least six months' standing in the party, which in a period of rapid expansion was more severe than it seems. Moreover, the requirement of probationary service as a 'candidate' was then introduced into the rules for the first time, and here there appeared a point of discrimination against the intellectuals, in that while workers and peasants were required to serve for two months, six months were required of persons of other social origins. The figures of membership for the period indicate that these principles were not so rigorously applied as to exclude at least the lower strata of the non-manual workers and intellectuals. The Tenth Congress of March 1921 raised to one year both the six months' standing required of sponsors and the six months' probation imposed upon the less-favoured class of recruit, and inaugurated a purge which in twelve months reduced the total membership

[1] *KPSS v Rez.*, I, 520.

(with candidates) by over 200,000 to some 532,000, according to present official figures.[1] But it was only on the conclusion of the civil war that the party was able to indulge in the luxury of discrimination on class grounds between the workers and their peasant allies. The Twelfth Party Conference of August 1922 produced some tightening up all round, raising the minimum period of probation from two to six months and the number and standing of the sponsors required to three of three years. For the first time the requirement of confirmation by higher authority was incorporated into the rules. Here new elements of discrimination appeared. Admission upon the minimum terms so defined with confirmation by the next higher party committee, that of the *uezd*, was confined to workers and Red Army men of worker or peasant stock. Other peasants required similar sponsorship, but were to serve as candidates for a full year and required confirmation by a still higher party committee, that of the governorship. People with other social backgrounds were subject to this last rule as to the confirmation, but were to find five sponsors of five years' standing—a very difficult requirement to fulfil in the circumstances—and were to serve two years as candidates. Former members of other parties might be accepted only upon approval by the Central Committee—a provision which remains in the rules to the present day, though it can hardly now apply to anyone except inhabitants of recently acquired lands and perhaps a few refugees from other countries. Subsequent successive revisions of the rules continued the trend of increasing discrimination on class grounds by adding to the number of categories and defining more and more narrowly the most favoured one. The Fourteenth Party Congress in December 1925 distinguished among the workers those engaged permanently in physical work for wages, while other workers and Red-Army men of worker, peasant or farm-labourer stock formed a separate and lower group. The Seventeenth Party Congress at the beginning of 1934 reformulated the distinction among the workers; those who had been so engaged for five years or more now alone constituted the first category, and all other workers were placed in the second together—by a development which foreshadowed future change—with engineers and technical workers, who had previously been in the lowest. Within the categories the formulation of the terms of entry for all except the least-favoured category, the intellectuals, was somewhat eased in 1925. The first category required only two sponsors of one year's standing, the second two of two years' standing, and peasants three of two years. But here,

[1] *KPSS v Rez.*, I, 514, and I, 599. As there was no cessation of new admissions the number of exclusions was larger. But purges were at that time still non-violent.

too, the 1934 rules produced a drastic stiffening: the most favoured workers required three sponsors of five years' standing and were to serve a year as candidates; the other workers required five sponsors of five years' standing, and the peasants required, in addition, the recommendation of the heads of the political departments of their machine-tractor stations or district party committees. All other applicants required five sponsors of ten years' standing. All except the new privileged first class had to serve for two years as candidates. At the same time there was instituted a category of associates inferior in status even to the candidates. These were the sympathisers' groups, described as 'the nearest to the party of the non-party activists who have shown in action, in production, their devotion to the party, but are not yet fitted to join the party'.[1] The factory and similar party committees and political sections of machine-tractor stations might admit people to such groups on the recommendation of two members of the party. The sympathisers were required to attend all open party meetings, and might speak but not vote. There was no specific provision in the rules for their ultimate reception into the party as there was for candidates; but, nevertheless, that was the intention. The Central Committee at a plenary meeting of the 21st–25th December 1935 described the groups as 'the most important reserve for filling the gaps in the ranks of the All-Union Communist Party (Bolsheviks)'. They took party organisations to task for superficiality in their treatment of the sympathisers and failure to screen them carefully with this end in view.[2]

These latest developments were an obvious manifestation of the forces of their period: that of the purges. These in the form of private calumniation of most, public inquisition of all and summary expulsion of many had arisen early in the party and had largely done their work before they reached their climax in the state at large in 1937. A resolution of the Sixteenth Party Conference in April 1929, based on a recommendation of the Central Committee and the central control commission meeting in joint session earlier in the same month, had decreed a general purge, and a further wave of this protracted process was initiated by another resolution of the last two bodies in January 1933. In the phase initiated by the murder of Kirov, the Central Committee by letters of December 1934 and May 1935 ordered the general withdrawal and the reissue after due checking of all party cards and a revision of the party records. One result of this was that the new stringent admission rules of 1934 did not come into effect until November 1936,

[1] Rules 15–17 of the party rules as formulated by Seventeenth Congress, 1934; *KPSS v Rez.*, II, 778.
[2] *KPSS v Rez.*, II, 329.

for all admissions and advancements had been suspended since the end of 1932; and despite the professed intention of the congress and the Central Committee to get them going again,[1] it was not until then that anything was done. By that time the total membership, including candidates, was down by a million and a half from its pre-war peak at the beginning of 1933 of three and a half million, and in consequence of continued expulsions accompanying the new recruitment a further slight wastage continued until about the beginning of 1938, when it stood at 1,920,000.[2] As was to be expected in the circumstances of the period, the main victims had been the peasants and the new workers with strong rural connections, but in the process Stalin had also got rid of most of the leading 'Old Bolsheviks' (pre-revolutionary party members). In 1939 only 20,000 of the 1917 members were still in the party—according to one reasonable estimate only about 10 per cent of those who must have still been living,[3] the rest having been pushed out to the bleak life of the ex-member. Another observer calculates that by that time the ex-members already numbered a million more than the members,[4] though this, perhaps, overestimates the expectation of life of the ex-member. The membership by this time was just under 2,500,000 members and candidates together;[5] that is to say, a million less than in 1933, but already half a million more than in 1938. The wastage was being made good, but with a different sort of material. The members were better educated on average; some 127,000 (5.1 per cent) had had a higher education and 335,000 (14.1 per cent) a secondary education as against 9,000 and 110,000 in 1928.[6] But few had been educated in any tradition other than that of Stalin. Of the members 70 per cent had joined since 1929[7] and these were in no obscure positions; already they provided 43 per cent of the congress delegates. These new recruits were predominantly young men.

By the time of the Eighteenth Party Congress of 1939 there were thus few motives for discrimination left. Stalin's power and the collectivisation of agriculture were accomplished facts. The regime had at its

[1] *KPSS v Rez.*, II, 822–31 (resolution of plenary session of Central Committee, December 1935).
[2] Fainsod, op. cit., p. 224.
[3] G. Bienstock, S. M. Schwarz and N. Yugow, *Management in Russian Industry and Agriculture* (1944), pp. 28–9.
[4] A. Avtorhanov in *Vestnik Instituta po Izucheniju Istorii i Kultury SSSR*, No. 12 of 1956, p. 12.
[5] *KPSS v Rez.* (II, 877) gives the figures as 1,588,852 and 888,814 respectively.
[6] Malenkov's report to Eighteenth Party Congress, *XVIII S'ezd V.K.P. (b)*, p. 148.
[7] Malenkov's report, p. 149.

disposal a managerial class of its own creation on which it felt it could rely. The traditional criteria of class origin had ceased to be significant in the new society where function alone—utility to the regime as manager, as maintainer of prestige, morale or security, or as exemplary worker in production or other approved purposes—was important. Consequently that congress abolished the social class categories regulating the entry of new recruits, and with them the short-lived sympathisers' groups. By the new rules all aspirants to party membership required three sponsors of three years' seniority in the party and were to serve for one year as candidates. The only special provision, apart from that concerning former members of other political parties, applied to persons between the ages of eighteen (the minimum age for candidate membership of the party) and twenty. Entry at such ages was restricted to members of the *Komsomol*. Any member of that organisation might present the recommendation of its district committee as equivalent to the recommendation of one party member. These regulations remain unchanged.[1] The period of the war of 1941-5, however, brought certain temporary concessions. A decision of the Central Committee of the 19th August 1941 provided that soldiers should require only three sponsors of one year's standing, and another decision of three months later provided for those who had distinguished themselves in battle a reduced candidate stage of three months. Wartime concessions were allowed to continue until 1947, though they were less generously applied after the cessation of hostilities. There occurred a rapid rise in membership. This was not entirely a product of the circumstances of the war period. In the society as refashioned by Stalin recruitment to the party had obvious attractions for both recruit and regime; the advisability had been discovered of bringing all persons of importance within the party where in exchange for privileges and prospects they could be induced to accept obligations and a degree of supervision greater than could conveniently be imposed upon ordinary citizens, though it was realised that a watch must be kept for the arrant careerist. Early after the resumption of admissions, and repeatedly, local party organisations had to be warned against recruiting drives pressed as ends in themselves and to the neglect of individual fitness. Nevertheless recruitment went on apace, and during the war it seems that the party so far overcame its objections to seeking members as to persuade the officers and recipients of decorations to join, presumably in order that it might have the benefit of their prestige. At the beginning of the war the membership (with candidates) was just under 3,900,000.[2] By September 1947 it was

---

[1] Rule 5 of the current rules.
[2] *Bolshevik*, No. 3-4 of 1941, p. 56; speech of Shatalin.

6,300,000,[1] far higher than ever before, and in consequence of war casualties or other cause only some 2,000,000 pre-war members (i.e. about half) survived among this number.[2]

This development gave rise to the expectation outside Russia that a weeding-out of the unsuitable would follow, and some colour was lent to the supposition by authoritative hints of revision of the membership rules to be introduced at the Nineteenth Congress in 1952. In fact, no general purge has occurred, though there have been local checks, with expulsions, sometimes on a fairly large scale. There is evidence of this from Belorussia, Kirgizia, Esthonia and Moldavia up to 1952, and in 1948 the Georgian party, in reaction against previous over-generous recruiting, seems to have expelled more than it admitted.[3] Some local party organisations apparently put a stop on all recruitment in this period, but this has been ruled incorrect.[4] At the Nineteenth Congress Malenkov claimed that the party had since the war been applying a policy of restricting admissions and devoting more attention to training, and would continue to do so. But the only material change then made in the rules in this respect—and none was made in 1956—was the insertion of a provision limiting to one year the additional term which an unsatisfactory candidate could be required to serve. If thereafter he had still not justified himself he was to be expelled. Previously some aspirants had been allowed to cool their enthusiasm for the cause through protracted periods of probation. As usual the change of policy does not seem to have produced any immediate change of practice. In 1954 some party candidates in Armenia were reported to have remained as such for twelve years, and more than half of those in Georgia and Belorussia, as well as 45 per cent in the Ukraine and Lithuania, to have exceeded the official term.[5] Some success, however, as well as the non-occurrence of the purge in the grand manner, is reflected in the proportions of the membership as announced at the 1952 and 1956 Congresses. At the former it was given as 6,013,259 full members and 868,886 candidates; at the latter it was 6,795,896 members and 419,609 candidates. The enlarged party seems to have come to stay, and the wartime recruits to have taken root and flourished—providing 21.6 per cent of the 1956 Congress delegates, with another 13.4 per cent for post-war recruits.[6]

[1] *Pravda*, 9th December 1947.
[2] Rigby, Thesis, p. 131.
[3] Ibid., pp. 120–1.
[4] D. Bahshiev, *Partijnoe Stroiteljstvo v Uslovijah Pobedy Sotsializma v SSSR* (1954), p. 84.
[5] Rigby, Thesis, pp. 126–7.
[6] *KPSS v Rez.*, II, 1096; *Pravda*, 15th February 1956 (Khrushchov), 17th February 1956 (Aristov).

The checking commission reported that since the previous Congress there had been a general recall and reissue of party cards, necessitated by the change in the party's name, but it does not seem that use was made of this occasion for a general critical review of members' records.

Over the country as a whole the full party members thus numbered 3.34 per cent of the population. On a very rough calculation from the particulars given by Aristov (in the report of the mandates commission) for the six largest republics by population outside the R.S.F.S.R. Georgia (with 4.75 per cent party full membership) and Azerbaidjan (with 3.82 per cent) were ahead, as in 1952. The others ranged between 2.8 per cent (Kazah) and 2.05 per cent (Uzbek). For all republics this represented a rise and apparently some levelling out. In 1952, when the proportion for the country as a whole was 3 per cent, the R.S.F.S.R. had 3.5 per cent, Georgia 4.4 per cent and Moldavia, at the other extreme, 1 per cent. The party is an institution of the whole Union, not in any significant sense 'at home' in the R.S.F.S.R. and 'in occupation' in the other republics. Nor is it a peculiar preserve of the Great Russians, from Russia proper or elsewhere. Non-Russian names predominate in the central committees of the republican parties and, as far as the evidence takes us, among regional first secretaries in the republics. Nevertheless, there are always a large number of Russians as well, while there is not a corresponding contingent of non-Russians in office in the R.S.F.S.R., and for most non-Russian first secretaries there seems to be a Russian in the almost equally powerful office of second secretary.

It is still, on the whole, a man's party. Aristov reported 1,414,456 women in the party—apparently including candidates—95,488 more than in 1952 and 1,080,635 more than in 1939. Even now the women do not hold many of the leading offices, though there are now a few of them serving as regional first secretaries and, latterly, a woman member of the Praesidium. They are more prominent in such lesser offices in the party's gift as those in the trade unions and the youth movement. That they should be in a minority is not surprising. The party is a party of active participants in politics, not one of supporters, and the most actively influential offices in the Soviet state are still held by men.

In general character the party seems to be, as it was becoming before the war, a form of co-optive aristocracy of the new society, representing primarily the managerial element of the system. In 1956 1,877,773 members and candidates had some form of specialist training of higher (university) or middle (secondary) standard. In all 2,651,745 had received higher or middle education, and another 2,127,862 partial middle education—making two-thirds of the whole membership available for posts of some influence. As early as 1936 it was stated that nearly 99 per cent of the factory managers were members, and the position was apparently similar in the higher ranks of the army. On the other hand, a report of 1939 indicated that the rural areas, with 65 per cent of the population, did not contain 20 per cent of the membership, and of these members only half were on the collective farms. Here there has been some change, partly because as a matter of policy recruiting has latterly been directed towards the rural population, and particularly the rural intelligentsia, and partly because of the intensification of the long-standing practice of posting urban communists to rural areas, mainly in the attempt to provide agriculture with managers capable of achieving the results which Moscow believes possible. By the Congress of 1956 the total rural membership had increased, but the balance within it was much the same. The rural districts, Mr. Khrushchov reported, had more than 3,000,000 party members and candidates, but less than half of them were working directly in the collective farms, the machine-tractor stations, or the state farms. There are some 87,000, 9,000, and 5,000 of these institutions respectively; each requires a head and a number of senior officials; most accounts which we have show at least the intention of filling these posts with communists, so that there is little room in the party ranks for the working peasant, though we have accounts from some farms where there are such members. A report from Smolensk region immediately after the congress mentioned one district where only seventy-four of 400 members were on the collective farms, though the region as a whole had shown a 20 per cent improvement since 1954, to 12,573 in the farms and stations out of 20,080 members and candidates.[1] In the coal industry Mr. Khrushchov had similarly reported 90,000 communists, but only 38,000 of them working underground.

In the local soviets we have seen the party diluting its élite, which even now it has to some extent to limit in numbers in order to preserve its quality, with less satisfactory though still serviceable non-party material in the remoter places and less important posts for which considerations of economy and public relations require local recruiting.[2] But, as we have suggested, the degree of dilution does not indicate the degree of party control. Nor perhaps do the same particulars indicate who is who in the party. Since the soviets, as distinct from the executive committees which are supposed to be answerable to them, do not ordinarily exercise much influence on the course of events, the members of the party assigned to serve in such bodies are not necessarily of more consequence socially or in their political influence than those engaged

[1] *Kommunist*, No. 3 of 1956, p. 65.   [2] See p. 98.

on the party's business in some other capacity which does not require them to stand for popular election. About party representation in the inner bodies, such as the Executive Committee, we have little direct information, but all the signs are that it is very high.

As in the Supreme Soviet, so also at the local level there is some interlocking of membership of party and state deliberative bodies. The first secretary of the party committee is normally a member of the soviet executive committee, and the chairman of the soviet executive committee is normally a member of the party bureau. An article of February 1956 declared that, in consequence, 'in the recent past... leading workers of region and district spent almost their whole time at sessions. Scarcely had a meeting of the bureau of the regional committee of the party been concluded after several hours, and not infrequently after several days, when a meeting of the executive committee of the regional soviet began.'[1] It was claimed that this position was now somewhat eased by the reduction in the frequency of meetings in both types of body, but it seemed that it remained usual for the local leading officials to serve in both. They are, however, few in number and, in their executive functions, either in one hierarchy or in the other. To entrust office in the two systems into the same hand—to appoint, for example, the same person as both party secretary and soviet executive committee chairman —would not be consistent with the purposes which the two hierarchies serve, though the Yugoslavs in their Stalinist days appear to have overlooked this objection. Only at the very top has there been effective merging in the simultaneous tenure by the same person of office in the Praesidia of the party Central Committee and of the council of ministers. The effective cabinet, alone of all bodies in the Soviet structure, was not checked by a parallel body within the party structure but was merged with it. It is, however, now more common than it used to be for officials to move from one to the other in the course of their careers, and those who reach the top in the state structure seem usually to have held some party office at some time.

What Membership Means

The revision of the party rules in 1952 gave marked attention to the duties of members. This was directed, Mr. Khrushchov suggested in his report to the congress, against the disposition of members, and in particular of holders of leading offices, to regard their position as one of privilege, and the failure of organisations to call them to order for this. The existing obligations were brief: to master the foundations of

[1] P. Doronin in *Kommunist*, No. 3 of 1956, p. 63.

Marxism and Leninism, to obey party discipline and participate in party life, to be a model progressive worker in one's own trade, and to keep in touch with the masses, explaining the party's purposes to them, and their worries and needs to the appropriate authorities. These were retained, the clause on discipline being reinforced by specific references to obligation towards the state as well as towards the party, and to the application of both to leaders as well as to the ranks of the party. The new duties tended to assert further the military discipline of the organisation. Members were declared bound to preserve the unity of the party, not merely to acquiesce in but actively to promote the fulfilment of party decisions, to promote self-criticism and criticism from below, to inform the higher authorities, up if necessary to the Central Committee, of the shortcomings of others without respect for persons, to keep no secrets from the party, to be watchful in the preservation of all party and state secrets and always to follow the party's personnel policy in any field without regard for friendship, kinship or personal inclination. To obstruct a member in his duty of delation, or to transgress in any of these respects, were stated to be serious offences, specifically declared in the case of the two requirements last mentioned to be inconsistent with continued membership of the party.[1] There was not in substance here anything new. Though the party has enlarged its membership, it remains a disciplined body as Lenin made it, and its discipline is an exacting one.

Since 1939 the rules have also specified certain rights of the party member, and these were not modified at the 1952 Congress or subsequently.[2] These are the right to discuss policy at party meetings or in the party press, to criticise any member at its meetings, to elect the party organs and be elected to them, to be present when his own conduct is under discussion, and to put questions or declarations of views to all party authorities, up to the Central Committee. But in practice the obligations of a disciplinary character operate so as to negate these rights. According to the principle of democratic centralism issues of policy are subject to discussion only until the party has made up its mind, and since 1934 the party rules have made it clear that discussion and criticism were to be offered only as invited. To discuss important issues in all the party primary organisations, Stalin declared in 1923, would be to carry them out into the street, to reveal plans to the enemy and lose the advantage of surprise over him, to be involved in endless debate,[3] and this the conspiratorial tradition of the party precluded.

---

[1] Rule 3 of current party rules.
[2] Rule 4.
[3] Speech at Twelfth Party Congress, April 1923.

Criticism in this, as in any other rigidly organised hierarchy of authority, can always be represented as breach of discipline. The evidence which we have suggests that a member will normally only venture to criticise a leading official at his own level or at any superior level if he has or thinks he has the support of persons of still higher status in the direct line or in any parallel line of authority. Thus when, as before the 1956 Congress, the transport system had its separate party organisation, it was apparently possible to play off higher levels in this and in the ordinary territorial organisation of the party against one another. It is presumably possible to criticise without having obtained prior support in the hope of rallying such support later, but this is a somewhat perilous undertaking. The right to an open trial for party offences was certainly not observed in the purges of the 'thirties, when the presence of the accused was commonly required only for purposes of self-criticism. Whether this is true of normal times it is impossible to say, since the Soviet Union and its party have never known normal times. As regards self-criticism and criticism from below, which always go together, as in the rules of the party, the former is the obligation to public confession of guilt in respect of any charge brought against a member with the authority of the party. Its object is apparently to enable the authorities to point moral lessons for the edification of the members and the public at large, and particularly the basic moral that all that goes wrong is the fault of an individual and not of the system. In consideration of this service such self-criticism is apparently commonly accepted in mitigation of the offence, real or fictitious. The term 'self-criticism' is also frequently used of organisations as well as of individuals, in which connection it comes very close to the sense of criticism from below. The latter is the denunciation by subordinates of their superiors in the party or state hierarchy. The suppression of criticism, the attempt to prevent news of such denunciation reaching higher authorities, and refusal by the person denounced to acknowledge his own fault, are among the offences most commonly reprehended in the press, and visited with some degree of party reprimand, but it has been pointed out that the prevalence of the practice itself argues that an official in an important office has normally reason to suppose that he has a good chance of getting away with it. There is evidence that the ability to recognise when a criticism has official authority is one of the great techniques of the art of Soviet official living. The obligation to the payment of membership dues is mentioned separately in the rules. These are assessed according to a progressive scale on the basis of the members' or candidates' salaries from $\frac{1}{2}$ to 3 per cent, payable monthly. There is also an entrance fee of 2 per cent of the monthly salary payable on admission as candidate. The greater part of the cost of membership lies in less material burdens. On joining the party a citizen forfeits many of his personal freedoms, even those guaranteed by the constitution. Thus 'if religion is a private affair as far as the state and the citizens of the Soviet Union are concerned, it is not a private affair so far as the party and its members are concerned. The Communist Party is not indifferent to its members' attitude, for the outlook of the party is dialectical and historical materialism which is irreconcilably opposed to religion and idealism'.[1] He is obliged to be respectable according to the rigid ideas currently held by the authorities and scrupulously honest. As his party standing is likely to bring him into contact with persons of influence he may be in a better position than others to avoid censure for lapses from such standards, but if detected in them his condemnation is likely to be greater. Also he is required to give heavily of his time, not only to work hard in his own calling but to be available to assist in any of the numerous campaigns and drives instigated by the authorities, and not only to be obedient but to display an active, constant and quite inhuman zeal. 'Proper channels are for official business. If I'm a communist absolutely everything concerns me,' says the elderly overworked doctor in Ilja Ehrenburg's novel *The Storm* to the party organiser who seeks to persuade him that there is no need for him to add to his burdens by acting as an unofficial housing agency. More than any other Soviet citizen he is liable to find himself uprooted from his home and work. In one case of 1953, typical of many, a thousand members are reported to have been sent by party and *komsomol* committees for permanent work in a steel-works construction trust in the north-west. Repeatedly there are similar drafts to points in the agricultural system, to posts which are often important but often also far away. Even if allowed to stay in one place, he is likely to be involved in various forms of party service to an extent which leaves him very little free time—as, for example, the woman worker, mentioned by the trade-union newspaper in February 1956, who was a deputy to the Minsk town soviet, a member of the party bureau of the combine in which she worked, and a member of the workshop committee of her trade union. In addition, she had latterly been appointed a delegate to the Twentieth Party Congress, and was also overfulfilling her work obligations under the plan in honour of that occasion, as presumably were all good workers. Even if he avoids any sort of office he cannot fail to put in an appearance at a variety of party or other meetings in support of, or in protest against, or for information about, things remote from his interests. If he attempts to evade his responsibilities, as obviously many members do, he lays himself open to censure.

[1] *Kommunist Tadjikistana*, 27th June 1954.

The party member is also subject to special dangers which do not confront the ordinary citizen. Prominence in the Soviet Union, and especially perhaps party prominence, involves a special liability to blame, since the system never takes the blame for anything, and to sudden unexpected presentation in the role of scapegoat. In the party records a member's career is documented in detail as that of a non-party citizen is not. This may be to his advantage in securing for him early consideration for any of the many posts to which the party has the presentation, but it could be turned against him. In addition to the sanctions of the law he renders himself liable to party disciplinary measures, reprimands of various degrees or ultimately expulsion, which can blight his career. The state of the ex-communist, it is said, is appreciably worse than that of the citizen who has never been a member. As in other fields of Soviet penal action, there is apparently more thunder than lightning. Ministers are criticised in the press for serious party offences yet remain in office,[1] and at least one writer of memoirs claims to have been expelled from the party three times and on each occasion to have argued himself back.[2] But if a Soviet citizen refrains from joining the party when he has the opportunity—as it seems that many do—it is of such inconveniences that he is likely to be thinking. It is improbable that he wishes to dissociate himself from the official philosophy or current policies or, unless perhaps he holds strong religious views, from any part of them.

The incentives to assume these burdens are no less obvious than the burdens themselves. A party card is almost indispensable for advancement to the highest posts in all walks of life. Without one probably no army officer could hope today to get beyond junior rank, no worker in industry or commerce to attain a managerial post in an enterprise of any size and significance, unless his technical abilities were quite exceptional, and even then considerable material inducements and moral pressure would be applied to persuade him to join. Latterly, the peasant who is not prepared to associate himself with this product of the townsman's political speculations has as little hope of ever being chairman of a collective farm. For a post of any effective influence in the administrative organs of the Soviet system the requirement is the same. For the really ambitious there is the prospect, at the price of accepting even greater restrictions and even greater risks, of paid full-time office in the administration of the party itself. Apart from these more tangible attractions the social cachet of belonging to a unique élite organisation of which the prestige is built up by all the resources of official propaganda must count for something.

[1] e.g., the case of Mr. Dygai mentioned below, p. 177.
[2] G. A. Tokaev, *Betrayal of an Ideal* (1954).

For the ordinary member, who is not prepared or able to make a career as a full-time party official, influence within the party is probably very narrowly limited. The large issues of policy never come up for discussion, and as regards decisions of detail the principal local party officials bear too much personal responsibility for it to be at all probable that they will stand much interference from the rank-and-file members. The power of election, too, is probably not much more effective within the party than outside it. At the beginning of March 1937 the Central Committee ordered that the party's electoral practices should be brought into accordance with those of the state as established by the new constitution. Secret balloting upon individual candidates was to replace open voting on a list. The practice of co-opting, instead of electing, a large part of the membership of party committees, which was declared to be widespread, was condemned, and regular holding of elections was prescribed. Nevertheless it was not intended to give the local organisations an entirely free hand. In August of the following year the appointment of all first, second and third secretaries down to district and town level was placed in the gift of the federal Central Committee, though without removing the local power of election.[1] Since the war there have been further complaints of neglect of the electoral principle. In 1947 it was complained that there had been no party elections at district, town or regional level in Belorussia since the war. In any case, since all appointments by whomever made require confirmation by higher authority, the scope of selection of the local bodies must at least be limited by knowledge of what would be acceptable. Moreover, the cadres secretary of the next higher level attends all election meetings and apparently always has a candidate to recommend as secretary or head of department, who is always elected. He is supposed to persuade rather than to coerce; the cadres secretary who informed a conference that 'In the practice of party work it is not the accepted thing to nominate for the list of candidates for secret voting any candidates in excess of the number which it is necessary to elect to the membership of the district party committee',[2] was held to be at fault. Nevertheless he is expected to get the right man in, and does. We have accounts of posts of first district secretaries being as a general practice filled from among the junior secretaries and departmental heads of the regional party organisation. The ordinary party member generally has his reward in the form of influence, but outside the party, not within it.

[1] *Partinoe Stroiteljstvo*, No. 19–20 of 1938, p. 78, quoted in Rigby, Thesis, p. 338, who suggests that the requirement has probably lapsed. See p. 181 on appointment and election to party and other office.
[2] *Partinaja Zhizn*, No. 1 of 1948, pp. 27–8.

For the party office-holders the position is very different. Their place is one of real influence and real personal responsibility. In particular the first secretary of a party organisation from district upwards is the general agent of the government for his area. The success or failure of that area in fulfilling the assignments set it by current government policy, particularly in agricultural production and deliveries, is set to his account. To succeed he must know the resources of his area and the character of the people with whom he has to deal, take decisions and exercise persuasion. Instructions from above can never be sufficiently detailed, and a regular target of attacks in the Soviet press is the party secretary or other party official who spends all his working hours in his office, or in meetings passing on the instructions which he has received, and issuing commands instead of developing and applying a sense of circumstance and personality in the field. The advice is much the same as that given to prefect or district commissioner in other systems of government. How far his influence can be exercised on those above as well as those below, to urge a slower or more rapid process of local industrialisation, better supplies to consumer goods or the commitments of a large proportion of the country's resources and attention to the exploitation of a promising industrial or agricultural technique of interest to his area, it is hard to say, depending as it must on the personalities involved. It is possible that Mr. Khrushchov may have discovered for himself the possibilities of maize cultivation, but it may also be that the idea was conceived by an official who thought he could earn credit by growing it well in his own area. Clearly in the Soviet Union as elsewhere it is impossible for any one mind to know all things, and to think out all things, without influence from outside. Even Stalin must have needed to consult at least the politbureau on some matters, and it is highly probable that he was obliged to accept the word of regional party first secretaries and of the Central Committee members drawn largely from their ranks, as well as of the ministers and heads of other principal agencies on the state of affairs in their own areas or fields of action, though not necessarily without corroboration. With his probably less self-confident successors the need may well be the greater; merely to meet the top leaders or their immediate advisers is to have some influence.

The number of officials on the paid establishment of the party was stated in the report of the checking commission to the Twentieth Congress in 1956 to have diminished since 1952 by 24.7 per cent, but it has not been officially stated what the figure then was. A common, though not very confident, estimate at that time was a little under 200,000,[1] which would give some 150,000 in 1956. The chairman of the

[1] e.g., Fainsod (op. cit., p. 178), suggests 194,000.

commission reported that the great preponderance of the established party workers belonged to town or district committees and primary organisations; that is to say, the levels at which the greater part of the operative work is done. The establishments of regional and territorial committees and republican central committees, it was stated, did not amount to more than 12.2 per cent of all the local staffs (i.e. of our hypothetical 150,000 less perhaps some 800 in Moscow. This gave these widely varied units an average of 108 officials each. Districts (some 4,000, each with a staff of two or more secretaries and some dozen department and sector heads and 'instructors' for work in the field) must have at least 60,000 'responsible workers'. These may include many of the 30,000 working in May 1955, presumably as full-time paid officials, in the party instructor groups in the machine-tractor stations, though some have gone to farm directorships or chairmanships. Towns of various sizes and the largest primary organisations —they are mostly small enough to have only a part-time secretary— can easily make up the further 60,000 or so—if these figures mean anything. With closer control of agriculture—since early 1958 no longer through machine-tractor stations—and of industry through councils of the economy there can be little room for staff cuts.

There is little certain evidence of how one rises into and through this select corps within the party, for the careers of the leading officials generally become known to the outside world only when they have well established themselves; the significant earlier stages are missing. It has been stated that organs of the party and soviet systems and the economy are staffed largely from among secretaries of primary party organisations, and the duty laid by the Central Committee in February–March 1937 upon every secretary to select and train two deputies for possible advancement to his own office is still quoted as actual, and probably applies in the sense that all leading officials are supposed to keep an eye open for talent. Readiness in a member to give largely of his time and self-advertisement to those in whose gift the post lies are probably the usual ways to these and equivalent initial appointments. Formal educational attainments now evidently play a large part in the selection, and the party's own training schemes are related to them. It has been suggested of late that this criterion is over-emphasised to the exclusion of consideration of character and organisational ability. In 1954 24.3 per cent of the district-committee first secretaries, 14.7 per cent of the junior secretaries at the same level, and 14.6 per cent of the chairmen of district soviet executive committees, who for obvious reasons are commonly put in the same category in Soviet writings, had a full higher education; for incomplete higher education and middle-school education together the figures in the same three categories were respectively 70.4 per cent, 79.1 per cent and 69.6 per cent for 1952, the latest year for which details were available. In all cases this was a marked increase over the figures for 1946 or the pre-war years.[1] Given the necessary educational standard, or even without it, since it is likely that quite a number of exceptions are still made in the formal requirements, work as an ordinary member or unpaid official, particularly in connection with some successful campaign, is probably the best way of showing the requisite qualities of character and organisational ability to obtain a permanent place in the party administration, and to procure advancement within it. Similarly, association with failure, inability to raise production, a tendency to antagonise unnecessarily and produce resistance must have undone many officials and returned them to their places in factory or collective farm. Typically, it seems, the party official is not a technician, a master of any particular process, even of the propaganda process for which the party is peculiarly responsible, but an organiser, a mover of men, able to secure results in any field of activity. Whereas there are specialisms in wide variety developing in Russia, and a man can live out his life and obtain distinction, and probably even ministerial rank, in a single industry, the type of official in whose career party office has a large place is distinguished by ability to move from one field to another, within the party or outside it—as chairman of the local trade-union organisation, as chairman of the soviet executive committee and particularly latterly as chairman of a collective farm—or as a party first secretary to marshal all fields. Territorial, as well as functional, mobility is a feature of this career, probably because of this adaptability and the desire to have the best men at the points where trouble of whatever kind happens to require action rather than from any fear on the part of the authorities of their establishing a local connection, though that motive is not to be excluded. It is apparently a perilous career, but for one who can play it properly may be brilliant. If he can rise to the status of a regional first secretary he will receive emoluments and perquisites and influence such as are rare in any system, perhaps obtain a place on the Central Committee, and collect an Order of Lenin—or, at worst, the lower order of the Red Banner of Labour—upon his fiftieth birthday.

The Party as Administrative Machinery

The function of the Communist Party of the Soviet Union is comprehensive, as the constitution itself indicates, and it has repeatedly

[1] Particulars for 1954 and 1946 in article in *Partinaja Zhizn*, No. 9 of 1954, pp. 6–7. Those for 1934 and 1939 are in Fainsod, op. cit., p. 321.

been said, in one form or another, that its concern extends to the whole life of Soviet society. This life is conceived mainly in economic terms by those who have most influence in shaping it, so the economic motive predominates in definitions of the business of the party. 'Party committees as organs of political leadership,' it was said in a *Pravda* editorial (5th January 1955), 'are responsible for the condition of the economy. The party appraises the work of its local agencies on the basis of actual economic result.' It added, however, 'the solution of economic tasks should be approached by methods characteristic of party organisations. Party workers cannot narrow their work to the sphere of economics only. They are first and foremost social and political workers. What is required of them is the ability to combine political and economic work.' For the performance of this administrative or managerial function the party has one of its most valuable means in its individual members, many of them placed in the key positions in ministries and soviets, in the factories and the intermediate bodies between them and their ministries, and in the similar links in the chain of agricultural management from the collective farm upwards. All of them are indicated by the very fact of their membership as among the most ambitious in the community, and a number of them zealots. Such as are not holders of office are thus likely to be contenders for office in the party or elsewhere, and accordingly watchful for faults among those above. Such considerations of interest are supported by the voice of duty as expressed in the party rules; and though evidently the lower office-holders often make the task difficult and sometimes perilous, the higher management is not sparing in its efforts to circumvent them. The more enthusiastic and even the merely intermittently enthusiastic party members form a band of trusties with a stake in the established order.

It is not enough that members should be energetic and intolerant of sloth and inefficiency in the part of the machine with which they are charged. They are concerned not merely with expeditiousness of performance but also with the correctness of the decisions taken, and of that correctness the party itself is the measure.[1] Consequently, for example, it is reasonable that 'the party gives the soviets directing instructions determining the political line and orientating their work'.[2] It is not a matter of a few general guiding principles laid down at the centre. The party repeatedly insists that the correct decision must be 'concrete' and based on knowledge, both 'scientific' (i.e. theoretical, or

---

[1] 'To decide a question rightly means to decide it in full accord with the policy of the Communist Party and of the Soviet government . . .' (G. I. Petrov in *S.G. i P.*, No. 8 of 1955, p. 23.

[2] V. Borisov in *S.G. i P.*, No. 12 of 1947, p. 11.

Marxist-Leninist) and practical. It is to provide this concreteness, to relate the central policy to local circumstances—though, the centre in practice always insists, without rejecting any part of it—that the chain of local party organisations exists, and it is consequently from them that the soviets receive the 'directing instructions', and as elaborated by them that these are binding upon the soviets. It is suggested that this should be achieved 'not by commanding but on the basis of the influence exerted on the activities of these organisations by the communists working in them'.[1] This influence, however, in a matter of such importance cannot be left to individual conscience and public spirit. We find the Drogobych regional party conference in the Ukraine criticising two of the regional party secretaries for failure to attend sittings of the regional soviet executive committee of which they were members. In their work, we have seen, they are required to operate in disciplined groups. Such practices are not peculiarly Soviet, but it is evident that the process sometimes takes peculiarly direct administrative forms. Thus we find *Pravda* (7th January 1953) reporting without any indication of disapproval that the bureau of the Primorski (Litoral) territorial party committee, in the far east of the R.S.F.S.R., had twice charged the head of the territorial soviet executive committee's commerce section to attend in one of the towns of the territory and help local organisations with reforms, and had censured him for doing nothing about it.

There exists also another form of supervision which is distinctive of the Soviet system: a standing inspection—not ideological but mainly economic and organisational—conducted by paid officials of the party with acknowledged right of access to the records. Committees of the party, or their bureaux, are required to exercise a constant supervision over the soviets and their executive committees at their several levels, and to report to the next higher level of the party up to the centre. There the ministries have their own party committees, with a similar right of supervision vested in a secretary paid from party funds and so independent of the ministry payroll and of any influence exercised from within the ministry. In a case reported in May 1954 the secretary of the party organisation in the federal Ministry of Building was found to have been receiving pay from the ministry for filling a fictitious post of deputy minister. 'Minister Dygai,' it was reported, 'irresponsibly fixed rates of payments to party officials, and by thus corrupting them tied their hands.'[2] The Central Committee of the party removed the party secretary from his post; and others, including the minister himself, received reprimands. He nevertheless retained his ministry—somewhat truncated

---

[1] Borisov, op. cit., p. 10.
[2] *Partinaja Zhizn*, No. 3 of 1954.

by later reforms until the May 1957 changes, held a high R.S.F.S.R. planning post and re-joined the Union government in August 1959.

Locally, too, the party, in so far as it acts institutionally rather than through its individual members, does not confine itself to the general regulatory organs of the state, the soviets. The party committees in the larger enterprises have their own officials enjoying a separately financed independence similar to that of the corresponding bodies in the ministries. 'The party exercises strict supervision to see that the independence of party officials is not infringed, that nothing hinders them from developing self-criticism and criticism from below. Party officials who are excused from production duties, as is known, are paid from party funds and are forbidden to receive payment under any pretext from economic organisations. The party Central Committee most strictly forbids economic executives to award bonuses or otherwise reward party officials. Party officials are similarly forbidden to accept any bonus or emolument from economic organisations.'[1] Secretaries of smaller party organisations who continue to hold productive posts—often it seems as foremen or in similar capacities—seem to have the same duties as paid secretaries. These officials answer to the industrial department of the party organisation at the appropriate level. In 1939 this link and the departments themselves were abolished as detracting from the management's authority, but in 1941 they were restored. They seem to form an essential link in the industrial-administrative structure. The party organisations should not, however, wait passively for the reports of the factory committees and their secretaries. Party organisations at the responsible level and in all higher levels are empowered and expected to carry out regular inspections and to give directions. The Soviet press regularly complains of bad planning of such inspections so that the management is troubled by visitors from too many levels within a short time, superficiality of interest in some places and a tendency to keep entirely to the managerial level instead of combining the inspection with political work among the workers at large. All that one enterprise has seen of the party officials during the past year had been one visit from the first secretary and two or three from the secretary for the industrial department, which, it was implied, was not enough. They had been concerned merely to collect facts for production at the next meeting of the party bureau, plenary session of the committee or conference, and had not taken the trouble to check the accuracy of the information which they had been given. Here, as in all fields, the standard which the authorities have in mind is the constant retention, by various means, of a finger on the pulse of activity in the area, not an occasional inspection.

[1] *Partinaja Zhizn* No. 3 of 1954.

In the councils of the economy of the economic-administrative districts the party as such is apparently represented without regard to the theoretical objections to direct intervention in management. It was envisaged that the reform 'will increase immeasurably the responsibility of the party organisations' at region for economic affairs.[1] Regional first secretaries at once and repeatedly agreed in print; neglect of their instructions could not in future be justified by a plea of ministry orders from Moscow. The council chairman—perhaps from industry, but of republican central committee or equivalent party status—ranks below the secretary and state chairman of his area.

In agriculture the party's responsibility was already of a peculiarly direct administrative kind. Exhortation and censure were conventionally addressed in the press, and probably elsewhere, jointly to 'party, soviet and agricultural organs', the last being those of the Ministry of Agriculture, in general the management of machine-tractor stations, in respect of collective farms and of the Ministry of State Farms for its smaller domain. Soviet executive committees were here more fully involved than in industry because of the absence from co-operative —though not from state-farm—agriculture of the enterprise directly subordinate to the federation or union republic which made up a large part of the structure of industrial management; the party because of the lack of an expert corps which it could trust even as little as industrial managements. The district soviets were safely in party hands, but the Ministry of Agriculture seems to have been in something of a struggle for competence ever since the days of collectivisation, and as the principal force of experts it was in a rather strong position. But the party has usually led, and of recent years it has tightened its hold. The plenary session of the party Central Committee concerned with agriculture in September 1953 included among its resolutions one 'to have in the district committee a group of workers for each machine-tractor station headed by a secretary of the district party committee, which should conduct party political work in the machine-tractor station and in the collective farms which it serves. The general direction of all these groups shall be carried out by the first secretary of the district committee'.[2] In connection with this development it was decided to abolish the post of deputy director of the machine-tractor station for political affairs, which had been the previous channel of party work in this field. Mr. Khrushchov suggested at the Central Committee meeting that the secretaries of these groups should live on the machine-tractor stations to which they were assigned, and the press in subsequent

[1] Mr. Khrushchov's theses, *Pravda*, 30th March 1957.
[2] *KPSS v Rez.*, II, 1195.

months regularly reported more or less successful efforts to get them to do so, in spite of their own preference for living and working in the district centre. The secretaries employed to this end were apparently additional to the previous establishment of their party committees but have much the same backgrounds of party and other experience. Of the 118 secretaries of such groups working in Penza district already at the end of 1953, seventy-eight had already worked as secretaries of district party committees, eighteen had been heads of departments in such committees, and ten were secretaries of party organisations in machine-tractor stations. The 'instructors' who made up such groups were each responsible for a group of collective farms. In addition to political instruction they had 'responsibility for carrying out party decisions'.[1] With the dissolution of the machine-tractor stations from early 1958 the district committees resumed control from the district centre, but were still probably stronger than they had been before 1953 by the concentration of the collective farms into fewer units, by the loss by the Ministry of Agriculture—as by other ministries—of much of its managerial function and by the increased 'instructor' staffs in their own organisations. State farms, now under the councils of the economy, are presumably a concern of the regional party committees.

A principal concern of the party from the first has been staffing, or, as the terminology has it, cadres work. This is not merely the provision of a civil service. The party's concern with cadres extends to the political posts, both representative and administrative, as known in other countries, to managerial and technical posts in industry and to key posts in all other walks of life and, to some extent, to lesser posts as well. The Soviet Union is best regarded as a single concern with vast commitments and limited resources of educated manpower. The party is not the sole agency concerned with this problem. Ministries and enterprises have their own cadres departments, and in fact it is usual for the responsibility for appointment or election to any important office outside the party's own staff to be divided among as many as four authorities: the soviet or economic organ to which the appointment is to be made, the appropriate ministry or other superior authority and the party committees, or the responsible departments in them—at present, as we have seen, divided according to the kind of activity rather than united in a single cadres department—of both levels.[2] But the party as the 'leading nucleus' bears, as in other business, a greater responsibility than the other organs. We find the good district party secretary moving his party forces about 'to the decisive sectors of production'. The work

[1] *Pravda*, 11th January 1954. [2] Rigby, Thesis, p. 367.

is of the first importance, and seems to have formed the basis for the earlier career of Mr. Malenkov.

The party committee at each level has a schedule of appointments (*nomenklatura*), for which it is responsible as appointing or confirming authority, including those of leading officials of machine-tractor stations, factories and other enterprises, banks, agricultural procurement agencies and collective farms, in addition to official posts in the soviets or in the party. Like most other organisational matters in the Soviet Union, the allocation of responsibility for appointments varies with time and place according to a debate in the party mind between the voice of necessity, which demands centralisation, and the voice of conscience, which speaks for decentralisation. For instance, until early in 1954 appointment to posts as chairmen of collective farms was apparently in the gift of district party committees, but perhaps because these were evidently apt to be moved by improper considerations such posts were then removed to the regional *nomenklatura*.[1] Vice-chairmen, field-work-gang ('brigade') leaders and livestock-farm managers were left to the district.[2] At a moment of large-scale emergency recruiting for such work the district seems still to have been important as a provider, if not as appointing authority. Thus it is reported that in the Smolensk region, 'In the spring and summer of 1954, 825 district and regional workers were sent to leading work in the collective farms. Among those recommended for posts as chairmen of collective farms were fifty-six secretaries of district party committees, more than 200 heads of departments of district committees of the party, and deputy chairmen of executive committees'. Under such special circumstances there may even have been some public consultation to learn of suitable persons: 'In all towns and districts of the region assemblies of the party activists have been held. At them selection was made of the most authoritative and experienced comrades for work in the capacity of chairmen of collective farms',[3] but it seems clear that more normally such appointments are made by the party as a routine administrative matter. On the

[1] *Pravda*, 6th March 1954, decision of a plenary session of the party Central Committee in February–March 1954.
[2] I. V. Pavlov (in N. D. Kazantsev, I. V. Pavlov, A. A. Ruskol (eds.), *Kolhoznoe Pravo* (1955), p. 305) speaks of this assignment of the presentation to posts of chairman and vice-chairman as if it were a devolution down the administrative line 'to raise the responsibility of local party organs'. It may be that there is now less interference from the centre, but the recent mass drafting of suitable people from the towns into agricultural management hardly suggests it. On the concern of party organs with the appointment and dismissal of the lower office-holders on collective farms, see H. Dinerstein, *Communism and the Russian Peasant*, p. 89.
[3] *Kommunist*, No. 3 (February) of 1956.

basis of reports submitted by their own inspectors, examination of subordinate officials, and reports from the public the responsible departments at all levels are expected to maintain records of persons suitable for appointments to any post which may occur within their *nomenklatura*. These are not confined to members and candidates of the party, though they are an important and flexible resource. As the composition of the soviets suggests, non-party men may be used in positions of considerable prestige and even, it seems, of real importance. At the least the district *nomenklatura* seems to have included some hundreds of types of posts and that of a union republic some thousands.[1] As usual, however, party responsibility is not limited by formal assignment, so that party organisations at any level are required to keep a general eye on all cadres matters, and are liable to blame for failure to draw attention to suitable persons for even the less important posts which are not formally theirs to fill. Nor can they count on being left alone to exercise their power of presentation. The source quoted on Smolensk region reports that 'in 1955 upon the call of the Central Committee of the Soviet Party of the Soviet Union and the Council of Ministers of the U.S.S.R. a further 380 persons were selected for the region and sent by the Moscow party organisation for work as chairmen of collective farms', and it is probable that such assistance by the centre is general. Probably the principal party posts of all levels—secretaries, from primary organisation upwards, and heads of all the main departments —are on the *nomenklatura* of the next higher level with or without higher confirmation. The appropriate party authority is held responsible for the quality of those whom it appoints. Its reconciliation of its own responsibilities in connection with appointments with the rights of others—the members of a soviet or its executive committee in the appointment of their officials, the members of a collective farm in the choice of their chairman and a ministry in its selection of staff—is a matter for its own tact. Here, as in many other fields, the party evidently values the ability of an official to enforce the party's will without causing avoidable hard feelings, and will not long tolerate one whose action in this respect repeatedly raises a storm.

Similar considerations of tact and also, it seems, a reluctance to waste the higher organising and co-ordinating abilities of the party officials in matters of detail which can safely be left to a lower grade of staff in soviet

---

[1] Rigby (Thesis, pp. 332–3) gives about 220 for districts and towns in Kirgizia, about 800 for regions and 2,700 for the republican Central Committee (quoting *Sovetskaja Kirgizia*, 21st September 1952, as the basis of his calculation). Kirgizia, as one of the less-developed republics, probably has fewer categories than most.

or other organs, are evident in official criticism of other aspects of party work. Stalin's dictum that 'The party is the nucleus of . . . [state] authority, but it is not, and cannot be identified with, state authority'[1] has been quoted or paraphrased time and again as a ruling that it is incorrect for party organs to displace organs of the state, though exception is made for times of emergency such as the war and, apparently, for areas of special urgency, such as agriculture now seems to be. They should in principle develop, encourage and assist the latter, arrange for the training of their officials, keep them informed on policy and, above all, keep them under supervision. But they must not use them as their mere agents, and they must not involve themselves needlessly in details. Thus two periodicals of April 1948 criticise a regional party committee for employing the chairman of the regional party executive committee upon work in one of the districts for months at a time and a district party committee for issuing detailed instructions to a village soviet upon the procurement of wood, the repair of club-houses, and the cleaning of seed. At the end of the previous year it was held unsatisfactory that a district party committee should be in direct telephone communication with a collective farm whereas neither the district agriculture administration nor the district executive committee was so provided, so that for information about the affairs of the collective farm they had to get into touch with the party secretary. Such a case might not now incur criticism. There is an occasional complaint that the party is too much involved in economic matters generally, but this is hard to avoid in Russia's circumstances of permanent crisis.

These administrative functions demand of the party administrators qualities which, whether admirable or not, are certainly rare, and it is evident from criticism in the press that they are not always up to the required standard which their party requires. The offence of 'familyness', readiness to do a deal for personal advantage or an easy life with those whom they are supposed to be supervising, apparently exists even in the élite, where it is particularly reprobated. Indeed the system of appointment which virtually makes all the principal functionaries in an area clients of the local first secretary, probably tends to promote it. Against this vice the supreme virtue of 'partyness' seems to have a hard fight. Moreover, officials of the party, and especially the prominent, show a human resentment of criticism which at times clearly takes the form of extreme vindictiveness. The party, apart from any concern which it may feel for justice, is interested that they should not get out of hand, and to that end it enforces upon them an obligatory humility. In

[1] Stalin, *Voprosy Leninizma* (Problems of Leninism), 11th Russian edition (1945), p. 124.

view of the very substantial power which the system places in their hands, this is difficult; it involves a complexity of supervision which is very wasteful of manpower and a severity of retribution which, because many cases are never known to the higher authorities, cannot but appear arbitrary. This is hardly conducive to the smoothness of operation of the political system.

Even without avoidable fault this maintenance of a duplicate, and rather higher-powered, administration is a substantial addition to the cost of running a country which is still poor by the measure of its ambitions. The cost is somewhat diminished, presumably by the contrivance of the system so as to attract much voluntary unpaid service from the ambitious in the hope of future advantage, but this can only cover part of the field. The desire of the authorities to keep this area of enthusiasm and voluntary action as large as possible, and consequently the field of bureaucracy as small as possible, is understandable. So is the desire of the established officials in both state and party—or, to put it in more realistic terms, in the general state service, and in that select corps of organisers within it which is called the party apparatus—to widen the area of established procedures and of predictability.

The Party as Organised Faith

Probably even now some of the Soviet leaders are so far imbued with the principles of primitive Marxism that they would prefer to concentrate on the indoctrination of the people and then leave to them the 'administration of things'.[1] But certainly in practice they lack sufficient confidence in the force of indoctrination to influence action, and with good cause. Nevertheless ideology is still evidently felt to have a place of first importance in the system. Russian official pronouncements repeatedly insist that 'party work is, above all, work with people', even in its administrative aspects, and, as we have seen, the inspection of factories and the direction of collective farms alike are supposed to be combined with 'political work', the promotion of right views. The party retains from its conspiratorial days the function of all political parties, even of those in parliamentary countries, of keeping the ideology up to date, bending it to fit developments of circumstances and of the faction fight, reconciling divergent interpretations of it, proving its consistency with its alleged principles and winning support for it. It differs from parliamentary parties in its monopoly of power and, by reason of its control over the machinery of state, its penal sanctions extending beyond

---

[1] This is, in principle, the position of the League of Communists of Yugoslavia.

expulsion even for purely ideological offences, and in being the authorised and sole agency of the state for such work. Though the several ministries, especially those concerned with education and culture, have propaganda functions in their own fields, there is no ministry charged with propaganda or information work in general. The practice of some local party organisations in earlier days of turning over their agitation functions to the soviet executive committees at their several levels was denounced as an error and would almost certainly be so regarded now. Here as elsewhere it is pointless to discuss whether the party has taken command of the state or the state of the party; they are integrated so that the party is merely a specialised agency of the whole system by which the society is organised. As we have seen, it does not, like parliamentary parties, have to campaign as such for election.

The process of reaching agreement—that is to say, the political process as we have defined it—is obviously easier if all accept the same things as good. Thus ideology is an important political institution. If it is generally accepted within the political community it will enable the leadership to silence criticism by the unanswerable argument, and often to convince inconvenient persons of their own error and guilt, which for its exemplary effect on others is better than merely persuading them of the advisability of professing it. The evidence which we have of Soviet purges, 'self-criticism', and criminal proceedings, suggests convincingly that the official ideology is thus deep-rooted. Ideological exercises, like military drill, instil the habit of ready response to orders, and keep the mind occupied to the exclusion of other ideas. Because the official ideology of the Soviet Union offers a complete explanation for all the circumstances of life and is taught in a vacuum of other ideas, those educated in it have great difficulty in entirely rejecting it at any time.

Ideological uniformity, however, has its cost. The minimum responsiveness of all is purchased at the cost of apathy in a part of the intelligentsia, a lack of initiative among those whose business is the understanding of human affairs. This is evidenced by the constant complaints of the failure of Soviet playwrights and other literary men to produce works which, besides being ideologically unobjectionable, are also reasonably interesting. Further, the Soviet intellectual world at large is often denied the opportunity to take account of fruitful trends of thought in the non-Marxist world, though it is apparently also saved from the temptation to explore some philosophical and other intellectual dead ends there in fashion. Moreover, the propagation of the official faith is a further burden upon the administrative system, in this case primarily upon that part of it which is known as the party.

The most important method by which the member is kept in touch with the latest trends in the party line is the regular meeting of his primary party organisation and of any conferences at higher level to which he may be elected, but also all members are supposed to devote some attention to their own political education. Since 1947 regular attendance at ideological meetings has not in principle been compulsory, but all members who do not attend are apparently expected to undertake some course of private study. It is evident that they do not always do so in any form acceptable to party authority, and that in particular they try to avoid the investigation of political themes which might conceivably involve them in trouble. An article by Mrs. Furtseva, the new candidate member of the party Praesidium, published in February 1956, complained of a preference among members for the study of remote periods of history, and particularly singled out for criticism the party members in the Ministry of the Fuel Industry of the R.S.F.S.R. who had elected to study medieval history. The ministry party committee, she suggested, should have directed them to some course of study more relevant to their work. The same article directed attention to the lack of local political schools in one of the districts of Moscow and to the poor attendances. The report of the central checking commission at the Twentieth Party Congress in the same month, however, stated that short courses and seminars run by regional and territorial committees and republican central committees had in the course of the year been attended by 50,000 propaganda workers, and the party's 288 evening universities of Marxism-Leninism by 149,000, 80,000 of them party members, 33,000 *komsomol* and 36,000 non-party, apart from the work of the major training institutions. In addition to such means of education there are also the party publications, which include *Pravda*, the principal national daily paper and critic and leader of the rest of the Soviet press, together with a large proportion of the provincial daily press, and a number of specialist organs, including in particular the Central Committee's 'theoretical and political journal' *Kommunist* and its organisational journal *Partijnaja Zhizn*. In the contents of these the practical nature of the system's concerns is clearly indicated. Discussion of concrete tasks in the organisation of industry and agriculture is much more frequent than are speculations on the nature of society in general. Comments on foreign affairs, where the scope of manipulative action by means which can be publicly discussed is more limited, make a greater use of the categories of Marxist theory. Even there they are very obviously directed to striking home the lessons which happen to fit in with the latest turns of practical policy. The daily press in particular, and to some extent *Partijnaja Zhizn*, devote much of their attention to shortcomings on the part of individuals in the fulfilment of the tasks assigned to them. To the foreign observer it must remain something of a mystery why anybody regularly reads some or perhaps most of these journals, in view of their very poor and very inexplicit news coverage. It may be assumed that the career party official, those who hope to be so, and persons in leading positions in other fields, will wish to know what themes are particularly engaging the party mind at any given moment, so that they may give due attention to them in their own writings and utterances. Since it is practicably impossible to keep a watch on everything which is supposed to receive their attention, they must seek to show themselves particularly watchful against the shortcomings of others in those fields where slackness on their part is, for the time being, particularly apt to involve themselves in official censure. The total circulation of the Soviet press is limited by the standards of other countries. The total circulation for one issue of each of the 7,537 newspapers, ranging in frequency of appearance from the unique seven issues of *Pravda* a week and perhaps 500 others which may roughly be called dailies, to the weeklies, is given in 1957 as 53,500,000. Issues are usually of four pages each. Publications of periodical form are given as over 2,500 and their total annual circulation as 418,500,000.

The activities of propaganda and agitation named in the designation of the responsible branch of the party's administration are distinguished in official terminology. Lenin quoted with approval Plekhanov's statement that 'a propagandist presents many ideas to one or a few persons; an agitator presents only one or a few ideas, but he presents them to a mass of people'. This distinction fits in with the regime's recognition that different ideological standards are appropriate for the leaders and for the people at large and even the general run of party members. The rules of the party now only require members to 'recognise' (*priznatj*) its programme. A previous requirement, that before admission as full members they should 'assimilate' (*usvoitj*)—that is, fully understand—it, was dropped in the revision of 1939 on the authority of a statement of Stalin in 1937 that its application would 'leave only intellectuals and learned persons generally in our party. Who wants such a party?'[1] Zhdanov, introducing the revision, pointed the contrast with the leaders who still needed to 'assimilate'.

Doctrine need play only a small part in the thinking of those who are not professionally committed to it as propagandists or in similar capacities. But whatever is presented must be swallowed whole. The admission of disagreement on points of doctrine which diversified party life in the early years after the revolution ceased with the rise of Stalin

---

[1] Stalin in *Vlastj Sovetov*, 6–7 of 1937, pp. 26–7, quoted in resolution of the Eighteenth Congress of the party, 1939; *KPSS v Rez.*, II, 912.

to power and has not been revived with his death and partial denunciation. If the cult of individuality is now proscribed, the cult of infallibility of a collective management consisting, apparently, mainly of Mr. Khrushchov is no less in force than before.

The department of propaganda and agitation under the Central Committee of the party is much more an operative agency in itself than are most of the other departments which are concerned to supervise the work of the ministries in the state structure. It included, according to an analysis of 1950, twelve sectors: central press, local press, publishing houses, film, radio, fictional literature, art affairs (including theatre and music), cultural enlightenment institutions (i.e. mass education), schools (i.e. formal education), science, propaganda and agitation.[1] This structure, like most in the Soviet Union, has changed from time to time, but the total range of functions remains much the same. The structure at the lower levels is simpler, but always includes as an important part of its organisation a press section and a section for schools.

The party control of the press extends beyond the publication of its own journals. A number of the ministries, and also the youth organisation, and such approved specialist and learned organisations as the Writers' Union, produce their own newspapers and periodicals, but all are under the supervision of one or other of the press sectors of the party Central Committee and subordinate levels. Editors of all journals, party or otherwise, are appointed on the *nomenklatura* of some party committee, as are most other officials in positions of influence. As we have seen, special attention is devoted in the organisation of the party schools to the training of editors at all levels down to the local, and emphasis is laid upon the necessity of a regular guidance of them in the course of their work. 'The increased role of local newspapers in economic and cultural work wholly depends on the level of party guidance of the press,' said an article of April 1955, adding, with an echo of Lenin, 'Where this guidance is competent, the newspaper is a true propagandist and agitator, a militant organiser of the masses. . . . The party Central Committee persistently demands that local party agencies work with newspapers not as occasion arises but systematically and fundamentally, and direct their work from day to day'.[2] The local party committee should examine the editorial plans for some time ahead and suggest subjects. The same article, however, criticised the uniformity of style in Soviet newspapers, a theme which is constantly recurring in official

[1] Louis Nemzer, 'The Kremlin's Professional Staff: the "Apparatus" of the Central Committee of the C.P.S.U.', *American Political Science Review*, No. 1 of 1950, p. 72.
[2] *Kommunist*, No. 2 of 1955, p. 13.

pronouncements, and to the eye of the foreign observer obviously provides ground for criticism. Where the whole of the press is geared to the single machine of the state and party this fault is probably inevitable. Failure of local newspapers to devote attention to the principal themes which for the time being the government is seeking to propagate is another regular theme of criticism in the national newspapers. Specific instructions are from time to time issued to the press, as for instance the instructions from a plenary session of the party Central Committee of September 1953 to direct attention to socialist emulation and experience of progressive techniques. The demand that editorial plans should be inspected some time in advance can only be understood in the circumstances of the Soviet press, which is not bound by consideration of competition to publish news at the earliest possible opportunity, but can and does keep it for days or even for weeks. How far any individual editor can defy the instructions of a particular party official clearly depends upon much the same considerations of relative influence with higher authorities as determine other situations of power in the Soviet Union. We read of regional party committee officials in Gorki region, the assistant director of the industrial department, the director of the press department and the secretary of the Gorki town committee, allegedly seeking to prevent publication by the local newspaper of a satirical article on misappropriation of funds in a local factory. In the last of a number of telephone calls to the editor the town committee secretary said, 'I don't forbid it but I don't recommend it. I advise you to be more precise and weigh the pros and cons.' Apparently the newspaper did not publish; but *Pravda*, with which the editor was already presumably in touch, did, and the officials earned a rebuke.[1]

It is a frequent subject of complaint that the party is neglecting the ideological side of its work to concentrate upon its administrative, and particularly its economic, tasks. This, though reprehensible from the point of view of a party which has always laid much emphasis upon ideology as the foundation of its claim to sole power, and which makes no concessions to the limitations of human capacity, is nevertheless quite understandable. Officials are aware that failure in their more material tasks will the sooner be detected and visited upon them, and therefore they tend to concentrate on them. Many of them, it is frequently complained, bring to their ideological work the same trust in 'results' which can be set out statistically in the report of the party committee to its conference—'so many propagandists and agitators were selected, so many reports, lectures, talks and readings (even readings!) were carried out, so many thousand persons were "covered"'.[2]

[1] Feuilleton in *Pravda*, 31st March 1955.   [2] *Kommunist*, No. 18 of 1955.

One town, the commentator noted, had the impressive record of one agitator to three inhabitants; but it was not explained at the conference that none of them had done any explanatory work.

The Party as Symbol

An important function of the Communist Party is to be the embodiment of the Leninist revolutionary tradition, the link with the ideals of primitive Marxism, and the living justification of the authorities' claim to have possession of a philosophical method affording a unique insight into the causes of things. It is a mark of distinction from the outside world not favoured with this insight, a badge of the special holiness of Russia, and the embodiment of orthodoxy in a country which has always had, and appears still to need, a comprehensive official creed. For this reason, if for no other, the party must continue to be represented as something with a life of its own and not merely a part, however essential, of the state's administration.

The party has also an international significance. It is the embodiment of the hope of world revolution—of the hope, expressed in the heading of all the principal Soviet newspapers and periodicals, that the proletarians of all lands will unite. The Comintern, the Third International which until its abolition on 22nd May 1943 was specifically charged with this side of Soviet policy, and the Informburo, or, as the West knew it, to emphasise the continuity of aims and methods, the Cominform, the organisation of certain European Communist Parties formed in 1947 and dissolved in 1956, were comparatively unimportant bodies. The work could, did, and presumably still does go on even without their existence. Their purpose was symbolic, to remind foreign countries that they had Russia's friends in their midst, and in the case of the later organisation that Russia now had dependencies. In fact the party itself, even as a symbol—apart from its material contacts—has probably always been more important in this respect. It provides something with which communist parties abroad can feel kinship, as perhaps they could not with the Russian state, an inspiring vision of what it is like to be in power. Even so, it is unlikely that any very great weight is given in the minds of the Soviet leaders to this aspect of the party's role. It is essentially a practical instrument of rule.

CHAPTER V

The Web of Management

Organisation in Industry

Industrial enterprises (*predprijatie*), factories, mines, oil wells, chains of shops, etc., are, like towns, classified according to their 'subordination'. Hitherto there have been three categories: Union, Republican and Local, managed respectively by ministries at the federal level, ministries at republican level, and executive committees of local soviets, usually of regional, but sometimes also of district status. The ministries for enterprises of union subordination were either all-union or union-republican in structure, while those for enterprises of republican subordination might be of either union-republican or republican structure. Thus two levels of a union-republican ministry might be found running similar enterprises in the same place, the enterprise coming under the federal ministry being so managed, in principle, because of its greater importance as compared with the enterprise coming under the republican branch. Sometimes, understandably, the distinction became a little thin. Thus in 1954 two fisheries trusts were reported to be in business at Rostov both buying up fish from the collective organisations of fishermen in the Sea of Azov, yet one of them coming under the federal ministry of the fishing industry and one under the R.S.F.S.R. ministry of the same name. It was said that the two ministers could not agree upon a merger.[1] Little has been left in local subordination, though in principle local soviets have been given increased freedom of planning since the war, and therefore increased power to form such enterprises. Local industries have, in general, been concerned with consumer goods, to which, with very occasional exceptions, the authorities have always given a low priority. Even in this field there was little reason and less generosity. Rostov region executive committee had a hand in the management of six breweries and two confectionery factories, but its winemaking factories and bakeries, among other enterprises, were run from Moscow.[2] The favoured heavier and extractive industries have shown

[1] *Izvestia*, 17th July 1954. The fishing industry seems to have a particularly bad organisational record. See *Pravda*, 17th July 1955 (report of Mr. Bulganin) and 19th April 1957 on costs and administrative reduplication in the Far East.
[2] *Pravda*, 20th March 1957.

a constant tendency to move up the line into the direct management of federal ministries. This in general has meant their transference to the all-union category, but need not necessarily do so. Some mills and other minor enterprises for the processing of agricultural produce and enterprises for the production of bricks and tiles and other building materials are run by the collective farms, themselves generally comparable to enterprises of local subordination, and these 'are not forbidden to dispose of their surplus production to the local population'.

The main cause of high-level concern, and so of change, seems to have been the disposition of ministries to keep everything within the firm, to have transport, telephone lines, timber reserves and, above all, supply and constructional organisations of their own duplicating other systems.

It is declared that under the 1957 reorganisation there will be only two subordinations: to the council of the economy of an economic-administrative district, and to a local soviet executive committee. For most republics these are likely in fact to be the old republican and local subordinations. In the R.S.F S.R. the Ukraine and Kazahstan subordination is thus to two organs at regional level—one connected with the soviet executive committee, the other not. The surviving ministries, and where no ministry survives the State Planning Commission, are not to manage but to plan and supervise. Probably to date most enterprises have been run from federal level, though it has been reported that in 1955, in contrast to preceding years, the greater part of production came from ministries of union-republican structure. It has been said that under the new system the soviet executive committees will get most of the enterprises hitherto under republic, leaving the councils for the economy with those now federal.

The enterprise might be connected with its ministry through a number of intermediary bodies, trusts (*trest*), combines (*kombinat*), federations (*federatsia*), sectors (*sektor*), departments (*otdel*), administrations (*upravlenie*) and chief administrations (*glavnoe upravlenie*, commonly called *glavk*). Few chains of command had all these links, but it was stated in 1954 that such cases could then be found in the lumber, coal and oil industries. In fact there is a constant reshuffling in progress to meet new needs and, in intention, to eliminate unnecessary stages of management and so unnecessary staff. Cases, some unsuccessful, of direct subordination of trusts to chief administrations are reported. One article in this campaign in 1956 stated that 'the structure of many ministries and authorities on the three- or four-link system (chief administration—administration—department—sector) has given rise to an enormous number of small subdivisions and has led to an inflation of the staff, an increase of the cost of its maintenance, irresponsibility, formalism and an office-minded approach to the business'.[1] The ministries particularly mentioned were non-industrial—the Ministry of Agriculture, the Ministry of State Farms, the Ministry of Agricultural Procurements and the Ministry of Commerce. This statement of the position does not mean that the lower levels of the full range as mentioned above—the trust, the combine and the federation—did not exist in these fields. Such bodies are regarded as, like the enterprise itself, legal persons acting under authority of the ministry but with some independence of action and legal responsibility of their own, rather than as stages in the administration. The extent to which they can, in fact, live an independent life without thereby infringing the independence of the several enterprises is not clear. The word 'trusts' appeared in the Soviet terminology during the period of the New Economic Policy at a time when there was some imitation of the practices of the private-enterprise economy and an attempt to suggest competition with it. When in 1927 a new basic law on trusts was enacted this suggestion was dropped, and the trust became an administrative organisation subject, like all others, to the national economic plan.

The localised councils of the economy need a less massive connecting system, but seem sometimes to have needed some persuading of this, and there is little sign that the change goes beyond omission of the chief administration. It lives on, however, in the supply and disposal system under the State Planning Committee and Commissions. The problem of co-ordination remains.

The Men in the Machine

Apart from the minister himself, appointment to posts in the service of the several ministries, whether at headquarters or in the field, rests with those ministries, subject to the rights of the other participants in the system of dual subordination, the local soviet executive committees, and the parallel responsibility of the party. Establishments require confirmation by higher authority throughout the system, with presumably the advice of the State Establishments Administration of the Ministry of Finance, and general proportions of pay for each grade are fixed by the federal Council of Ministers. Ministries generally have specialists trained in their own schools or by courses provided to their requirements in schools of the general educational system. In general the best pupils of the schools of that system, as tested in the state's examinations, are admitted to ministry schools of higher educational standing without further tests, and others on the result of a special examination, much as

[1] E. V. Shorina in *S.G. i P.*, No. 8 of 1955, p. 17.

has been done with university admissions. At a lower level there is the system of Labour Reserves, begun apparently mainly as a drive to get surplus labour away from the farms. An edict of the Praesidium of the Supreme Soviet of the 2nd October 1940 provided for the mobilisation, by means of a quota from each collective farm, of up to a million young people annually for training for from six months to two years in essential industrial skills, after which they were required to serve in the appropriate branch for four years. Conscription seems no longer to be required since voluntary recruitment has proved adequate, but as a system of training schools which 'supplement vocational training with the regular ideological and political education of the students' and 'on instructions from the government redistribute the country's labour resources among the economic regions' it goes on. It was said in May 1957 that since its foundation about 9,000,000 skilled workers had been trained, including, apparently in the last three years, 900,000 mechanics for agriculture; in October 1955 there were over 3,000 schools in the scheme, 900 of them agricultural-mechanical.[1] Until the death of Stalin it was directed by a separate ministry, then merged in the Ministry of Culture, and is now apparently run by a chief administration directly under the federal Council of Ministers. The distinction between vocational and general schools, however, is not a sharp one. Institutions under the educational ministries, no less than those under the managerial ministries, are concerned with the training of cadres for more or less specifically envisaged posts. To minor posts as clerks or manual workers the head of the unit has apparently a substantially free power of appointment, and there have been frequent allegations in the Soviet press of lack of discretion in the exercise of this power, particularly failure to consult the labour books and other records concerning persons who subsequently proved to be dishonest or particularly unreliable. The labour book, instituted by decree of the Council of People's Commissars in December 1938, is a personal career record maintained for every Soviet citizen in employment and containing, among other details, records of posts held, reasons for leaving them and rates of pay received. It moves with the employee from post to post. In addition, since 1940 all residents in urban areas and within a wide radius of Moscow, Leningrad and Kiev are required to have internal passports, issued by town or district militia (police) headquarters upon application certificated by the soviet executive committee, which have to be registered with the police before they are allowed to take up residence, and these also record changes of employment. Cases are reported where with the aid of gullible officials wrong-minded citizens

[1] G. Zelenko (Director of the Chief Administration) in *Pravda*, 7th May 1957.

can get round even this obstacle to mobility. But if the system works properly the Soviet citizen should be well documented, and officials engaging staff are expected to take account of the fact.

The problem posed by the admission of trainees is less one of selection than of finding people of something like adequate quality, and training, posting and retaining them. A particular difficulty in respect of posting obviously arises from reluctance to serve on remote stations. Accounts are commonly given of intrigue among students completing their courses in ministry training schools and among officials already in state service to secure town posts or posts in the more advanced parts of the country. Personal contacts play a large part in this process of intrigue, and leading officials intervene to obtain satisfactory postings for their children. It is complained that excessive lenience is shown with the insubordinate and unreliable at all levels, such as the graduates who flatly refuse the postings offered. This is probably in consequence of the shortage of manpower, and especially educated and skilled manpower, in the Soviet economy. Where a course of training leads to a formal qualification refusal of appointment may apparently lead to its forfeiture, but trainees presumably understand the protective value of their indispensability. Once appointed, moreover, officials seem to have a tendency to drift back to the principal urban centres, or, with less obvious illegality but still contrary to approved policy, to continue to live in town while holding a rural post. Collective-farm chairmen and technical specialists and soviet executive committee chairmen seem particularly to offend in this respect. This results partly from habituation of leading officials to the middle-class comforts which their position enables them to enjoy in the towns, but it is akin to a similar problem of scarcity and instability of labour generally. An edict of the Praesidium of the Supreme Soviet of 26th June 1940 made the wilful abandonment of employment or absenteeism by any worker or official a criminal offence, but by an edict of the 25th April 1956 the criminal penalty for those offences was abolished, allegedly on the ground that the conscientiousness of labour had improved. Sanctions of a less drastic sort were still retained to induce labour to remain at its post. Persons changing their places of employment at their own request, with certain exceptions, and those dismissed for persistent absenteeism were to lose for a period of six months all service bonuses and the right to benefit for temporary incapacitation for work, and for the latter offence an entry was to be made in their labour books. Incapacitation benefit was restored to them in cases of industrial injury or occupational disease by edict of 31st January 1957, and in all other cases by one of 25th January 1960.

On his visit to Yugoslavia in June 1955 Mr. Khrushchov expressed very cautious interest in workers' participation in management as practiced there. At the end of a visit to one factory he said, 'I do not know whether we will be able to apply any of this in our country, for we have got used to a different system,' though he added that the Soviet Union would study the Yugoslav system and adopt from it anything which might be applicable, as it had already shown itself prepared to learn from American practice. Wide and constant consultation of workers directed by the party and trade union organisations and use of any practical ideas suggested is now in favour, but the 'different system' of individual authority and responsibility, established since early enthusiasm gave place to the planned economy has been little qualified by it. The director seems to be personally commissioned to obtain and maintain the equipment and materials, to engage and discharge staff, raise financial resources, handle moneys, conclude contracts and agreements and conduct legal proceedings as necessary to discharge the firm's production task, and the responsibility for shortcomings is his. But he is under considerably more restraint than his counterpart in a private-enterprise economy. Apart from the party organisation in the factory and the more specialised supervision of other networks, such as that of the Ministry of Internal Affairs, his range of action is limited by the financial conditions decreed in the state economic plan, by the rigidities of the system of allocation applying to many of the raw materials which he needs to complete his assignment and by wage rates and provisions of specialist staff to his departments fixed at higher levels. Articles by enterprise directors published in *Pravda* in 1955 complained that applications for materials were required to be submitted before precise instructions had been received from higher authorities on the range of goods to be produced in the following period, that the annual planning period was too short for many processes, and that it was difficult to provide incentives for special competence because the director's freedom to allocate the wages fund did not extend to administrative and technical personnel, because the maximum and minimum rates for other posts had often not been fixed and especially because the maximum for foremen had been fixed at a lower point than that for the best workers. The director was free to acquire a new item of equipment only up to the value of 300 roubles, and above that had to involve himself in the complexities of an application to the Industrial Bank. The agencies of the Ministry of Finance regulated minutely the sums which might be spent, even from the firm's own amortisation fund, for purposes of capital repairs. A business journey by a member of the staff required the approval of the chief administration, and a transfer of raw materials required that of the minister. These criticisms, like most appearing in the Soviet press, had obvious official endorsement. Mr. Bulganin, at the plenary session of the party Central Committee in July 1955 mentioned some of the same grievances, and added that 'The director of an enterprise cannot independently accept and execute orders placed by other organisations, even in cases where some productive sections of the enterprise are not working to capacity and the order could be executed without interfering with the basic programme of the enterprise'. The committee passed a resolution demanding the extension of directors' powers and the Council of Ministers duly produced a decree of the 9th August 1955. In the middle of 1957, however, the same grievances were still there; the measure, it was said, did not go far enough, the ministries failed to observe it, and the Bank interpreted it very restrictively. An enterprise could not obtain a supply of metal outside its allocation to meet a rush order, even where it could find a supplier with a stock of it. Nor even a ministry could release additional stocks of cement. Yet the enterprise's own allocation might not be fully met. Moreover directors hesitated to take on casual orders, lest in future years they find them added to their plans. Powers to pay bonuses or to spend money out of the enterprise's amortisation fund were still very restricted—the decree of August 1955 allowed expenditure on new equipment only up to 500 roubles—and plans were still made for unrealistically short periods and subject to arbitrary amendment during the year. If, however, the director is often set an impossible task, the inducements to find a way out may be considerable. Bonuses payable only if all obligations in the plan have been fulfilled, and increased greatly for any over-fulfilment, may amount to a substantial proportion of his salary. But, on the other hand, impossibility of performance because of conditions created by higher authority or external circumstances is considered no excuse for non-fulfilment of the assignment.

In this situation industry has to find unofficial methods, ranging from the semi-legal to the plainly illegal, of regulating its affairs. 'The Soviet industrial executive should never behave cunningly towards the state and put narrow interests before those of the state. Nevertheless, it is known that certain executives intentionally submit incorrect plan fulfilment figures in order to win bonuses or conceal defects.'[2] Apart from plain cooking of the record there are such methods as concentration on the more easily produced lines, so as to give a good overall result, and this is done on such a scale as to show up markedly in the figures for

[1] A. Krylov (a factory director) in *Kommunist*, No. 6 of 1957, pp. 44–9.
[2] L. Slepov in *Pravda*, 4th September 1955.

whole industries.[1] Influence again plays a part here. Many, or perhaps even most, enterprises maintain under various titles their purchasing agents and contact men to discover supplies, circumvent the usual channels and avoid unpleasantnesses. Some are virtually in private practice of their irregular profession. Satirical articles in the press mention the known pluralist obtaining from his various employers 5 per cent of the value of the supplies which he procures, plus expenses, and other agents, dealing in agricultural produce, monopolising the telephones at a town's post office. Probably the regime finds it advantageous to have the unorthodox ways of making the system work explored at the peril of individuals. Illegal practices which work can subsequently be legalised and generalised; those which do not can be denounced and punished. Apparently, however, the managers' propensity to the discovery of irregular but effective methods is not limited to ways of achieving regular ends, of making their business work, but extends to providing additional perquisites for themselves. On these the regime looks less tolerantly. A particularly frequent subject of denunciation in the press is the ingenuity of leading officials in contriving for themselves the additional prestige and comfort of a private motor car at the expense of their factory or department, and so of the state.

Agriculture

The nature of the processes of agriculture, the mingling of different crops on the same farms, has left less scope for the minute and shifting division of ministerial responsibility than in industry. Ministries for technical crops and for cotton-growing have made their appearance, but have proved short-lived. On the other hand, attempts to concentrate the whole of agriculture in one ministry have fared no better, lasting, in the period of the present constitution, only from March 1946 to February 1947, and from March 1953—the death of Stalin—to September of the same year. There have usually been three ministries. Two amalgamated on the 30th May 1957, ran the farming. They were the Ministries of Agriculture—responsible for the collective farm system—and of State Farms. The division is fairly obvious; the state farm is in effect a rural factory with a management and paid workers, while the collective farm is technically a co-operative association, though its land belongs to the state, which grants it the perpetual use of it. It was not, however, quite clearcut. The Ministry of State Farms had in fact control of only about three-quarters of the state farms. Specialised ministries, including the Ministry of Agriculture with, mostly, fruit nurseries, ran

[1] See p. 235.

the rest.[1] Since the administrative reforms state farms answer to councils of the economy, collective farms to district authorities. The third agency has been the ministry concerned with the surrender of agricultural produce to the state and its marketing—generally a Ministry of Agricultural Procurements (*zagotovki*), which in May 1956 became the Ministry of Grain Products. This is now a State Committee.

The early years of the Soviet state produced several types of collective farms differing in the extent to which members retained control of the land and equipment. The favour of the state came to be given to what was in form an intermediate type, the *artelj*, in which cultivation is collectivised but consumption is not. In fact the differences between the system of management in such farms and those in enterprises in other parts of the economy are few and the differences between the position of the collective-farm member and that of the worker in an enterprise are not, in general, to the advantage of the former. Unlike the state-farm worker, he is not entitled to a fixed wage, but only to his share, as calculated by a method prescribed by the state, of such portion of the produce of the farm as the state thinks fit to leave to it for distribution. A model charter for agricultural *arteljs* was adopted by a congress of collective-farm shock workers—that is, exceptionally productive workers in agriculture—held in February 1935 and immediately confirmed by the government and the Central Committee of the party.[2] Thereby it is held to have acquired the force of law,[3] and the charters of the several farms may depart from its wording only at the points envisaged in the model itself or in subsequent state or party ordinances imposing particular tasks on collective farms in particular areas. The model leaves to be determined only such details as name and statement of location, the number of members of the managing bodies, the size of the members' private homestead plots and their maximum holdings of livestock. The two last may be varied according to the character and conditions of farming in the various parts of the country, within prescribed limits and subject to the general requirements that such private agriculture should supplement the peasant's income from collective farming, but not make him independent of it. Variation, however, is not at the discretion of the members. The local forms of charters were originally worked out by authorities at regional level in accordance with ministerial and party

---

[1] Details in *Narodnoe Hozjajstvo SSSR*, p. 133.
[2] Text in Gsovski, *Soviet Civil Law* (1948), II, 441–462. Apparently standard charters exist, and are similarly binding, for all permitted associations and organisations (see W. W. Kulski, *The Soviet Regime* (1954), p. 254).
[3] A. M. Turubiner in N. D. Kazantsev, I. V. Pavlov and A. A. Ruskol (eds.) *Kolhoznoe Pravo* (1955), p. 74.

instructions from the centre, and with a few exceptions were uniform throughout the area of each administrative district. Thereafter changes could be made only by the federal government. A charter must be adopted at a general assembly of the members of the farm to which it is to apply, and registered with the soviet executive committee of the district, which is under obligation to satisfy itself that it is in full conformity with the model charter and any other relevant regulations.

The chairman, who by reason of the theoretically co-operative character of the farm is not called a director, is closely comparable with one in function. The vice-chairman's post is apparently a full-time one only in the largest farms and otherwise combined with other duties. The other organs of management of a collective farm are the general assembly of the members, which meets only occasionally, and the management board (*pravlenie*) of five to nine members, which is required to meet not less than twice a month. The members of the latter body are drawn mainly from among the leaders of work gangs ('brigades'), the managers of livestock farms within the collective farm, the party secretary—who is usually free of other duties—and other specialists. The vice-chairman is always a member, being elected to that office by, and from among, the members of the board. The chairman, though elected to office by the general assembly, presides *ex officio* over meetings of the board. As we have seen, the appointment of chairmen and experts is not in fact freely made at the discretion of the members. Official Soviet sources admit of cases where the official nomination to such posts in a backward collective farm has been received with indifference and even hostility, but refusal to elect is apparently rare, and probably allowed to succeed only in cases where the authorities themselves know that they have a weak candidate.

As usual in the Soviet Union everything is checked and rechecked. Thus in addition to the management board there is a checking commission of three to five members, which is also elected by the general assembly, though subject to confirmation by the district soviet executive committee, and to which the officials of the farm are not eligible. This is required to make a check on the work of the management four times a year, to keep a general watch and report to the general assembly on the financial operations of the management board, and to keep in touch with the local agencies of the ministry. The machine-tractor stations and procurators are required to develop it and help it to stand up to the management board which it has often been reluctant to do. Certain personal responsibility for the accuracy of information given to higher authorities is placed upon a bookkeeper who is appointed by the management board subject to confirmation by the general assembly and may be dismissed only by the general assembly upon the motion of the management board. Care is taken to avoid any victimisation of him by the members. He is under obligation to draw the attention of the chairman to any irregular order, and if it is confirmed in writing he should appeal to the checking commission and, if necessary, to supervising authority and the district procurator. If by performing it he would be committing a criminal offence he must go to the procurator. One of the many sinister alliances for which the authorities show themselves constantly on the watch is that between him and the chairman. It is not clear how far the shift of immediate responsibility for the control of collective farms from district to region and from state to party has changed this system of management.

On the respective merits of state farms and collective farms there was early a shift in official policy. The state farm was the obvious course of development for a regime of communist political opinion, and the regime in fact attached itself particularly to this form in its earlier days, and in such schemes as Mr. Khrushchov's project for 'agro-towns' still shows its inclination towards the assimilation of conditions in agriculture to those of the factory. The change to reliance upon the collective farm proceeded mainly, it has been suggested, from a realisation that collective farmers did not have to be paid whilst state-farm workers did, and that it was not in fact within the regime's power to ensure the means of paying them in bad years.[1] State farms, all specialised in particular crops, unlike many of the collective farms, were retained as supplementary to the collective-farm system and as models of progressive methods, though in fact in this respect many state farms early showed themselves inferior to the best collective farms as marshalled by the machine-tractor stations, and apparently still are.[2] It has latterly come back into prominence as the chosen form for the development of the virgin lands of Kazahstan, upon which Mr. Khrushchov has set his heart as one of his two solutions for Russian agriculture problems. In that case, however, it could hardly have been otherwise, since there were there virtually no peasants to collectivise. At the end of 1955 the number of state farms stood at 5,134, an increase of 260 over the previous year—247 of the increase being in Kazahstan[3]—as against the total of 87,500 collective farms.[4] It does not seem that the distinction of form is now a very

[1] Bienstock et al., op. cit., pp. 177–8.
[2] *Izvestia*, 2nd October 1955.
[3] *Narodnoe Hozjajstvo SSSR*, p. 137.
[4] See page 75. The state farms, however, were in general larger. Their agricultural land amounted in November 1954 to 77,600,000 hectares—while another 11,100 belonged to 124,000 other state-owned agricultural enterprises, such as those of experimental and subsidiary character, as against 389,700,000

serious one. The members of collective farms have proved as easy to manipulate as the workers of the state farms, 'completely removed from control in the organisation of production' and playing 'merely the passive role of a labour unit'.[1] The manner in which collective farms shall recompense their members for their services have been uniformly regulated according to the ideas of the central authorities as to the best method of inducing them to work collectively rather than devoting their attention to their own personal plots, and the central authorities of the party have decided uniformly for the country as a whole, though with repeated changes of mind from time to time, on the best size for the working team in the collective farm, just as they decide the size of the farm itself.

Perhaps the principal distinction of the collective farmer at the moment is the possession of his personal plot guaranteed in the constitution, but it is an insecure right, exposed to shifts of policy, since though very small—usually only a quarter of a hectare (half an acre), sometimes twice as much—they are a constant temptation to the peasant to neglect his obligations in respect of collective-farm work, at the cost of sacrificing the very small earnings which the system allows him from such work, to grow something of his own of which he can at least be certain. A joint decree (*postanovlenie*) of the party Central Committee and the Council of Ministers in March 1956 held it to be 'essential to recommend and advise collective farms, proceeding from the main task of ensuring a steep rise in agriculture and animal husbandry, themselves to supplement and amend the several provisions of the charter accepted by the agricultural *artelj*, having regard to the local concrete conditions of the collective farm'. One of the principal matters to which their attention was directed was the efficient use of land, with particular reference to homestead plots, in determining the area of which they must 'start from the point that collective-farm families in which there are collective-farm members fit for work but not working in the collective farm, or taking an inadequate working part in the social economy of the *artelj*, should have shares of homestead-plot land smaller than families of collective-farm members who work conscientiously in the collective farm. In this the increase in the quantity of land applied to homestead plots at the cost of the common lands of the collective farm must not be allowed; on the contrary, an effort must be made for its reduction, since the utilisation of land in common cultiva-

---

hectares communally farmed (i.e. apart from the peasants' homestead plots) by the collective farms (*Narodnoe Hozjajstvo SSSR*, p. 105).

[1] *Pravda*, 8th April 1930, and *Izvestia*, 6th May 1930, quoted in Bienstock et al., op. cit., p. 155.

tion, seeing that the machine-tractor station has a large quantity of technical equipment and high mechanisation, will be incomparably more advantageous, and in the final reckoning the collective-farm members will receive substantially larger incomes'. On the other hand, the decree sought to provide additional incentives for collective work by requiring the farms to make part of the payment to members for their collective work monthly instead of, as hitherto, annually upon completion of the harvest.[1] Latterly the plots seem to be back in official favour.

The collective farm was required to deliver to the state at an artificially low price a quota of produce determined in the plan. There was also a tax element in the payment in kind to the machine-tractor stations for their services. Where there was no machine-tractor station farms paid an additional tax instead. Further sales to the state could be made by contract, and with the elimination in the Khrushchov period of both stations and compulsory deliveries this has become the basic means of procurement. Members share in proportion to 'labour-days'—time worked heavily weighted, according to a state-prescribed scale, for the importance of the job held—in what remains.

In the early days of the régime there was some discussion whether collective farms might, as do state farms, own agricultural machinery. The decision was, and until 1958 remained, against this, and for the concentration of such machinery serving collective farms in the machine-tractor stations (M.T.S.). These came into being in 1927, originally as co-operative enterprises to which the peasant contributed part of the cost, receiving in exchange shares in the capital. This form was originally favoured as against ownership of the machinery by the individual farms, mainly, it seems, on the ground that it was unsafe to entrust valuable equipment to the mechanically incompetent peasants. But another motive was soon discovered for the establishment of M.T.S.s, in that they provided a very effective means of state control and party influence over the farm, and it was as such that they came to be principally developed. The practice was early evolved of sending selected bolsheviks to work there, which fitted in well with the requirement for technical skills, and this continued. The joint-stock organisation of the stations was not in any case readily acceptable to the communist mind, and by a resolution of the party Central Committee of the 11th January 1933 the stations were made state organisations upon the budget of the Ministry of Agriculture, and the collective farms were required to sell to them all complex equipment. A further resolution of the same date set up in each M.T.S. a political section under a deputy director to deal with opposition to the government's agricultural plans. It gave place

[1] *Izvestia*, 10th March 1956.

after September 1953 to resident party secretaries and instructors.

The concentration of machinery in the hands of the M.T.S.s went on until the sudden decision early in 1958 to sell it to the now enlarged farms and dissolve the M.T.S.s. Stalin's last published work firmly refused to countenance such a concession to the collective farms; their growing resemblance in discipline and efficiency to state farms was not held decisive. The annual contract which the farm concluded with the M.T.S., and which was almost uniform in all cases and based upon the obligations defined in the plan, was the main regulating instrument determining the farm's production. By 1952, it was claimed, 99 per cent of collective-farm land in production was being served—and consequently supervised—by M.T.S.s. It was stated in 1955 that the average administrative district contained 2 M.T.S.s, twenty-one collective farms and about 30,000 hectares of land in cultivation.[1] Local conditions, however, varied widely from the average. At the end of 1955 5.3 per cent of the country's 9,009 M.T.S.s had over twenty collective farms in their zones, but 8.3 per cent had three or fewer. The official policy was to bring the average number down, both by establishment of new M.T.S.s and by consolidation of farms. By the time of the decision to start the dissolution of M.T.S.s it was being revealed that many in the most developed areas had only one farm, and sometimes a common management with it. Some tractor teams had been permanently attached to particular work brigades.

The M.T.S. management was similar to that of an industrial enterprise, but the director was assisted by a council which included not only the leading officials of the station itself but also the chairmen and other leading workers of the collective farms which it served. Official writings on the subject indicate that discussion in their meetings ought not to be narrowly managerial but rather generally educative in progressive agricultural methods. By a decision of the party Congress of 1956 the stations were further to conform to the practice of industrial enterprises in their financing; they would cease to be borne on the ministry budget and become self-accounting and self-financing. The feasibility of this was hardly put to the test before their dissolution.

Originally the quota of produce to be surrendered by a farm to the state was assessed individually for each collective farm, but from 1940 the system was adopted of relating the quota to the farm's area of arable land, as a spur to the less efficient and an incentive to the more efficient. The delivery of livestock, which had previously been assessed as a percentage of the farm's herd, was at the same time similarly changed

[1] Ja. Storozhev in *Partijnaja Zhizn*, No. 9 of 1955.

to a prescribed weight of meat per acre. The obligation is a heavy one, and cases are recorded where in bad years the farm has had to buy produce on the open market to sell again to the state at a loss in discharge of its obligations.[1] By an order of February 1947 this arrangement was modified so as to allow district officials to vary the delivery quota on the basis of the extent of development in the individual collective farm, the intention being, apparently, to favour the stronger, more efficient farms. In July 1958 quotas were abolished. Already farms were urged to contract in advance with the state agencies for the supply of produce against immediate payment of part of the purchase price which is higher than for the obligatory state deliveries, but still considerably lower than the price on the open market. This provides the farms with a large part of their disposable funds during the year. The payments to be made to the peasants during the course of the year under the governmental instructions of March 1956 will presumably be made from funds acquired by such contract sales or from bank advances. Anything remaining after meeting obligations under delivery quota or contract may be sold by the farm on the open market or shared out among the peasants, who receive no other payment, and similarly sold by them.

Organs of Detection and Regulation

The ministries and the industries or other services which they operate are only parts of a whole, and there exists elaborate machinery to ensure that they and their agents do not lose sight of this fact. Apart from the duality of state and party and the dual subordination of most organs in each, the state system itself, like that of the party, is well provided with organs of general oversight. In a state which is also, and primarily, a business concern this category brings together in a way unfamiliar in liberal states such familiar mechanisms as audit, banking and police as well as others belonging more peculiarly to the Russian tradition, old or new. That we consider them together does not mean that each has not functions in which it diverges from the rest. Banking is a providing, as well as a regulating, service, and the police are concerned with the private citizen's propensity to larceny or homicide no less than in other countries. But we draw attention to the similarity of function which might the more easily be overlooked.

Annual audit by the several ministries of the accounts of all enterprises and services under their direction was instituted in 1936. In the following year the Ministry of Finance was charged to duplicate these services through its audit administration (*kontroljno-revizionnoe*

[1] Quoted in Dinerstein, op. cit., p. 45.

upravlenie).[1] It has the right of access to all financial records throughout the system. All approved establishments and salary scales are registered with the same ministry or with its subordinate branches in the soviet executive committees, and regular returns of expenditure are made by budgetary institutions for all, and by self-accounting enterprises for most, of their funds. Letters in *Izvestia* in 1955 complained that such supervision was so minute as to discourage local initiative and progress.

Another organ, the Commission of Soviet Control, known from 1940 to August 1957 as the Ministry of State Control, parallels and to some extent duplicates the work of others, especially the Finance Ministry. Mr. Khrushchov warned the Supreme Soviet in May 1957 that the Ministry, then under Mr. Molotov, had gone too far in that direction. It remains a specialised corps, though because of its influence its ministerial head is usually chosen from outside its ranks. Its task is not purely inspectorial; its powers extend to the giving of obligatory directions and, with the government's permission, to the infliction of penalties for irregularities detected.

All enterprises, co-operative organisations and permitted associations are required to keep accounts with the State Bank, and to settle their accounts with one another only through its books. The Bank collects and transfers their tax obligations to the state, meets demands on their funds in accordance with a prescribed order of priorities in which obligations for wages and salaries and liabilities to the state budget have first place,[2] and gives short-term credits to cover deficiencies in their circulating capital, since this is not intended to cover all contingencies. In this it works upon a monthly credit plan fixed by the federal Council of Ministers. The terms on which the Bank grants credits are intended to promote adherence to the requirements of the state economic plan, by varying the period of loan according to the planned rate of turnover in the industry concerned and similar considerations, and since August 1954 the Bank has had power to impose special conditions on enterprises which do less than they could to get their costs of production down, or which hold excessive stocks or otherwise offend. In this it is considered to act not as a person in civil law—an enterprise dealing with other enterprises and settling disputes with them through the courts—but as a part of the state's administrative machine. The result is claimed to be 'a system of bank control on the use not only of loans but also of the economic organisations' own means'. In giving credit to cover a relatively small part of the firm's operations, the Bank establishes a check on the

[1] On the terminology see footnote on p. 150.
[2] See list of categories in M. H. Zhebrak, *Kurs promyshlennogo uchjota* (1955), p. 267.

rest. 'Thus the Bank places under supervision the whole course of economic-financial activity of the organisation and the fulfilment of its plan as a whole.'[1] For the granting of longer-term credits there are specialised banks for industry, for agriculture, for commerce and for 'communal' (public works and services) activities.[2] These banks are apparently still under the Ministry of Finance. Like the State Bank, they act as agents of the government, and their own function, it is asserted, is only to ensure that the conditions prescribed in the credit plan have been complied with by the borrower. It seems that the banks generally are not always as strict as they should be about such requirements. It has been suggested that the existence of a variety of long-term credit banks leads to difficulties of co-ordination in such fields as the building of housing in which enterprises of all branches and also local soviets engage.

The designation of the ministries responsible for police work has changed considerably over time but the function has throughout been kept particularly under the control of the party. In the earlier years consideration of the most important cases, regarded as threatening the security of the state, was separated from the general ministerial structure and placed in the hands of a body known as the special commission or *Che-ka*, subsequently known as the State Political Administration or G.P.U., which with the formation of the federation became the Unified State Political Organisation or O.G.P.U. In 1934, when a federal People's Commissariat for Internal Affairs was set up, it took over the functions of the O.G.P.U. in addition to the general police work previously performed by the republican People's Commissariats for Internal Affairs. In 1941 part of its function was removed to a separate Commissariat for State Security; and in 1946, like the other People's Commissariat, these two bodies became ministries—the Ministry of Internal Affairs (M.V.D.) and the Ministry of State Security (M.G.B.). In March 1953, upon the death of Stalin the two ministries were merged into one under Beria, but upon his fall state security was again detached from the ministry and placed under a commission responsible to the Council of Ministers. A few months later, however, the chairman of the commission was admitted to membership of the Council of Ministers, so that in effect, although not in name, it became a ministry again.

Though the judicial and correctional functions of the Ministry of Internal Affairs are now apparently somewhat diminished from what they were at their greatest, it is still evidently a key ministry as another channel for the checking of performance generally. As such it has a network extending to the economic field and the armed forces, and locally

---

[1] M. A. Gurvich, *Sovetskoe Finansovoe Pravo* (1954), p. 317.
[2] There is also a specialised bank for foreign trade.

its representative is one of the leading figures, at least equal to the chairman of the executive committee and apparently needing to be treated with care and respect even by the party first secretary. For routine police work it has the force known as the Militia, which appears to be purely an enforcement body without most of the functions of maintenance of records and criminal investigation and prosecution included in the work of British police forces. For such work the ministry has maintained its own officials separate from the Militia at local levels, attached to but independent of the local soviets. An instrument (*polozhenie*) confirmed by edict of the Praesidium of the Supreme Soviet of the 24th May 1955 declared the investigators to be in the procurator service and under its orders. Appeal against their action was to lie to the procurator. It is not clear what functions remain to the internal affairs administrations as now transferred to regional soviet executive committees, except to supervise the militia administrations similarly placed at district level. The case has been officially made for changes in the system by which any investigation done by the militia was done again by the ministry investigators.[1] But these investigators remain, still out of local hands. Internal affairs is a distinct career service. The concentration of power which it represents makes it a precarious one at the top. Beria and his three predecessors have all met violent ends and carried some of their immediate subordinates to destruction with them.

The procurator service, which in designation and function recalls the pre-revolutionary system, is another such distinct corps. As under the Tsars, the procurators are the direct representatives of the centre without any concession even to the form of federalism. The head of the service, the Procurator-General, as he has been designated since March 1946, is appointed by the Supreme Soviet, but the procurators of union republics and lower units are designated by him, with formal appointment by the Praesidium of the Supreme Soviet for the three highest ranks in the service, without reference to any local agency. The titles of the ranks in this service are variations on the theme of 'counsellor of justice', but at no level are the procurators subject to the Ministry of Justice or any other ministry. They are principally concerned with such forms of improper conduct as may involve judicial proceedings, and conduct many of the prosecutions coming before the courts as well, apparently, as participating in the judge's preliminary hearing of all criminal cases,[2] but they are not solely public prosecutors. They are

---

[1] M. V. Barsukov (Head of Chief Administration of Militia), *S.G. i P.*, No. 2 of 1957.

[2] A. Kiralfy, 'The Soviet People's Court—A comparative review', *Soviet Studies*, vol. iii, No. 4, pp. 396–7.

charged to intervene in proceedings in order to protect the state's interests and empowered to 'protest' against decisions, without any limitation of time, up to the level of the federal Supreme Court or, if necessary, the Praesidium of the Supreme Soviet. They must apparently attend all hearings of certain classes of cases—such as those involving labour relations and employees' rights to compensation—in any court, and give a legal summing-up for the guidance of the bench.[1] If they think fit they may initiate or continue civil proceedings on behalf of other individual or corporate parties where these do not proceed. They are, however, not confined to the preparation and presentation of cases discovered by other agencies, but have a general right and duty of inspection of the work of all public bodies, and accounts are given in the press of appeals made to them by the public for redress of grievances. The constitution itself gives to them as to the courts the power of arrest, and they are also empowered to detain. They are mainly a control over the officialdom, but other citizens too may suffer from their activities. Accounts have been given in the press of citizens being detained by the procurator for such offences as 'slander of an official'; that is to say, for a complaint which the prosecutor chose to consider malicious. In one such case reported as having happened in Azerbaidjan in the spring of 1955, the parties—two brothers, one of them a collective-farm work brigade leader who had criticised the chairman of his farm—were kept in custody by the district procurator even after the republican Supreme Court had ordered their release on the ground that a new charge was being framed. It needed a letter to the national newspaper of the youth movement and action by the Assistant Procurator-General to get them released and a severe reprimand administered to the district procurator and a warning to the regional procurator who had supported him. An edict of the Praesidium of the Supreme Soviet of the 7th April 1956 provided for the establishment within the procurator's service of the following departments: Department of General Oversight, Investigation and Administration; Staff Administration; Department for Oversight of Investigation work in the organs of State Security; Department for Oversight of the Consideration of Business in Criminal Courts; Department for the Oversight of Consideration of Business in Civil Courts; Department for the Oversight of Places of Deprivation of Liberty (that is, prisons); Department for Affairs of Juveniles; Control and Inspection Department; Section for Systematization of Legislation; Statistical Department; Economic and Financial Administration and the General Office and Reception, both with the status of departments. It was also to include the principal military procurator's service and the

---

[1] See cases in Marshall MacDuffie, *The Red Carpet* (1955), pp. 51, 59.

principal transport procurator's service. Attached to the Procurator-General personally were to be 'Investigators for specially important business', and a Methods Council. There were also to be attached to the service an institute for detection research and a journal to be published jointly with the Ministry of Justice and the Supreme Court. Previously, it seems, this service was remarkable for its complexity even by Soviet standards; in some branches its federal organisation duplicated its own republican organisation, so that investigational work in the R.S.F.S.R. was done entirely by a section of the Procuracy of the Union, which had no other functions, despite the existence of a procuracy for the R.S.F.S.R.

Organs of Adjudication

As in other fields of Soviet government, the economic theme is dominant in the work of the courts and other organs of adjudication. One of their principal functions is to complete the work of the administration of which they are, in fact, a part by determining the order of priority of the divergent instructions which enterprises and other economic agencies may have received through the multiple channels of management and general oversight to which they owe obedience, and sorting out the obligations in which they may find themselves involved.

Where the conflicts of obligations are between state-owned enterprises a special system of courts is involved, the arbitration tribunals within the several ministries for their own enterprises and the State Arbitration (*Gosarbitrazh*) for disputes between enterprises of different ministries. The latter is established at federal, republican, territorial and regional level, and in Moscow, Leningrad and Kuibyshev towns under a Chief Arbiter for the federation, empowered as a last resort to vary the judgment of his own tribunal, which is independent of any ministry and subordinate directly to the federal Council of Ministers. These bodies, when founded in their present form in 1931, were conceived as administrative tribunals guided exclusively by considerations of public policy, especially as embodied in the economic plan, but the arbiters who, though not necessarily lawyers, are all full-time specialists in the work and have legal assistance, have come in time to function very much like courts, applying both the Civil Code and a considerable case law of their own devising. Their procedure is expeditious and reasonably informal, and they are prepared to give guidance before damage is done and liability incurred—for example in the case of a dispute on the making of a contract.[1] This is only possible because the contracting parties are not in fact free agents, but already bound by obligations

[1] H. J. Berman, *Justice in Russia* (1950), pp. 248–9.

which a tribunal can assess and reconcile. But in Soviet circumstances it is a useful service. It is suggested that they provide the most convenient means by which officials of state enterprises may obtain a reconciliation of the conflicting instructions which they are apt to receive from the various co-ordinate authorities placed over them by the complex Soviet administrative system.[1] The arbiters are appointed by the Councils of Ministers and executive committees at their several levels.

Courts of the general judicial system are established at all levels of the administrative structure from the district or town up to the federation. At the lowest level they are known as People' Courts, above that as Area Regional or Territorial Courts, and in all units designated as republics, whether autonomous or union, as Supreme Courts. There is a Supreme Court of the U.S.S.R. as a whole. Judges of people's courts are directly elected for terms of three years,[2] and judges of all higher courts elected indirectly by the soviets or Supreme Soviets at their several levels for terms of five years.[3] In addition to the judges who are paid full-time officials there are also elected by the same procedures panels of assessors, of whom no individual is supposed to sit for more than ten days in the year. A court in most first-instance proceedings consists of one judge and two assessors; in cases involving technical knowledge one assessor may be a specialist,[4] but otherwise both are taken from a panel. Thus a people's court, which does only first-instance work, has a panel of between fifty and seventy-five assessors and only one full-time judge.[5] At the election in Latvia in December 1954 it was reported that ninety-four judges of people's courts and 6,935 assessors were up for election. During the absence of the professional judge one of the assessors is appointed by the local soviet—presumably by its executive committee—to act in his place. During such service the assessor is paid at not less than the rate of the regular judge's salary. Otherwise he gets the equivalent of his own usual salary for each day on which he sits. Some attempt is apparently made to provide by the publication of textbooks and by short courses for the legal training of assessors, and Soviet publications periodically insist that greater effort should be made in this direction. The professional judges of people's courts themselves seem not to be all legally trained; apart from the law faculties of the universities (in which probably only a bare majority of the judges even of the higher courts have been trained) such training

[1] See case in John N. Hazard, *Law and Social Change in the U.S.S.R.* (1953), p. 55.
[2] Article 109 of federal constitution.   [3] Articles 105–8
[4] Case in Berman, op. cit., p. 89. He notes, however, that this provision is little known.
[5] Kiralfy, op. cit., p. 388.

is available in schools run by the Ministry of Justice, or at worst by correspondence course, and official publications suggest anxiety to remedy defects in this respect. The status of the professional judge and the assessors is equal on the bench and the verdict is reached by majority vote of all three. No dissent is expressed in court, though the judge may note it on the record for use in the event of an appeal. It seems that in general the assessor defers readily to his professional colleague. He is apparently not always treated by him with much respect. It is complained that assessors are regularly summoned only on the day before they are required, and rarely sent the papers in advance. Certain classes of cases are heard by benches composed entirely of professional judges without assessors. These include all appeals, which come before the same system of courts, but mainly in the upper ranges. Labour discipline cases—though not other cases involving labour relations—were also tried entirely by professional judges, but this class of business seems to have been entirely abolished by the legislation of April 1956. Thus the superior courts have much smaller assessor panels than the people's courts; the federal Supreme Court elected in 1946 had twenty-five to sixty-three judges. At the 1957 election there were twenty; the number of the full-time judges was reduced to a chairman, two vice-chairmen and nine members, together—in the current fashion of respect for federal rights—with the fifteen chairmen of republican supreme courts. All courts above the people's court have more than one judge. They are divided into collegia, or groups, on civil and on criminal cases.

By an edict of the Praesidium of the Supreme Soviet of the 14th August 1954 a further level of appeals was provided 'in order to increase the role of local judicial agencies in the matter of court review'. These are the praesidia of union and autonomous republic supreme courts and of the courts of territories, regions and autonomous regions. They are to be formed of the chairman of the court, the vice-chairman and two members of the court, and the selection of people to them is to be confirmed by the Praesidium of the Supreme Soviet or the soviet executive committee at the appropriate levels. As the procedure has been defined by a subsequent edict of 25th April 1955, protests against the entry into force of sentences and decisions may be made by the federal Procurator-General or the chairman of the federal Supreme Court and their deputies to the praesidia of all courts, and by the corresponding officials at lower levels to the praesidia of courts at or below their own level. The protests may be made against a judgment on appeal regardless of the motives for which it is given. A member of the court who has sat upon the case at an earlier instance is disqualified from hearing the protest as a member of the praesidium. If in consequence there is no quorum the matter goes to a higher court. The decisions of a praesidium may themselves be protested up to the level of a collegium of the federal Supreme Court. This has no praesidium. It has, however, a military collegium, and until February 1957, when the instrument defining the structure and powers of the court was revised, had also collegia to deal with appeals from the rail transport and water transport courts. These last, abolished at the same time, were formed to deal mainly with breaches of labour discipline and other acts tending to disorganise the transport system. There were formerly transport procurators, and is still a military procurator, under the Procurator-General, with the power of protest. The Supreme Court, like all other courts, hears cases on ordinary appeal from the level of courts immediately below, in addition to those brought to it by the Procurator-General. With assessors it may even take cases of special importance at first instance, but it is unlikely that it gets much such business.

The civil proceedings before these courts are largely concerned with much the same sort of disputes on economic matters as engage the State Arbitration, but where one of the parties is not a state enterprise. This brings them into cases involving the collective farms and other co-operative organisations and approved societies, as well as disputes of private persons with these or with enterprises and other emanations of the state. An edict of the Praesidium of the Supreme Soviet of the 14th March 1955 removed from the competence of the people's courts, which deal with the greater part of such civil business, disputes involving sums of less than 1,000 roubles between state organisations, co-operative organisations other than collective farms, and 'other social organisations'. These were now to be settled by the hierarchic superior of the organisation against which the claim was made. Disputes in which the parties on both sides are private citizens are probably comparatively few in consequence of the omnipresence of the state. Disputes between fellow-occupants of a residential building, for instance, generally involve an enterprise or the housing administration of the local soviet executive committee as their common landlord. A large part of the business which in other countries would come before the courts of civil jurisdiction as disputes between individuals, is thus settled in the Soviet Union through administrative channels. Minor property cases, including those arising from wills, and family matters evidently engage the courts. Divorce cases are more apparent to the observer than most because of the requirement of notice in the press between consideration by the people's court, where they start, and completion in the higher courts, which alone are empowered to determine them. Citizens may sue enterprises or other public agencies, including ministries, or collective farms and other co-operatives for damages for wrongs done to them, for reinstatement in case of wrongful dismissal or transfer and for the recovery of wages or share of collective-farm produce due to them. They can be sued for failure to fulfil their production norms, though it seems that they rarely are. The first recourse for the settlement of disputes and complaints between management and workers has been to the norms and conflict commissions (R.K.K.) representing equally management and the (official) trade unions. A director who prevented the establishment of such a commission on the ground that there were no disputes in his factory was held to be at fault.[1] Recourse to the people's court, it seems, was by leave, or action, of the trade union. An edict of January 1957 established an intermediate appeal to the full factory or local trade-union committee, if any, made both appeals matters of right, and stated the periods for application and defined the considerable limitations on the powers of the R.K.K.—which it renamed 'commissions on labour disputes'. Holders of a very wide range of responsible posts are excluded from recourse to the commissions and courts and can look only to higher authority in their branches.

All cases heard in the courts may be appealed to the next higher court within a set limit of time. There they end unless taken higher by the procurator or the higher courts themselves.

Criminal cases come before the same courts. The procedures seem to differ only at the preparatory stage; the judge, in ascertaining whether there is a case to answer and what witnesses should be called, acts on his own in civil cases but should call in his assessors in criminal matters.[2] The criminal code is distinguished from those of most systems by extreme vagueness both in its definition of offences and in the sentences which it prescribes for them, and there is a similar failure to prescribe which levels of the system shall be competent to deal with which offences. Even the most serious offences by Soviet standards are all placed within the competence of the regional and equivalent courts. It seems that the procurators have among their tasks that of deciding at which level it is convenient to bring any particular case, though it rests with the court to accept or refuse it. The vagueness in the other respects gives the courts wide discretion in which they are expected to be guided by analogy from similar classes of offences in a way which would not be found in any other judicial system, by regard for the whole motivation and record of the accused rather than the mere fact of commission, and by considerations of public educative effect in view of the administration's concern, for the time being, to suppress particular forms of conduct and inculcate particular attitudes.

[1] *Trud*, 29th December 1955.   [2] Kiralfy, op. cit., p. 396.

This changing penal policy and the machinery of retribution by which it is implemented we shall consider briefly in our concluding chapter among the other means by which interests are manipulated to secure performance of the authorities' decisions. The educative and exemplary purpose of court proceedings—to make policy clear to the citizens—is evidenced in the reporting of them in the press. The reports are brief and make few concessions to professional interest in legal complexities or to general public interest in the personalities involved. They are exemplary and concentrate on the offence and the penalty imposed. Thus since the war, when the authorities have been particularly concerned with acts of violence, and at all times when they have been troubled by official malpractices, cases of prosecution for such offences have become prominent in the daily press. Civil proceedings, having no exemplary quality, are not reported. For the same reasons trials of especial relevance to some message which the authorities wish to drive home may be held in a public hall or in the factory or farm where the offence was committed, rather than in the regular courtroom. The great show trials of the late 'thirties and, less spectacularly, since then, with their public confessions of the improbable, can be explained only by similar considerations. Such events as these, and the general readiness of the prosecuting and judicial authorities to impute to an accused person the logical consequences, by Marxian analysis, of his actions, even if he had himself never envisaged them, may cast some doubt on the statement that Soviet criminal law is exceptionally concerned, or concerned at all, with motivation. But in fact the motives which engage its attention are those which have made the accused the person which he is rather than those which have impelled him to the act with which he is charged. The belief is probably genuinely held by many in authority that a propensity towards acts disruptive of the socialist order of Soviet society can be revealed by acts not themselves amounting to definable offences, though they may need to be represented as such for public edification, and that it is important that such a propensity should be eradicated. Certainly the courts go to great length to enquire into the circumstances, attitude and character of those who come before them and seek to adjust the sentence to what they think they find.

Cases of a criminal nature—though not so described in Soviet terminology—may, like much civil business, be settled administratively without reference to the courts. In addition to the punitive powers of the Commission of Soviet Control and the power of factory directors to deprive some unsatisfactory workers of certain social welfare benefits, there are the village soviet powers and various minor departmental powers to inflict small fines. But the most important of such powers has hitherto been that of the Ministry of Internal Affairs to hear political cases, in a very wide sense of the term, in private, without the presence of the accused or any of the safeguards of the general judicial system such as the right to legal representation or the right of appeal. The decree of the Central Executive Committee and the Council of People's Commissars of 10th July 1934 setting up the federal People's Commissariat for Internal Affairs created a 'special consultation' (*osoboe soveshchanie*), consisting, as subsequently defined, of the minister, his deputies, the head of the police service, and the minister of the appropriate republic, which 'shall be granted the right to apply in an administrative procedure banishment from certain localities, banishment with settlement in a locality, confinement in a correctional labour camp up to five years and deportation abroad'.[1] Despite the limitation of sentence to five years the lack of any public proceedings meant that further sentences might be imposed as soon as the original one had expired. In practice similar powers were exercised both by local tribunals of the ministry and by special tripartite commissions (*troika*) composed of a representative of the state authorities, one of the party and one of the Internal Affairs Ministry. In February 1956 it was announced that the special consultation had been abolished in 1953, and its business transferred to the regular courts.[2] Emphasis has of late been repeatedly placed upon the right of citizens to a fair trial. No precise indication has yet been given of what is changed, and on experience there is still room for doubt whether the system can entirely dispense with the more expeditious and convenient exceptional procedures.

As we have suggested, it is impossible to attach any clear meaning to the guarantee of judicial independence in Article 112 of the constitution. It is expressly stated in Soviet writings that it does not mean that the judge shall not be subject to the policy of the Communist Party. Apart from the manner of the judge's election and the short term of his office, and also the possibility of his being recalled at any time during that term (as six judges of the federal Supreme Court were by decree of the Supreme Soviet at its meeting of February 1955), he is subject to constant pressures in his work which are opposed to the ideas of judicial independence held in other countries. Thus the press repeatedly comments on unsatisfactory verdicts and carries threats of disciplinary penalties upon judges for excessive leniency in the treatment of offences

---

[1] Gsovski (op. cit., vol. ii, p. 23) gives in English the relevant article from this measure; Kulski (op. cit., pp. 233–4) gives *in extenso* an English text of the consequent decree of the same authorities concerning the organisation and jurisdiction of this body.

[2] *S.G. i P.*, No. 1 of 1956, p. 3.

which the authorities are, for the time being, particularly anxious to suppress. Judges have at times been specifically instructed by the Ministry of Justice to take account of comment in the press and to meet periodically with its representatives to discuss the investigation of complaints. Any greater concessions to judicial independence would, in fact, be surprising in the Soviet setting, where government policy, which means the policy of the Communist Party, is not the purpose of a transient administration but, in principle at least, the spirit underlying the laws themselves.

Within their limits the ordinary courts seem to be consistent in their practices, to take their tasks seriously and to seek to give effective protection to the citizen from these forces in society against which he may need it. By the definition of its functions as supreme protector, the state as a whole, always correctly interpreting the instructions of the party, cannot be one of these forces. It is said that opening of criminal proceedings before the courts generally stays any further administrative action, and that this is a fact known to, and counted upon by, the comparatively large section of the Soviet population, whose daily activities are apt to bring it sometimes into conflict with the law.

The Armed Forces

The regular armed forces, formerly known as the Red Army and Red Fleet, but since 1946 as the Soviet Army and Naval Forces, do not appear to be a regular means of supervision and manipulation in Soviet internal politics. For any such purposes the Ministry of Internal Affairs has throughout had its own troops, including its own Air Force, and probably still has. Nevertheless, owing to the concern of the regime from its earliest days with consideration of external security, the regular forces are a presence which the citizens can hardly ignore, with a network of garrisons covering the whole country and represented by senior serving officers on the local and central elected bodies of the state and party in a way which contrasts markedly with the practices of most other countries. Moreover, as in most other countries at present, it is a system through which most of the younger citizens have themselves at some time passed. Military service, originally restricted to the approved social classes, has since 1939 been compulsory for all for terms varying with the arm of the service from two years up to five in the navy, with periods of reserve service of diminishing frequency and duration up to the age of 50. Leave is rare, free time limited and the amenities provided in the service superior to those outside; control over the men is therefore far-reaching. The party through its political administration makes full use of its opportunity for the indoctrination of the citizen thus brought within its reach. Political studies according to a centrally prescribed syllabus are required of all, apart from the special obligations of members of party primary organisations as such. Hours of instruction on political matters and state and party history seem to have amounted to about five a week immediately before the war—or perhaps more if general informative talks be included—and to continue on much the same scale. All commanders are charged with political work in their units as a regular part of their military duties, and are responsible to the *zampolit*[1] at the next higher level for it. Usually, it seems, the *zampolit* conducts the political education of the higher ranks under his charge, leaving to his subordinates and to the regimental officers the education of the lower. In addition he is required to report every few days on the state of morale of his charges. Recreational facilities, clubs and reading-rooms are all within the responsibility of the *zampolit*, and down to regimental level he is provided with subordinate staff to manage such activities.[2] On the whole the army is probably popular, and serves to win some support for the regime. It seems that it is still one of the party's best recruiting grounds, and though many of its recruits are among the officers for whom membership is a professional requirement, it is likely that many conscripts are caught in the net, if not of the party at least of the *Komsomol*.

But besides the opportunities for winning popularity and shaping minds the services offer, as do other approved organisations to a less extent, a chance to build up detailed information on the character of individuals. This can be done both through the party network and through the counter-intelligence sections (or Special Sections), the agents of the Chief Administration for Counter-Intelligence in the Armed Forces (linked with the Committee of State Security) attached to formations down to division and independent brigade, and with individual officers in all units down to battalion and an extensive staff of informers of all ranks at all levels,[3] and exercising surveillance over all, including the party.

The Soviet Union is more generous than most countries in its granting of exemption from military service to those whose services are valuable to the state in other ways, including, it seems, all those with

[1] See p. 155.
[2] Summarised from Zbigniew Brzezinski (ed.), *Political Controls in the Soviet Army—a study based on reports by former Soviet officers* (who are named and severally contribute sections to the book), Research Programme on the U.S.S.R. (1954), and comments of Raymond L. Garthoff on it in *Problems of Communism*, No. 1 of 1955; see also Fainsod, op. cit., pp. 408–13.
[3] Brzezinski, op. cit.

higher-educational qualifications. This is hardly surprising where all occupations are forms of disciplined state service. The political indoctrination which people so exempted thus miss is made up in other forms, as for instance in the compulsory political instruction at universities and other institutions of higher education. No provision is made for exemption on grounds of conscience.

The officers of the armed forces seem all to serve on longer engagements than that of normal compulsory service, and a great preponderance are professionals. In theory rank designations were abolished at the time of the revolution, and they did not begin to be introduced again until 1935, after which they gradually penetrated through the system until by the time of the war the complete conventional structure of ranks had been reintroduced. In practice, however, clearly recognised graduations of rank, and the distinction between officers and others in status, authority and living conditions had existed throughout. The distinction is now considerably more rigid than in most armies. Entry into officer rank, as into the higher grades of the state and party bureaucracy generally, is apparently now based very largely on educational qualifications and completion of exceptionally thorough courses of training. Political soundness, as judged by the party, is a condition, but not a sufficient condition, of advancement. Political leaders without military attainments were given high rank during the war of 1941-5, but this is not typical of the system. The military career still seems to be open to ability; there is no clear evidence of the establishment of any form of hereditary military caste, although in 1943 schools were established to train boys—originally war orphans, the sons of men with distinguished military careers—for entry to the services in officer rank, and these may offer the higher ranks the means of perpetuating themselves. Most of the present generation of high-ranking officers, however, are of a different background, being products of the revolution and civil-war period. The Tsarist officers, who formed a substantial element in the army of the 'twenties and 'thirties, and were a cause of some suspicion to the Soviet leaders, are now almost extinct, in consequence of time and the purges.

We have seen that military representation in the Supreme Soviet is high by the standards of most other countries, and it seems that much the same applies to elected bodies lower down the Soviet system. Until recently the same has not been true of the party structure, though in this respect there seems to have been some change of late. The senior ranks of the army are now represented, rather more fully than hitherto, on the Central Committee and the Central Checking Commission, and in the person of Marshal Zhukov one briefly appeared for the first time as a member of the party Praesidium. This, however, probably does not represent any current danger of military dictatorship. The well-read Marxist is aware of the danger of a Bonaparte, and the powerful apparatus of party and police control permeating the army is the answer to it. The military figures who achieved prominence and personal popularity during the war, including Marshal Zhukov himself, were reduced to obscurity and unimportance in Stalin's last years. After his death they achieved a new prominence as an element in the ruling junta's appeal to the people, and perhaps increasingly in its internal balance of power. But they are probably still not a much more considerable factor than the factory managers, the scientists, or the administrative officials, and as fully integrated into the party.

Education and the Educated

The state-party structure is the sole provider of education, and the power which this gives for shaping the dispositions of the participants in the system has been jealously safeguarded. Resources, especially of teaching manpower, have throughout been very limited; and the revolution, with its early distrust of formal schooling and of a teaching profession, which, though largely socialist, was often not Bolshevik, did not help. Since the beginning of the Stalin-Zhdanov period there has been a drive of increasing intensity to improve facilities, but compulsory seven-year education (normally for ages seven to fourteen) written into the constitution in 1956 as a citizens' right,[1] had been declared achieved only in 1949. In practice it seems that even now some children in undeveloped areas receive only the first four years, provided by the elementary (*nachalnaja*) school, into which category in 1956–7 were stated to fall 110,300 of the country's 196,600 schools (though with only 4,100,000 of the 28,200,000 pupils). The 'seven-year schools' covering these same four years, and also the other three of the period of compulsory education, numbered 57,100 (8,600,000 pupils). The complete 'middle schools', which, despite their name, cover the whole of this period as well as an additional three years, were 28,300 (15,400,000 pupils). By the end of the last Five-Year Plan period (1961) this full ten-year course was to become compulsory everywhere, but this plan was clearly over-ambitious, and after widespread discussion in 1958, initiated by Mr. Khrushchov, for educational reform with general participation of pupils in useful work a more moderate plan was adopted, extending seven-year and middle schooling by one year, with compulsory eight-year attendance

[1] See p. 106.

by 1962-3 and some practical work in the later middle-school years.

Where, as in the larger towns, the facilities exist, middle-school education is probably virtually compulsory already. In some rural areas there may well be little compulsion to any education at all; the farm work required of children[1] may even act as negative compulsion. Figures suggest a falling-off in senior years of rural schools.[2] After full middle-school education students are admitted by examination to universities and other institutes of higher education providing a four-, five- or six-year course, or to teachers' training institutes providing a course of from two years upwards. Alternatively, after seven-year education they may be admitted to a so-called 'technicum', providing a vocational, though not necessarily technical, education. The four-year training of elementary-school teachers is at this level. On completion any student at university or technicum level must work for three years in the appropriate branch of the economy. The university student may proceed directly to post-graduate work, but for the technicum student, including the elementary-school teacher, further full-time education is excluded for the three-year period of compulsory service. In addition, the system provides for the continuation of education on a part-time basis by those already at work. The large numbers attending even the lower classes of these 'schools of working youth', 'schools of rural youth', and adult schools suggest continuing deficiencies in the general educational system. There were 723,000 external students of institutes of higher education as against 1,278,000 internal students and 351,000 of 'technikums' as against 1,660,000 in 1956-7.[3] Since 1957 those with practical experience in industry have had priority of university admission. As the system of general education of the ministries of popular instruction is supposed to be uniform in all elementary and incomplete or complete middle schools it is in principle possible for those who complete the earlier years of education in an area with limited facilities to continue up to the highest levels by moving elsewhere.

All schools have hitherto been day-schools, but boarding establishments (*internat*) are attached to many of them.[4] They have no necessary association of social superiority, but are principally the only answer to natural conditions which make for the very bad school attendance in

[1] Three collective farms in Frunze district are rebuked (*Sovetskaja Kirgizija*, 3rd July 1957) for requiring, in their revised rules, 50 'workdays' of children of 12-14 years and 75 of adolescents above 14. Whether the requirement was excessive or should not have been imposed at all was not stated.
[2] *Narodnoe Hozjajstvo SSSR v 1956 godu*, p. 246.
[3] Ibid, pp. 248, 250.
[4] In the R.S.F.S.R. alone there were reported to be in 1954 some 11,000 of them with about 440,000 residents (*Izvestia*, 5th October 1954).

some areas[1]—long a cause of concern to the authorities. Village soviets are often blamed for failure to get their children to school, but as often the imputation of fault probably covers an objective impossibility. Pupils living in remote districts must sometimes travel as much as ten miles to attend a seven-year school, over very bad roads and with a great shortage of means of transport. The *shkola-internat*, first envisaged by Mr. Khrushchov in his address to the Twentieth Party Congress—though he suggested that some new name would later have to be found—seems to be directed to other purposes as well as these, providing in addition to accommodation and instruction a full range of physical and other out-of-school activities. Yet despite his expressed emulation of such pre-revolutionary institutions as the pages' corps and the subsequent approving references in the Soviet press to the British public school, complete with housemasters and prefects, what is intended is still not a special form of education for an élite. The press indicates that it is intended ultimately to be the normal form of education, and the beginning being made in the school year 1956–7 seemed to be planned on a large scale, but its realisation will obviously take time, and much may be changed in the process. It seemed planned to be more strictly residential than the boarding school as typically known in Britain. Pupils were to be released only for their parents' summer holiday, but practice has been more liberal. Headmasters and group tutors (housemasters) are to keep parents regularly informed about the activities and problems of their children. The pupils are to participate in the running of the school—and presumably to learn the Soviet system of government—through their own elected councils, in which apparently the school *komsomol* branch is to play much the same guiding and organising role as does the party in the organs of the state outside.[2] It may be wondered how the means are to be found to provide these boarding schools, since it is evident that there were not nearly enough boarding establishments of the older type for lack of buildings and other resources. The closer supervision envisaged will presumably make further heavy demands on resources of manpower which have long been stretched beyond their efficient limits.

Tuition fees introduced in 1940 for the last three years of middle school and all higher education were abolished by decree of the federal Council of Ministers of the 6th June 1956. Boarding fees are charged, and will be at the new boarding schools, with relief for the poorer parents.[3]

---

[1] See, e.g., *Pravda*, 4th January 1953, and *Izvestia*, 11th October 1954 and 30th August 1955.
[2] G. Arnautov (sector head in the Academy of Pedagogical Sciences of the R.S.F.S.R.) in *Narodnoe Obrazovanie*, No. 8 of 1956.
[3] Mr. Khrushchov's speech, *Izvestia*, 15th February 1956.

A similar uniformity in the education provided at university level is maintained by the federal Ministry of Higher Education, or presumably in some part but not necessarily all of the field, by the corresponding republican ministries in those republics which have them. All courses require the ministry's approval, the allocation of students is apparently within its discretion and the maintenance of standards in the award of academic degrees and titles rests with it. Possibly, as in other fields, the rigidity of the system is not as absolute in practice as on paper. There is evidently some room left to local initiative even in the planning of courses, which may lead to conflict with the plans of other levels. Thus it was reported in 1953 that the University of Lvov had established, in the face of indifference from the Ministry of Culture which was then responsible for the universities, a course in State Law designed especially for future administrators in soviets or other agencies, but found that on completion its students were commonly assigned to the courts or procurators' offices for which their concentration on administrative matters and their lack of experience of criminal law and procedure unfitted them. Even where the subjects, hours and forms of teaching are prescribed, some scope has to be left to the teaching staff to vary the manner in which it is given, and advantage is taken of this.[1] Moreover, the ministry can be subjected to argument; we hear of regular annual encounters by correspondence on such issues as a ministerial attempt to force a university to take its quota of research students (*aspirant*) in subjects in which it has no qualified staff, to the neglect of the subjects in which it specialises, though the outcome is not clearly indicated. Nevertheless the assignment in courses common to a number of universities is uniform in all essentials and very heavy. Compulsory lectures should take up some thirty-six hours a week of the students' time, and some universities irregularly impose up to twelve more. The demand which this makes on the time of the staff has latterly led to complaint at the sharp division which has appeared in some subjects between teachers and researchers. Beyond the first course, which though constituting a recognised qualification does not lead to any degree, most universities and institutes of comparable status, including, as we have seen, the federal party school, provide courses of research study, normally of three years, leading to the degree of 'candidate', and beyond that to the doctorate. Rather under three-quarters of the research students are studying 'with break from production' (that is, full time),[2] and are paid a state stipend. The award of the higher degrees, upon assessment of the

---

[1] See S. V. Utechin, 'Moscow University—Reflections of a Former Student', *Universities Quarterly*, August 1955.
[2] Details in *Narodnoe Hozjajstvo SSSR*, p. 235.

dissertation or other work by the university council, is subject to the approval of a Higher Certificating Commission (V.A.K.) in the ministry, the powers of which are clearly no formality.[1] Cases have been observed of refusal of higher degrees even in scientific subjects for alleged servility to foreign achievements, though studies in the humanities are more subject to this political force. Understandably, political limitations are particularly severe in the social sciences including history, where research seems to be possible only on topics approved in advance by the ministry. The results may be seen in complaints in the Soviet press of the dogmatic scholastic approach of researches in this field, and also in the titles of the dissertations and published works which suggest almost exclusive concentration on subjects likely to produce conclusions of obvious utility for propaganda purposes. In the natural sciences, however, the results of the Soviet educational system are impressive. The regime's traditional attachment to science (though it has not always withstood the stress of practice), its concern with practical economic needs and its ability both to direct and richly to reward those whom it trains enable it to produce scientists and technologists as few free educational systems can do. Its problem at the moment appears to be how to support them with an adequate supply of technicians of a middle-school standard of education.[2]

The 'politechnicisation' of the educational system, a concept of rather indefinite content cherished by the regime since its earliest days and given renewed emphasis since 1952,[3] seems to consist mainly in a realisation of the need to do something to meet this requirement. In the school year 1956–7, 500 schools in the R.S.F.S.R. were supposed to work to a new curriculum providing for training in the elements of industrial and agricultural work. In the new boarding schools 'Every pupil... must receive not only a general and polytechnic education, but also a specialisation in production which will facilitate his inclusion in the process of productive toil in that region of material production towards which during his residence in the *shkola-internat* he has shown

[1] V. N. Sementovski (in *Vestnik Vyshej Shkoly*, No. 9 of 1955, p. 17) complains of the capricious standards of this body. It has proved particularly obstructive to nominations to doctorates on the basis of the candidates' work in general without defence of a dissertation. He suggests that the report made by the commission's referee on the dissertation should not, as at present, be secret, as it would be of use to teachers.

[2] *Izvestia* (17th September 1954) complained that in some branches of industry there were almost as many engineers as technicians. Mr. Bulganin, in his report to the plenary session of the party Central Committee in July 1955 stated that in industry as a whole there were less than two technicians to one engineer (*Pravda*, 17th July 1955).

[3] *KPSS v Rez.*, II, 1117–18 (directives for the fifth Five Year Plan).

the greatest inclination'.[1] Even in the non-scientific subjects Soviet education is markedly and explicitly directed towards the provision of trained staff (cadres) for the operation of the system, and for this and other reasons it is closely tied to the economic plan. In a revision of university courses towards the end of 1955, apparently designed primarily to eliminate over-specialisation which had occurred in both arts and sciences, the occasion was taken to include in all courses in the philological, historical, geographical, biological, physical-mathematical and chemical faculties compulsory lectures on teaching method and teaching practice. It was stated that from 1956 not less than 80 per cent of graduates in the first four of these faculties and not less than 60 per cent of those of the other two were to be directed to middle-school teaching,[2] which has always been a weak spot in the system.

Systematic Marxist indoctrination at the school stage has been given a minor place, as of less importance than such equipment for economic function and less easily imparted to the young mind. However, even as early as the fourth class the study of history, introduced at that level, is required to explain the rightness of the party and its leaders in the move towards communism and to 'arouse in the children a feeling of supreme love for the socialist homeland and an ardent hatred for all enemies and oppressors of the working class'.[3] Group tutors in the new boarding schools are to organise regular political and informational talks for their charges. All university and technicum courses include compulsory and specified instruction in party history, political economy and dialectical and historical materialism. The importance of political soundness and awareness in teachers at all levels is constantly emphasised.

Closely related are the country's central learned institutions. Of these by far the most important is the Academy of Sciences, an eighteenth-century foundation which has gradually been made into the principal channel for the considerable sums provided for projects of research in fields of learning likely to serve the authorities' purposes. It is a co-ordinating body directing through its eight departments some hundred institutes concerned not only with the several branches of the natural sciences but also with such fields as geography, economics, history, law and linguistics. All the research in history done in 1955 is said to have been done in the Academy's Institute of History, and not in the

[1] Arnautov, op. cit., p. 37.
[2] M. G. Uroev (Head of the Chief Administration for Universities and Higher Education Institutes of Law and Economics in the Ministry of Higher Education) in *Vestnik Vyshej Shkoly*, No. 11 of 1955, pp. 28, 32.
[3] E. N. Medinski, *Narodnoe obrazovanie v SSSR* (Moscow, 1952), p. 63, quoted in I. & N. Lazarevich, *Narodnoe obrazovanie v SSSR*. Institut po Izucheniju SSSR (Munich) 1956, p. 38.

universities. The Academy has fourteen branches throughout the R.S.F.S.R. and one in the union republic of Moldavia. The other union republics except the R.S.F.S.R. have their own academies of sciences watched and marshalled by it.[1] It answers directly to the federal Council of Ministers for its work, and of recent years has been under close control. Other learned bodies, such as the Academies of Medical Sciences, of Juridical Sciences and of Pedagogical Sciences, are established under and responsible to the appropriate ministries for their work. The Academy of Agricultural Sciences seems to have somewhat higher subordination. Another eighteenth-century foundation, the Academy of Arts, is of little importance and mainly a teaching body. The main channels of control over practitioners of the arts are the Unions of Soviet Artists, of Soviet Composers and of Soviet Writers, all established in 1932, with power to give directives, demand results and administer rebukes for non-performance, which usually (though less certainly in periods of relaxation such as the present) are sufficient to induce public repentance or lasting silence by the offender.

The nature of the assignments which through these channels the authorities instruct the educated to perform is fairly clear. For creative artists and workers in the humanities generally the task is to maintain contentment, promote a proper attitude and enhance national prestige; whether their activities bring them personal gratification and comfort is a minor consideration. For the scientist the task is to contribute to such purposes as productivity, national defence, health and well-being. Not all of this stress on obvious utility, it is clear, is stultifying to the scientist; he is restrained from the temptations which beset many of his fellows in other countries to follow mere fashion, to become a literary man or popular personality, or to withdraw from the world. The temptation which the Soviet system does offer him is to become, as for a time did Mr. Lysenko, a court magician. It is a temptation similar to that inciting factory managers to bid up plan-targets to impossible heights, a gamble with big prizes on the chance of being able to produce the results which the authorities desire. For a time Lysenko apparently established himself as dictator of all scientific activity, with the power, which he too frequently exercised, to blast the careers of others of whom he disapproved. This is obviously a fault in the circumstances of Soviet intellectual life, but the effect of the system in corrupting the scientist is probably not so serious as it looks; the sensible man probably considers

---

[1] A. V. Topchiev, Chief Academic Secretary of the Academy (*Vestnik Akademii Nauk SSSR*, No. 3 of 1955, translated in *Current Digest of the Soviet Press*, No. 29 of 1955), defines the nature of this relationship and also gives examples of the projects being undertaken in the various fields of the Academy's work.

well how firmly he may hold on to the regime's current line without burning his fingers. Party control is more likely to be stultifying for scholars in the field of human studies and for creative artists, concerned as they must be with understanding and epitomising the motivation of men—including their own—or evoking or expressing a mood. Not the utility of the results but the honesty of the pursuit is the excellence of practitioners in these fields, and in this the Soviet regime is not interested. This is more than just discouraging. The regime has a monopoly of the principal means of artistic expression. As we have suggested, only approved organisations may have newspapers, and the party keeps a particularly close control of their editorial personnel. All other publications, lectures, broadcasts and exhibitions require the approval of the Chief Administration for Literature of the Ministry of Culture, and may subsequently be banned by it. Private printing is impossible since sale, loan or the extension of use of printing, or even duplicating, equipment to private persons is forbidden, and its possession by organisations, themselves licensed and controlled, is registered and strictly supervised by the same chief administration and by the militia (police). Theatrical and concert repertoires are controlled on a federation-wide scale by a committee answerable to the federal Council of Ministers.[1] If the regime sees no utility in an artistic creation—and it usually looks for utility of a fairly tangible kind—that creation will travel no further into the world than the private conversation or the typed copy can carry it. The regime means the official on the spot, and he may well have some odd ideas of what may fittingly go into the local newspaper or review. But with the threat of denunciation, in *Pravda* or otherwise, hanging over him he is unlikely to err far on the side of daring.

We cannot say what is the political influence of the scholar; though his power, of his own motion, to influence public opinion at large is negligible, he may often have access to the greater or lesser makers of policy. Scientists at least must have the power to pronounce an idea unfeasible. It may be perilous to do so—under Stalin it evidently often was—but it is probable that despite a few obvious and immense errors the leaders have developed a fair eye for the sycophant and willingness to take honest advice tactfully expressed. If the Russian academic is at times and in some places remote from the world of practical action it is not by official design; the universities, it is insisted, must be fully integrated as regular consultants in the economic life of their several regions.[2] It is from the ranks of the holders of formal educational

[1] On these processes see Kulski, op. cit., pp. 251–3.
[2] Mr. Bulganin, in his report to the plenary session of the party Central Committee, 4th July 1955, deplored the fact that, although much important

qualifications, and especially technical qualifications, that the administrative leadership is largely and increasingly recruited. Mr. Khrushchov, Mr. Bulganin and Mr. Malenkov all have engineering training of a sort, though somewhat irregularly acquired under the disordered conditions of the early days of the regime, and such posts as leading party secretaryships, central or local, tend increasingly to fall to those similarly, but more orthodoxly qualified. Mr. Khrushchov has given his distinguished support to a tendency which seems general among political officials to put their sons into technology. This tendency does not mean that the specialist will tend to take over from the hustler and organiser, but it suggests that, like the military commander and the political officer, they will come to have a large common element of training.

Further Lines of Control

The English term 'trade union' has always had a contemptuous implication in Russian communist usage, suggesting the 'economists' of pre-revolutionary days with their readiness to negotiate with capitalism for material benefits. Nevertheless, trade unions—professional league (*profsojuz*) in good Russian and without any pejorative sense—are a useful, if subordinate, means of enlisting aid for the state's purposes and keeping a check on industry. They became important allies of the Bolsheviks in the latter part of 1917, once they had been captured from their earlier Menshevik allegiance, and gave promise of being a powerful influence in the new society. The 1919 programme of the party went so far as to envisage the eventual concentration in their hands of the whole administration of the economy, but in fact they had then already lost much of the administrative power which they had briefly held—particularly the management of the social-insurance scheme. The concern of the leaders of the movement to secure for the workers an adequate participation, by way of wage increases, in the country's growing

---

research work for the national economy was being carried out by members of teaching staffs of institutes of higher education, only a fifth of them were at that time so engaged. He added that the Ministry of Higher Education should organise such work, and the industrial ministries should be bolder in setting research tasks for the academics. He also deplored the lack of co-ordination: 'Scientific institutions, branch institutes and higher-educational institutions are out of contact with each other, which is absolutely intolerable in a socialist state where every possibility exists for co-ordinated activity' (*Pravda*, 17th July 1955). M. A. Prokofjev, Deputy Minister for Higher Education (in *Vestnik Vyshej Shkoly*, No. 5 of 1956, p. 10) stresses the importance of the integration of the universities in their regions as consultants.

industrial production brought them increasingly into conflict with the party leadership which was convinced of the need for absolute priority for investment and of its own superior competence to speak the real will of the workers, as against their transient inclinations. The adoption, from 1928, of comprehensive economic planning exacerbated relations. By fixing in advance the unalterable share of labour it rendered vain and obstructive any union representations; for its fulfilment it demanded a return to direction of labour and the identification of party and state with the new order of managers which they were building up, rather than with the workers. The party's technique of use of the party group for disruption was brought into play early and effectively, and in 1929 the trade-union leaders were drastically purged by Stalin for resistance. Mr. Shvernik was installed as chairman of the Central Council of the Trade Unions, which office he held until 1944 and again from March 1953 to March 1956. In the interval between his two periods of office the post was occupied by Mr. V. V. Kuznetsov, a professional engineer previously employed in a managerial capacity in the steel industry, and since March 1956 it has been held by Mr. V. V. Grishin, formerly a party official. The leaders at all levels have been appointed by the party, many from among its own subordinate officials. Into the safe hands of the Central Council of Trade Unions, were entrusted the remaining functions of the People's Commissariat for Labour upon the abolition of the latter in 1933—principally social insurance and the protection of labour against unsafe and inequitable working conditions. Recruitment of labour was left to the several industries in agreement with the collective farms which form the main source, though it is a function of the trade union to assist with propaganda and with care for the new workers' welfare. In 1947 they had restored to them the power of making local collective agreements on labour norms and conditions and wages which they had lost in 1933, though it was explicitly stated that all such agreements must conform with the collective agreement concluded for the whole industry at ministry level, which in fact left the local bodies on either the management or the trade-union side with very little room for manœuvre. Union functions are thus subordinate, but still important enough in the view of the authorities to warrant the maintenance of an elaborate organisational structure. The several unions provide for all workers, regardless of craft or standing, in an industry as defined by the existence of a responsible ministry—which has involved the trade-union structure in the fluidity of the state organisation—with committees elected by secret ballot at all levels down to the town and the factory, the last having under it separate committees for the several sections, where these have at least a hundred workers each, and below those groups of twenty members. The quality of these elections appears to be very much that of any others in the Soviet Union. Only as many candidates are put forward as there are places to be filled, so that if the voters reject one another election has to be held. The factory director should not seek to get his own men elected, or not in such manner as to arouse objection.[1] At federal level all the unions come together in an occasional congress—the latest, the eleventh, being held in June 1954, the tenth in 1949, and the ninth in 1932—an All-Union Central Council, which as elected in 1954 had 174 members and 55 candidates, its praesidium of 21 and a central checking commission of 17. Congress delegates seem to have been mostly full-time officials, as in the party. Since 1948 there have also been links at lower levels in the form of territorial, regional and town councils of trade unions elected for two-year terms by inter-union conferences at those levels. The delegates to these conferences were in turn to be elected at general union meetings in the several enterprises. The central organisations both of the several unions and of the movement as a whole maintain their own publications, research institutions and staffs for the running of the various services which they administer including the social-insurance service and welfare institutions such as hospitals and holiday homes, and a force of labour inspectors. Local and factory organisations, apart from providing a large number of full-time posts as union and inter-union secretaries, engaged in 1949 the services of some 9,000,000 out of the 28,500,000 members of the movement in unpaid part-time work, as group organisers, insurance delegates, labour inspectors and members of the commissions of factory or workshop committees or otherwise. Commissions then existed at factory level for social insurance, wages, protection of labour, cultural and educational activities, housing, workers' supplies (that is, canteens and similar facilities), workers' inventions and rationalisation, gardening and auxiliary farming, and assistance to servicemen's families. At workshop level they existed for most of these purposes. It is probably for its services in thus mobilising a large proportion of the working population as activists—persons involved in and committed to the system by personal activity—though only in respect of a limited range of concerns, rather than for any positive result achieved by such activity, that the movement is valued and retained by the authorities. Certainly it does not seem that in those of their ostensible purposes which are most relevant to the work of management the committees are very effective. But the authorities may also see some advantage in having yet another channel of communication in the industrial system, by-passing the local managements and forming

[1] Case in *Trud* 29th December 1955.

a potential check upon them. The 1954 membership of the movement (40,420,000) represented almost 90 per cent of the employed population. As non-members receive only half the sickness benefit paid from social-insurance funds to members it is surprising that it was not more.

The press, apart from being a pulpit for the party, and with the party's sanction for such other systems as the *komsomol* or the trade unions, is itself a channel of control of performance. The visit of a staff correspondent from *Pravda*, or even from some less authoritative organ, can hardly fail to arouse misgivings in factory manager, collective-farm chairman or other holder of such precarious authority as the Soviet system offers. He may be looking for an inspiring story of successful achievement, but it is virtually certain that his article will contain at least one or two slashing criticisms, and the matter may very well not end there. Every few weeks at least the feuilletons (satirical articles in semi-fictional form) and reports in *Pravda*—mainly on the party—and *Izvestia*—on the soviet system—and presumably also other papers, uncover some scandal of more than usual gravity, and this is always followed by a statement that the appropriate organ, if an individual has been under attack, or superior authority, if the victim was a collective body, has investigated the charge, found it fully justified and taken the necessary action, including reprimands and sometimes more severe penalties upon the culprits. Such cases have evidently been cleared by the party authorities in advance and the way opened to their successful conclusion, and it may be that the correspondent only sets out on his travels when the organs of the party or state system have found a case and some moral which can usefully be pointed by dragging it out to light. But it seems probable that the press, itself under strong party surveillance, works in independence of at least the general-purpose local network of party and state below its own level, that its inspection is, at least to some extent, a genuine one, though probably not all that it discovers finds its way into print. Much the same probably applies to letters from the public. Very few are published, and those often, it seems, inspired, and always so chosen as to fit into the paper's current campaign or perhaps to inaugurate a new one, but it may well be that many more are received and taken into account in the paper's own investigations. Certainly official insistence on the importance of the organisation in newspaper offices, as in party and soviet organs, for dealing with such business, suggests that it is of more value than the published matter proves. Such of this correspondence as appears is always of weight and usually informed by burning indignation without any of the amiable trivialities which appear in the correspondence columns of even the most august British newspapers.

No association, from the centre down to the local co-operative, sports club or cultural society, may be formed, and no meeting of any sort may be held, without license from the organ of the state authority for the area from which the participants are to be drawn. Where a model charter has been approved for the type of association as we have seen for collective farms, it must be followed; where there is none, the law requires the authority of the Praesidium of the republican Supreme Soviet for each foundation. Thus all legal organisational systems in Soviet society can be, and are, in some way made to serve the purposes of the Soviet state in organising the masses, the people at large, and so both redeeming them from uncommitted and unsupervised apathy and establishing a potential claim to their services against the other established hierarchies in case the need should arise so to use them. In general the authorities of the Soviet Union seem to distrust the unorganised as potentially dangerous. Most of their safeguards are to be found among the social, cultural and sporting societies which share with the party the honours of an appearance in Article 126 of the constitution. But it seems that now we should so account also the Orthodox Church. The order of the party Central Committee of 10th November 1954, forbidding actions offensive to religious believers and administrative action against the Church, though (as usual with formal declarations of rules in the Soviet Union) imprecise in its terms and at least partially propagandist in intent, seems to be an admission, and the clearest so far, of this standing of the Church. It cannot be said to be a body approved by state authority, for its basic teachings are obnoxious and its festivals and observances are apt to cause disruption in the process of production, but it is trusted and for some things valued; its traditional unworldly submission to the state in all things temporal and its character as the oldest symbol of Russian patriotism are useful to the state in the present conjuncture of its purposes. It is not for communists or members of the *Komsomol*, but it is a means of influence on the otherwise inaccessible. It may not teach, but it may hold its services and recruit clergy. It has most of the badges of a permitted organisation, including its own journal. Other religious communities are less favoured, particularly in so far as they are connected with stronger communities abroad and make heavy demands on the time of their believers. Mohammedanism has been open to both these objections, but it seems possible that with the Soviet Union's increased interest in its Southern neighbours the former may come to be seen as a virtue.

CHAPTER VI

Decision and Performance

Top-level Decisions

The sovereign decision-taking body in the Soviet system of government cannot be identified for all purposes with any particular organ of the state or party structure. Any formally constituted body is liable to the necessity of sometimes taking in a person who cannot be eliminated from the scene altogether, because his advice may occasionally be needed, or because he has influential connections, and who would be troublesome if left just outside the circle, but whose opinions are not in general of much account. After Stalin Mr. Voroshilov might attend meetings of the party Praesidium without the humiliation of having to ask for leave, but it is unlikely that Mr. Khrushchov often telephoned him to try out a new idea, which is probably a more significant process in the making of new policies than anything which happens at a formal meeting. There has of recent years seemed to be a central directing group sufficiently near equality for even Mr. Khrushchov to feel unable to settle the more difficult points in such matters of importance as his negotiations with Marshal Tito without some consultation, and generally in one another's mind. Probably it included most of the Praesidium of the party Central Committee and perhaps a few others in regular personal interaction. Clearly it was smaller than the whole Central Committee, the rest being only informed, called to witness and occasionally consulted. Mr. Khrushchov's use of it in 1958 was no recognition, but a unique engagement of forgotten forces. As reformed, the Praesidium seems to consist of advisers, rather than deciders, but possibly expert opinions will not be flouted without equally highly powered counter-opinions in fields not in the leader's eye.

There can be little on which the sovereign body can reach decisions entirely without advice from the outside. Probably the groups' internal relations fall most easily into this category; it probably needed no consultation of external opinion to decide that Mr. Malenkov should be relieved of the office of Chairman of the Council of Ministers, though in the case of Mr. Beria, where violence was involved, there must have been some soundings taken to find out who could be relied upon for support or, more important, who could not. Yet there is a considerable range of matters which can be said to be decided exclusively at this top level in the narrower sense that there is no overt sounding of opinion by a public announcement of the prevailing tendency of thought in advance of a final decision; the directing group merely calls in its official advisers and persons in its confidence, perhaps informs itself indirectly of the state of the public mind, and then forms its own judgment. Turns in foreign and military policy necessarily follow this pattern; Marshal Tito is a friend until one day the newspapers carry the news that he is a hireling of foreign capital and he remains an enemy and apostate until he is again hailed as a friend. But the same applies in the Soviet Union to the basic economic priorities; the Soviet citizen, like the foreign observer, must infer from the speeches of the leaders the degree of priority to be given to capital development over the production of consumer goods or the degree of severity to be applied to the peasants in the succeeding months. He is not consulted, he is told. Even the sixth Five Year Plan (of 1956) (though, unlike its predecessors, it was introduced to a party congress within a month after it was to take effect) had not been the subject of general discussion in advance, and could not be so thereafter. It had already begun to take effect in a budget passed by the Supreme Soviet at the end of the previous year.

Planning and Budgeting

At the Fifteenth Party Congress at the beginning of the period of the Five Year Plans in December 1927 Stalin announced that 'Our plans are neither predictions nor conjectures; they are directives.' Some element of prediction there must, of course, be—a reasonable guess of what is possible with the given resources of men and materials. But in general Stalin was right. The plan is primarily a general order to all enterprises and institutions in the system, a matter of law based upon sanctions rather than of science based upon an objective assessment of probability. It is in consequence of this that overfulfilment in any branch is always even more welcome to the authorities than exact fulfilment. The plan targets are indications of direction, or acceptable minima; the maxima are fixed not by them but by the resources made available, which in conditions of forced rapid industrialisation are always scarce. Decisions on such priorities of allocation, the real planning, are taken not in the formal planning procedure but by such 'top-level' decisions as we have mentioned in the previous paragraph. Fulfilment of the plan in its more formal aspects is evidently far from complete. 'In 1951,' said Mr. Bulganin, 'the proportion of enterprises which failed to fulfil their annual plans amounted to 31 per cent, in 1952 to 39 per cent, in 1953 to 40 per cent and in 1954 to 36 per cent. Moreover, the Ministries of Ferrous Metallurgy, Heavy Machine Building, the Machine-Tool Industry and Electrical Engineering, which in 1954 had overfulfilled whole major sections of their plan, had nevertheless fallen short on some of the most important products within those sections.[1] We cannot tell how far this happens over the long period: failures can largely be concealed by variation of the target, by overlooking variety and quality where these operate against production in quantity, and by quoting only particulars of those branches of economic activity which have succeeded. Yet it seems certain that in general the branches of industry in which the authorities are interested do succeed because at need the necessary resources in material, in managerial or technical skill or in labour power are always diverted to them. In the spirit of the economic bias of Marxism such planning extends to the regulation of the whole life of the community. Schools are among the economic enterprises comprised in local plans, both as making demands on local resources and as potential suppliers of labour power.

The instruments of long-term planning are principally the Five Year Plans for the whole of the economy, though there are also plans for particular branches and areas of which the terms may be shorter, longer or merely equal but not coincident. Officially mentioned examples are the Three Year Plan for the improvement of animal husbandry on collective and state farms to run from 1949 to 1951, the Ten Year Plan for the reconstruction of Moscow to run from 1951 to 1960, and the Five Year Plan for development of cotton-growing in Uzbekistan for the period 1954 to 1958.[2] Within these plans and breaking them down into greater detail on particular products and processes and often varying them to take account of unforeseen developments, there are short-term plans for periods ranging from a year to a month made for the various ministries, republics, administrative areas, and individual enterprises, all of which, it is officially stressed, form a single national plan. It is an elaborate pattern of inter-related instruments repeated and completed by budgets and plans for the allocation of materials, by the general contracts concluded between ministries for the supply by the enterprises of one of them of the equipment or material required by another, and by the local contracts concluded between the several

---

[1] Report to plenary session of the party Central Committee, 4th July 1955 (*Pravda* 17th July 1955).
[2] B. I. Braginski and N. S. Kovalj, *Organizatsija planirovanija narodnogo hozjajstva SSSR* (Moscow, 1954), p. 75.

enterprises and by the agricultural co-operative with machine-tractor stations and other agencies. Planning of one sort or another is a continuous process accompanied by equally continuous collection of details of the performance and capacity which form the basis of further planning. In practice, it seems clear, these details are often incorrect, through oversight or through deliberate misrepresentation by subordinates, and the planning little more than a reasonable guess at what these might be persuaded or bullied to within acceptable reach of performing.

There can be very little scope for initiative in the making of the lowest instruments of this system, but at least they serve as a solemn pledging of those who have to take the operative action on the instructions, and they may well in particular situations do more, mainly by providing to the lower levels the opportunity, and with the aid of the accompanying machinery of supervision the obligation, to reveal unknown resources and promise greater achievement. Consequently planning in this sense, as distinct from the fixing of basic priorities, is effected with protracted and widespread discussion. For the Five Year Plans the discussion is something of a formality. They come to the public eye in the form of 'directives' of the party generally issued in draft in preparation for a party congress and passed unanimously at it, so that the part of the public is confined to such reverential reading and organised expression of approval, as is usual with such congress material. The directives for the first plan and for the fourth were in form exceptional; the former were passed by a party conference (the Sixteenth, held in April 1929) instead of a congress and, unlike all others, also by a state organ, the fifth All-Union Congress of Soviets; the latter, prepared hurriedly on the conclusion of the Second World War, came before neither congress nor conference. All have so emerged only some time after they had already come into effect in the country's economic life; in this respect the month's delay of the sixth Five Year Plan of 1956 is quite exceptionally short. The first plan was the work of Gosplan (the state planning commission) which submitted a number of drafts to the party Central Committee before approval was at last secured, and when it appeared it was with the accompaniment of a mass of supporting material. Subsequently Gosplan does not seem to have taken the initiative, and the volume of published documentation has diminished markedly over the whole period of the plans, though with some revival in 1954.

Gosplan, as the State Planning Committee of the Council of Ministers is still briefly titled, has throughout remained responsible for the details of long-term planning, though for two years from May 1955 it lost current planning to the State Economic Commission. It is presumably consulted by the party organs which draft the five-year plan directives, which must in any case take account of its work on the analysis of performance under previous plans.

In the annual plans the process of negotiation is more marked, though of distinctively Soviet character, and within very narrow limits of time. The first stage is the preparation by Gosplan of 'control figures', the general framework on which the plan is to be based. These figures vary greatly in the extent to which they go into detail according to the importance of the various ranges of activity; only for capital works is there a full specification by ministries and union republics, and detailed industrial targets are given only for the most essential branches of production. In preparing them the commission is supposed to work in consultation with the ministries, to proceed from the basis of the Five Year Plan and governmental instructions and to take account of balances of stocks. This work begins some six to seven months before the start of the new year. Meanwhile the federal ministries and other authorities and the republics and territorial areas are preparing the preliminary draft of their own annual plans. In this they consult all levels subordinate to them, down to the factory and collective farm, a process designed to reveal all internal reserves—presumably in so far as the managers are not careful to retain them as a cushion for themselves against future circumstances—and to induce attention to progressive methods and the elimination of any divergence from them. The result over the system as a whole is the usual bidding up of targets, though experience must suggest to many managers that they are unlikely to be able to fulfil them. When details have been collected through the channels of the ministries, and for agriculture through the soviet structure, planning passes to the second stage, the preparation of the final text. The ministries and equivalent authorities and the governments of union republics prepare their drafts in accordance with all party and government instructions applying to them and submit them to the federal Council of Ministers with a copy to the commission by a prescribed date, which in 1952 was the 15th August and is always thereabouts, and the commission submits the complete version to the Council of Ministers—in 1952 by the 10th October—which finally passes it. In 1957 it was, unusually, presented also to the Supreme Soviet.

Budgeting accompanies the making of the plan, of which it is the financial expression. All budgets come within the plans at their corresponding levels, though not the whole of the material for the budget is to be found in the terms of the plan. All budgets, including those of the local soviets, are comprised in a general state budget for the country as a whole. This, in addition to providing for the central authorities' own services, makes available to the lower levels of the system the necessary funds for their budgets from the common revenues, and this process is repeated down the line, each budget providing for those of the subordinate authorities. Over the years of the present regime the proportion of the funds expended through local soviet budgets has declined and the services to which these local funds were applied have come increasingly to be of social rather than economic character.

The process of budgeting follows closely that of economic planning except in that it has always involved the soviet organs. Some four to five months before the beginning of the year[1] the Ministry of Finance warns all federal ministries and the republican ministries of finance of the limits within which they will have to budget, and on the basis of their proposals and in accordance with the state plan draws up the general state budget, which it submits simultaneously to the Council of Ministers and to the State Planning Committee. The former, taking account of the report of the latter, approves the budget, which is then presented to the budget commissions of the two houses of the Supreme Soviet, referred by them to preparatory commissions composed jointly of deputies and officials, and thereafter, as we have seen,[2] approved by them unanimously with identical amendments for presentation to the Supreme Soviet. The process at the union-republican level is similar and simultaneous. At the lower levels of the soviet system the process is simpler, and does not in the first instance involve consideration of the plans of subordinate bodies, but the consideration by commissions follows the same pattern.

The budget law provides no very detailed information on the financing of the Soviet system. The several divisions on the expenditure side specify the allocation to the several ministries for economic purposes and to the principal social and cultural purposes, such as education, regardless of the ministries by which they are provided. The paragraphs of the law further provide for the subdivisions of these sums between the several chief administrations of the ministries, institutions and services. The difficulty for the observer outside the system is to know exactly what services are affected by provisions to any particular ministry or agency. The local and ministerial budgets, which are more specific on these matters, are not normally published. The budget report of the Minister of Finance to the federal Supreme Soviet commonly gives rather more information than is contained in the law itself, but is not fully satisfactory, and the contribution of deputies to the debate is never in the direction of asking for fuller information.

[1] The Soviet financial year is the calendar year.
[2] See p. 102

The revenue section of the budget contains two main categories: taxation from the economy, which is the main resource; and taxation from the population—that is to say, the direct payment made by individuals—with separate sections for state loans and the income of machine-tractor stations and other minor sources. Since 1930 the principal source of revenue has been the turnover tax, a general levy on the product of the state-owned economy according to quantity, differential as between one branch and another, and falling particularly heavily upon food—taxed at its passage through the hands of the state procurement agencies—and consumers' goods. It is hard to tell how much of the selling price of such products is in fact taxation, since almost all the marketing is done through state agencies, which can in consequence largely fix their own price. In addition to this, the industry pays into the budgetary revenues of the state a proportion of its profits calculated separately for each enterprise so as to absorb whatever is left over after provision has been made for all recognised necessary purposes such as maintenance, investment and a contribution to the principal incentive to higher production, the enterprise fund. In the budget these tax receipts are specified according to the several ministries from the enterprises of which they come. Collective farms pay an income tax, partly in kind and partly in cash, at differential rates on produce sold to the state, produce sold on the open market and produce distributed to members. Co-operative organisations and social organisations, such as trade unions and sports clubs, each pay a graduated income tax, and enterprises providing services including entertainment pay a proportion of the takings. In addition the state derives revenues from the sale of property and, hitherto, from the work done by machine-tractor stations, which will now presumably be treated as are other enterprises. The main tax from the population is an income tax charged at rates varying with the type of employment and designed in general to discriminate in favour of state employees as against co-operative craftsmen and others. Collective farm and independent peasants pay an agricultural tax, falling not on the individual but on the household and levied according to the area of their private plots on scales varying from one republic to another. All persons without children pay an additional tax, and those with one or two children also pay it but at reduced rates.

The main source of revenue of the local soviets is a proportion of the several state taxes calculated for each authority by its superior authority in accordance with its supposed needs. It is left to the State Bank to make the allocation of funds to the accounts of the various authorities as they are collected. Provision is made for a limited number of local taxes, on building works, means of transport, land and cattle and collective farm markets, from some of which local executive committees are empowered to grant whole or partial exemption. No unauthorised tax may be levied, and maximum rates and certain obligatory exemptions are prescribed. The market tax is to be applied, as to 60 per cent, to the improvement of market facilities.[1]

The financing of industry and of the economy in general is mainly a federal matter, though industry and commerce of local subordination appears on the regional or territorial budget and to a very limited extent on those of districts and towns. Municipal economy—local public works—'is almost entirely carried on the town budgets'.[2] In agriculture a number of research and veterinary treatment establishments are mentioned as falling on regional and territorial budgets, while districts have some minor veterinary centres and the plant-protection service. Local roads are also mainly on regional and district budgets. Local social and cultural expenditure, it is stated, is mainly a district or town matter, while certain larger institutions such as teachers' training colleges, children's homes, homes for the incapacitated and specialised hospitals fall upon regional budgets. The concerns of the village, as we have already seen, are very small.

Low-level Decisions

Most of the matters on which the authorities require the benefit of local knowledge, such as the building of roads, schools or hospitals, as well as more purely economic matters, fall within the system of economic planning. Other matters which might appear likely to benefit by wide consultation, such as the teaching programme of the schools, do not in fact appear to receive it. Education is conceived of as primarily a matter of the training of cadres for the economic system as a whole, rather than for the benefiting of local life, and consequently it is highly standardised throughout the system. The public is consulted in the big demonstrations such as the making of the 1936 constitution and in a number of minor campaigns, although its advice is apt to be disregarded if it diverges from the line which the authorities have already worked out in their own minds. There can be little doubt that the central authorities feel strongly the need for detailed information from below and desire to carry the public with them rather than to enforce their will upon it. But their whole doctrine operates to persuade them that they know best and that those who are not enlightened by mastery of the Marxist

[1] V. Shavrin, *Gosudarstvenny Bjudzhet SSSR* (1953), pp. 37–65.
[2] Ibid., p. 21.

analysis are apt to be led astray and must at times for their own good be disregarded.

It is reasonable to assume that much which is done in the Soviet Union is done on initiative from below, though we can only say in very general terms how this happens. To get something done, to get a particular local road repaired, for example, or to secure some improvement in the local restaurants and canteens which have latterly been exercising the attention of the national press, it is probably best to approach some person well established in the party hierarchy even for matters which are to be taken up in the soviet executive committee. Letters to the press, which stands, as we have suggested, very close to the party centres of influence, may do some good by indicating to higher authorities a factual need of which they were previously unaware, and perhaps some unnoticed obstruction in the channel to its fulfilment. It is improbable that such letters influence the authorities by persuading them of the existence of a body of opinion to which, if they think it objectively incorrect, they are likely to be substantially indifferent. Executive committee or soviet members are likely to be of sufficient influence, or to know people of sufficient influence, to be useful points of first contact, but a direct raising of the matter in an executive committee meeting without previous clearance with the party would probably be fruitless, and raising it in a meeting of the full soviet even more so and possibly rather dangerous. For the improvement of amenities in a rural area there may be more to be hoped from the management of a well-run collective farm or the director of an appropriate enterprise, who can gratify particular interest under the guise of general economic purpose. Even in a large town we find citizens desiring the improvement of the local cultural facilities approaching the ministries to which the principal local industrial enterprises are subordinated. At such a high level the approach was legitimate; the criticism intended was of the ministries for their neglect, not of the petitioners for overlooking the local organs of state authority.[1] At a lower level, however, such an approach is precarious both for those who solicit favours and for those who grant them, and the resources at the disposal of such persons are commonly too much committed to enable them to confer more than small favours, usually against an equivalent counter-concession.

There is still some field for private agreement even in the Soviet Union. The disposal of private income and property for the purpose of pleasure is virtually unrestricted after payment of tax, and the rates of personal taxation are low. The principal restriction is the very limited supply of many of the things upon which successful citizens are

[1] *Izvestia*, 5th May 1956.

particularly anxious to spend their money—accommodation, motor cars and probably, even now, good clothes. Private-house building on plots with a limited lease is now possible but is out of the range of the great majority of citizens. There is no scope for private investment. Subscription to state lottery loans has been invited, and indeed enforced; redemption, however, is now suspended. Direct investment in particular state projects is not as yet invited, and investment in private projects would be capitalism and is therefore entirely excluded. Also, any form of 'speculation'—that is to say, buying for resale—is to be avoided on pain of criminal action, though it quite evidently is not avoided in practice. The press is frequently provided with material by the activities of shrewd citizens in buying up the available resources of scarce commodities in circumstances which suggest that they are not entirely for their own use. But discrimination between legitimate disposal of surplus property and such speculation is always difficult and must lead to many hard cases.

Securing Performance—Economic

A principal inducement to the fulfilment of economic obligations since 1936 has been the 'enterprise fund', a limited share of the profits of the enterprise retained for distribution in money or in the form of various amenities, between its managers and workers. The proportion of profits going to this fund varies from one industry to another, and as between planned and surplus profits. The industries which the regime is for the time being particularly concerned to promote, which in general means those concerned with the production of heavy producer goods, are allowed to retain a larger share than those in which it is not so interested —mainly those concerned with consumer goods, and the rather theoretical profits provided for in the plan yield much less benefit to enterprises realising them than do the genuinely unexpected profits achieved by extra effort or by discreet concealment at the time when the plan is being drafted. Until 1955 the fund was called the 'director's fund', but its application was not in fact entirely in the director's discretion. As now prescribed half of it is to be used for improvement of the firm's productive equipment or of the housing of workers and other members of the staff, since housing is a chronic problem in the Soviet Union. The rest may be spent on other social purposes and on bonuses as agreed between the director and the factory trade-union committee. In this and other forms—financial, social, honorific and others—all in industry are given an interest in unusually high productivity by themselves or by the enterprise. For managers this is almost the only way to promotion; hence plan-fulfilment rules their minds, and sometimes clashes with other government policies. A manager, reminded of his duty to provide employment for young workers, objects that he has a plan to fulfil, and that the restricted hours of work prescribed for young workers make it impracticable for him to employ them.

There is a negative side to all this. If in fact all penal deterrents to movement in search of higher wages are abolished without substitute it is likely that the problem of excessive mobility of labour[1] which has been dogging the authorities from the first, and which (apart from any peculiarities of national character) is the natural joint consequence of living in a land of opportunity where there are no normal trade-unionist remedies for unsatisfactory conditions, will again become so acute that something positive, even if not legislative, will have to be done about it. Managers failing in their assignments risk, at best, staying unpromoted in a hard-pressed, unprivileged and so probably discontented enterprise. At worst they may incur exile, whether so called or not, though, it seems, often still in a supervisory capacity. As far as one can tell, however, the resurgence of dismissed or demoted managers seems to have hitherto been remarkably frequent, probably in consequence of their continued scarcity. Apart from these consequences for the individual, the emphasis on plan fulfilment can be detrimental to quality, and the authorities are constantly exercised by the problem of how to take account of this factor, in the plan and otherwise, in a way which will enable it to withstand the worst excesses of the incessant and obvious demand for quantity. One fault which is regularly denounced in the press is that of 'storming' (*shturmovshchina*)—rushing at the end of a planning period to make up for the consequences of previous slacking, resulting in variations of quality and a disruption of the even tenor of the production process. Sometimes the pressure of the party operates so as to encourage this fault. The regional committee, instead of finding out how methods can be improved, sends a telegram demanding fulfilment in a few days' time. As a result all other tasks are dropped. Two coal-mines in one region were said in 1953 regularly to have five to six and eight to ten rush days a month respectively for this reason. The cause of unevenness may well be in the plan itself. One motor vehicle factory is said to have had its plan changed fifteen times during 1956 by the State Economic Commission and the Ministry. Collective farms apparently suffer similar revisions of plan.

[1] Mr. Bulganin told the party Central Committee in July 1955 that in 1954 2,802,000 workers left enterprises under all-union or union-republican ministries and 1,453,000 left construction sites, against 2,923,000 and 1,771,000 taken on. He mentioned housing difficulties as a principal cause of this.

Securing Performance—General

The regime's principal guarantee for the performance of the tasks which it sets the people for their own good as it interprets it is the universal inspectability from above, the general absence of any freedom from supervision. In principle this should not be, though Mr. Bulganin among many others has conceded that it too often is, a negative business of collecting reports on shortcomings and administering rebukes and other sanctions. 'To verify performance[1] means to organise people for a specific matter, to provide for the practical implementation of party and government directives, to prevent and correct errors on the basis of detailed study and to take measures for the future improvement of the work.'[2] But, whatever their intentions in this respect, the leaders' concern lest all channels of supervision and complaint should ever be blocked at the same time has led them to create a system of extreme complexity—or persuaded them to tolerate it if, as is probable, it has so grown without their specific intent. The cost is an obscurity of organisation and responsibility which must make it very hard for a citizen to know how the machine works, or how he is to play his own part in it without laying himself open to trouble. It makes excessive demands for scarce staff, duplicating the state organisation by that of the party, and the operative agencies within each by further purely supervisory agencies, for the supervisor must, if he is to be effective, have at least some knowledge of the techniques of the men he is supervising. The system probably also leads to a general lack of the trust which contentment—a sense of being free of, or attuned to, external forces—seems to require, although we should not underestimate the capacity of human beings for adapting themselves to what from outside may seem to be the most intolerable circumstances.

Apart from this system of regularly operating pressures, the Soviet political system, like any other, has a special apparatus of retribution for the intractable cases. The Soviet penal system, like that of the Russia of the Tsars before it, has always made comparatively little use of prisons in the general centres of population, and its equipment, apart from its intentions, would probably not permit it to do so now. The corrective labour camp has been the general form of detention, especially since the coming of the Five Year Plans in 1928, leaving the prison as a place of remand and transit and for the short sentence, which in Soviet practice is comparatively rare. Such camps have until recently been

---

[1] See footnote on p. 150.
[2] Mr. Bulganin's report to the plenary session of the party Central Committee, 4th July 1955 (*Pravda*, 17th July 1955).

widely distributed over the territory of the Soviet Union, though with a tendency for them to be in the less developed and less inviting parts of the country where free labour was least easy to obtain. A number of them was specialised in particular classes of work—mining, canal building, road building, lumbering, or cultivation—while some specialised in particular classes of prisoners such as women or children, and others were primarily organised with regard to the isolation and punishment of difficult cases rather than to any particular labour function. Release of prisoners has commonly been subject to various forms of restriction on place of residence and other civil rights, many prisoners being required to settle as exiles in the neighbourhood of their former place of detention instead of being allowed to return to their place of origin. This large element of semi-free citizens led to a wide divergence of opinion as to the number of the Soviet Union's prisoner population, but it has certainly been larger than most other states which require less of their citizens have found reasonable. Since the latter part of 1955 there have been indications of a tendency towards increased reliance on exile rather than on penal servitude—in the distinction of the pre-revolutionary days—with relative freedom of living conditions within a prescribed area. This may be the meaning of recent official statements that the camps are to be reorganised as corrective labour colonies, or these may be another form of punishment more closely resembling the old practice. The camps may have been briefly transferred to the management of the Ministry of Justice after the fall of Beria, but with the abolition of that ministry at federal level the Ministries of Internal Affairs are again, as formerly, charged with observing the regulations concerning the colonies—with the procuracy presumably still supervising. In addition to penalties involving displacement, regular use has been made of forced labour at the normal place of work, which in effect means a period on a drastically reduced rate of pay. For minor offences fines may be inflicted and, as in other countries, the courts have to be warned from time to time against excessive use of this form of punishment.

Capital punishment except in the form of the massacre, principally of political opponents—though the term has of late been very widely interpreted—has never had a large place in Russian penal practice. It was abolished in 1946, but restored in the following year for cases of treason, and in 1953 for murder resulting from the deliberate practice of violence; latterly the press has repeatedly reported cases of its infliction as part of the current campaign to suppress crimes of violence.

In view of the variety of prohibitions and the inhumanly high standard of social discipline which the system imposes upon its citizens much leniency seems to be shown, at least in small matters. The reprimand without further penalty is a common answer to minor offences, both in the formal judicial system and in the internal discipline of factory or farm. Soviet writings suggest from time to time that officials are too much given to this course, and that offenders have learned not to take much notice of it. Where, however, a form of conduct is considered in some way to undermine the system retribution can be very severe. Policy can change markedly, as it has done over offences against private property, once of little account but now guarded almost as jealously as the state's own property. It can also be openly discriminatory as between persons, in accordance with the exemplary purposes which we have noticed. It has been suggested, for instance, that in cases of misappropriation of state, or collective, property courts have commonly dealt appreciably more severely with peasants than with officials.[1] Possibly this is because officials are valuable in their posts and also subject to a degree of supervision such as cannot be applied to peasant pilferage. On the other hand, unreasonable delay and other offences by officials which in other systems would be likely to lead to nothing worse than dismissal, if that, may involve a criminal penalty in the Soviet Union; and if the offence is one which the authorities are for the moment particularly anxious to stamp out, possibly a severe one.[2] The same purposes explain the increased severity with labour offences in the legislation of 1940, lately repealed, or the present movement of repression against crimes of violence.

It is hard to say from outside how far all this makes up an effective penal system. Probably to most citizens it all seems too indiscriminate to have the desired deterrent or reformatory effect. The current attempt once again to achieve something recognisable as legality may make for greater efficiency, though it is hard to make any penal system fully effective in a society in which the law is largely unknown and most citizens must, to live and prosper, infringe it in some respect.

The system of the labour camps as it has existed hitherto has not been merely a penal system. The value of the work done by the prisoners, highly inefficient though it probably was, has been considerable in that the tasks were such in nature and location that it would have been hard to get them done at all without severe coercion. In 1941 the budget provision for capital construction to the Ministry for Internal Affairs which then managed the camps was larger than that to any ministry other than those for the oil industry and the aircraft industry.[3] There

---

[1] Dinerstein, op. cit., p. 121.
[2] Berman, op. cit., p. 272.
[3] Moore, *Terror and Progress U.S.S.R.*, pp. 28, 235n.

can be no doubt that in his latter years Mr. Beria had an industrial empire of his own which was unrivalled in the Soviet Union, and on which the regime was largely dependent for its capital works. This meant that, as in other fields, such considerations as sound administration were neglected in the pressing demand for results.

But retribution and contrived pressures are not the only motive forces in the Soviet system. Like any other system, it has its self-operating elements, though perhaps they are less prominent than in most. It is a system which offers considerable opportunity to the able and the ambitious, probably a less egalitarian society than ours, with larger differentials of net income—at least if tax-free perquisites on both sides be left out of account—and also high social mobility. Achievement is all, and for the capable there is the possibility of their rising by a conjuncture of their own efforts with official favour to considerable power and social distinction. There is as yet little evidence of the emergence of hereditary castes, though a citizen's position in life is largely determined by the standard of education which the representatives of the state with whom he chances to come into contact see fit to give him, and this in an influence-ridden society seems to offer highly placed parents the means of averting in most cases any extreme fall in social status from one generation to the next. Yet they can hardly hope to endow their children with such a fortune as will be more than a supplement to income from employment. Once he is in employment the pressure of the drive for production and whatever forces still operate against mobility of labour would seem to limit the citizen's chance of bettering himself. In particular, the peasants remain, as they were under the Tsars, both before and after emancipation, a people apart, more restricted in their movements physically and socially than other citizens by their lack of passports and by other limitations,[1] though economically not particularly downtrodden; Mr. Khrushchov's visions of urbanisation may perhaps in time wipe out this distinction.

The bright prospects are not only for the individual. The Soviet peoples have received some earnest of achievement in the extension of the common stock. The repeated promises of greater comfort have never been fully realised, ostensibly, and in part actually, by reason of external circumstances and notably as a result of the war, but largely because the authorities have been unreasonably ambitious in their planning and are determined that whatever else may suffer in consequence of their failure to realise all that they desire, the projects of industrialisation and national security on which they set their hearts shall not. But much of the product of the industry and abstinence which

[1] Kulski, op. cit., pp. 650–9.

the regime has imposed has been distributed. If many of its decisions were wrong, many were right, and have aroused no opposition, and the conditions of the individual citizens, if not perhaps better than they might have been had there been no revolution, are at least better than they were before the revolution. Moreover, the prospect of still better remains, and the unmistakable achievements of the country are a promise of this which the Soviet citizen must, and apparently in fact does, often appreciate. The ignorance of contemporary advances in the outside world, the suggestion, which seems somewhat ridiculous to the outside observer, that conditions in Great Britain, for example, are still much as they are described in the pages of Dickens, helps to heighten this sense of achievement.

The sense of danger may operate to much the same effect. The 'capitalist menace' is probably more real to most of the Soviet leaders than it is to most people in the world deemed by them to be capitalist. Whatever its reality, to them it has the practical utility of keeping up the tension. The Russian people after the revolution and civil war, after the violence of Stalin's march to power, and especially after the Second World War, has had enough of disorder, and the suggestion of the leaders that they are the sole pillars of peace against the threat of aggression from without may be supposed to be a strong inducement to their subjects to submit to and support their authority. There can be little doubt that the support which the government receives for its successive peace campaigns is substantially genuine. That the government itself may be one of the forces militating against peace is not brought to the attention of the people, and, as in most other countries, it probably does not occur to them spontaneously.

It must also be a support to the present regime and an element in Russia's political process that under its present management the country's influence in the world has been greatly enhanced. This is partly due to the external circumstance that there are now fewer great powers in consequence of the decline of possible rivals. There is, however, a more positive side to Russia's achievements. By all reliable indices of influence—industrial capacity, possession in quantity of the more destructive weapons of war, powerful presumptive allies, client states and friendly neutrals and sympathisers among the subjects of its potential enemies who can be expected to prefer its cause to that of their own countries, widespread interest in its ways of settling social and other problems and a conviction among leading people of some at least of the world's more considerable countries that they have much to learn from it—it is a country to which others must pay some attention in framing their policies, and more securely so than it was even in the years following the fall of Napoleon. It has a hold over central Europe and an influence in Asia such as the Tsars long sought but never achieved. In any case, whatever the cause of the increased influence, the regime in power gets the credit, as usually happens in such situations. Moreover, this rise in influence accords well with an official mythology which gives a pleasant sense of being on the side of humanity and inevitability.

In this system a large place belongs to fictions. Since the possession of an infallible key to the understanding and management of social processes forms the basis of the claim of communists to wield authority, error in the party itself or in the system of government which it has established can never be admitted. Consequently anything which goes wrong has to be imputed to the ill-will or selfishness of some form of rival influence explicable in terms of Marxist theory. The external menace is convenient, but cannot be stretched to explain everything; internal resistance, which in other countries could be ascribed merely to the tendency of all human beings to prefer their own interests to those of others, can in a society allegedly both Marxian socialist in its analysis and classless in its structure be accounted for only by supposing the existence of 'survivals of bourgeois mentality'. It may be necessary to keep this fiction in being after the extinction of the last of the generation which could possibly have belonged to any bourgeoisie other than that of the communists' own making. Even as it is, it is not applicable to all situations; it may be possible to explain the misdeeds of Beria by a fiction of contact with foreign influences and a desire to restore capitalism, but the misdeeds of Stalin can hardly be explained by anything other than defects of personal character unmotivated by any social forces, however deeply this may perturb foreign communists.

The elimination of all opposition of a party-political nature has been achieved at the cost of the loss of those services which a rival party normally performs for the one in power, in keeping its members up to the mark, pointing the finger of scorn at weak men and weak policies, finding a place as critics for the difficult men, thinking out alternative aims and methods which the ruling party can at a favourable opportunity discreetly purloin, and providing an identifiable enemy which can be blamed for shortcomings without poisoning the whole of social relations. In this and in the elimination of independent opinion generally the Marxist believers in the dialectic process have so sterilised their system that there is no dialectic operating, no mechanism to warn them when they are going too far on any tack of policy and to slow down and reverse trends before they degenerate from productive insight into destructive fanaticism. In consequence, it has been suggested, they have been obliged themselves to create an artificial dialectic.[1] This is probably not an entirely conscious process, but it has a distinguishable function in the system. It shows itself in the repeated sudden reversals of policy in all fields of the national life: on the rights of the peasant in collectivised agriculture, on managerial methods, on literary and architectural styles or the theory of language or otherwise. It is manifested, too, in the dropping of leaders, with or without violence, and the successive disownings of the past, one of which was recently seen in progress at the expense of the elaborately constructed prestige of the late Mr. Stalin.

[1] See 'O. Utis', 'Generalissimo Stalin and the Art of Government', *Foreign Affairs*, January 1952.

BIBLIOGRAPHY

For the reasons suggested in the introduction we can give no list of Soviet standard sources which will cover our whole field. The student of Soviet politics must read anything written by Russians for Russians which comes his way—texts of legislation, handbooks, newspapers and journals and even works of fiction—and hope for glimpses of the way in which things work. As, apart from its other faults, Soviet material is verbose and repetitious and hardly concerned at all with the purposes of the political scientist, this process is both tedious and expensive. It also has very narrow limitations; much which has been published in the Soviet Union has not been available abroad, except to the rare traveller who could fetch it himself, though latterly the position has improved. We must rely largely on the published works digesting and analysing this material which, mainly for reasons of expense, are mostly produced in America, and many of which make good use of these very limited resources. The following list attempts no more than to name a few of these which have been found acceptable to students, together with some of the more general and more widely available, though not necessarily the most valuable, Russian works.

NON-SOVIET

TEXTBOOKS ON POLITICAL INSTITUTIONS

Merle Fainsod, *How Russia is Ruled*, Harvard U.P., 1953. (Very good but rather forbidding in size.)

Michael T. Florinsky, *Towards an Understanding of the U.S.S.R.*, Macmillan (New York), 1951. (Being short, simple and comprehensive, finds favour with newcomers to the field of study.)

S. N. Harper and R. Thompson, *The Government of the Soviet Union*, Van Nostrand (New York), 1949 (2nd. edn.). (Has much the same virtues, though it is rather longer.)

Julian Towster, *Political Power in the U.S.S.R.*, O.U.P. (New York), 1948. (Like the previous work, it has suffered a little from time; this is probably still the best textbook for general use.)

There are also two useful short accounts in works of wider scope:

Vladimir Gsovski, *Soviet Civil Law*, U. of Michigan, 1948, Vol. I, Part I.

John Hazard, chapters on the Soviet Union in Fritz Morstein Marx (ed.), *Foreign Governments*, Prentice Hall (New York) (new edn.), 1952.

STUDIES OF THE WORKING OF SOVIET POLITICS

John N. Hazard, *The Soviet System of Government*, U. of Chicago Press, 1957.

W. W. Kulski, *The Soviet Regime*, Syracuse U.P., 1954. (Large, even by American standards, and markedly antipathetic to its subject, but very useful as containing a mass of otherwise inaccessible information and of direct quotation of sources, and conveying some sense of how the system works.)

Barrington Moore, Jr., *Soviet Politics, the Dilemma of Power*, Harvard U.P., 1951.

Barrington Moore, Jr., *Terror and Progress, U.S.S.R.*, Harvard U.P., 1954. (Much broader in scope than its title suggests.)

W. W. Rostow and A. Lewin, *The Dynamics of Soviet Society*, Secker and Warburg, 1953.

SPECIAL ASPECTS OF POLITICS

Law

Gsovski, mentioned above, is somewhat detailed for the non-specialist, but on particular topics he is very useful and readable. On collective farms and machine-tractor stations, for example, he is as good as anything published. Vol. II contains translations of legal tests.

H. J. Berman, *Justice in Russia*, Harvard U.P., 1950.

John Hazard, *Law and Social Change in the U.S.S.R.*, Stevens, 1953.

(Berman is primarily concerned with origins, Hazard with manner of operation, but neither exclusively so.)

The Economy (which, as we have suggested, is what Soviet politics are about)

G. Bienstock, S. M. Schwarz, A. Yugow, *Management in Russian Industry and Agriculture*, O.U.P., 1944.

H. S. Dinerstein, *Communism and the Russian Peasant* (in one volume with H. S. Dinerstein and Leon Gouré, *Moscow in Crisis*, which on its different subject—attitudes in Moscow to the withdrawal of leadership in the early days of the German invasion in 1941 is also interesting), Free Press, Glencoe, Ill., 1955. (Concerned with the peasants and their attitudes rather than with the management of agriculture, but sheds much light on both.)

D. Granick, *The Red Executive*, Macmillan, 1960. (An account of the world of the Soviet factory manager which also contains much of value on Soviet life generally and how to observe it.)

Trade Unions
I. Deutscher, *Soviet Trade Unions*, Royal Institute of International Affairs, 1950.

Propaganda and Its Public
Alex Inkeles, *Public Opinion in Soviet Russia—a study in mass persuasion*, Harvard U.P., 1950.

Armed Forces
Raymond L. Garthoff, *How Russia Makes War*, Allen and Unwin, 1954. (Its interest is military rather than political, but it is useful.)

Zbigniew Brzezinski (ed.), *Political Controls in the Soviet Army—a study based on reports by former Soviet officers*, Research Program on the U.S.S.R. (Praeger, New York), 1954. (The officers are named and severally contribute sections to the book.)

Political Personalities
George K. Schueller, *The Politburo* (Hoover Institute Studies), Stanford U.P., 1951. (An analysis of the careers of all who held office as full members of the politburo.)

Boris Meissner, *Sowjetrussland zwischen Revolution und Restauration*, Verlag für Politik und Wirtschaft, Cologne, 1956. (A useful collection of essays and character sketches and career studies of leading political and military figures.)

History (post-revolutionary)
E. H. Carr, *A History of Soviet Russia*, Macmillan, 1950. (The work has now, in its sixth volume, reached 1926.)

Isaac Deutscher, *Stalin, a Political Biography*, O.U.P., 1949. (Apart from its biographical merits provides one of the best shorter histories of the period.)

The Russian chapters in Hugh Seton-Watson, *The Pattern of Communist Revolution*, Methuen, 1953, are short and helpful. They are less charitable than Mr. Carr's account.

BACKGROUND

Geography

Georges Jorré, *The Soviet Union, the Land and its People* (translation by E. D. Laborde from the French), Longmans, 1950.

Pre-revolutionary History

Almost any of the general histories of Russia. Two recent publications are very useful:

Michael T. Florinsky, *Russia, a History and an Interpretation*, Macmillan (New York), 1955. (Two volumes, extending up to and including the revolution.)

Richard Charques, *A Short History of Russia*, Phoenix House, 1956. (Sketches in briefly the post-revolutionary period, and is generally directed towards the understanding of the present.)
Also, with a more limited period:

Hugh Seton-Watson, *The Decline of Imperial Russia, 1855–1914*, Praeger, 1952. (Of great assistance in the understanding of the conditions which the revolution inherited.)

Three specialised histories deserve the attention even of those not specialists in history:

M. Kovalevsky, *Russian Political Institutions*, U. of Chicago Press, 1902. (Partial in both senses, but accurate, illuminating and as a specialised history in its field almost alone.)

Nicholas Berdyaev, *The Origin of Russian Communism*, Bles, 1937. (An account of pre-revolutionary thought.)

G. T. Robinson, *Rural Russia under the Old Regime*, Longmans (New York), 1932. (An account of the principal discontent which destroyed imperial Russia in both its economic and its political aspects.)

BIBLIOGRAPHY

JOURNALS

Soviet Studies, quarterly, Department for the Study of the Social and Economic Institutions of the U.S.S.R., University of Glasgow.

Problems of Communism, bimonthly, United States Information Agency.

Osteuropa, monthly, Deutsche Gesellschaft für Osteuropakunde.

(The first is critically sympathetic and inclined to the theoretical, the second destructive but just, the third moderately inclined against the regime and very valuable for its detailed analyses of developments such as changes of organisation, personalities, etc.)

There are two main non-soviet Russian periodicals:

Sotsialisticheski Vestnik, a weekly Menshevik journal published in New York.

Vestnik Instituta po Izucheniju SSSR, published occasionally in Munich by the Institute named in the title. (Both journals are acute observers of the Soviet scene, and the latter publishes much scholarly analysis of Soviet material, as also do the frequent special publications of the same Institute, including a *Bulletin* in English.)

Important articles on Soviet politics appear from time to time also in the political journals not devoted primarily to the Soviet Union. Mention may be made of the work of Dr. T. H. R. Rigby based on a study of the Soviet provincial press: 'Changing Composition of the Supreme Soviet', *Political Quarterly*, July–September 1953; 'Local Government in the U.S.S.R.', *Australian Outlook* (journal of the Australian Institute of International Affairs), March 1954; and 'Soviet Government Changes since Stalin', *Australian Outlook*, September 1955.

Soviet Source Material in Translation

Current Digest of the Soviet Press, published weekly by the Joint Committee on Slavic Studies appointed by the American Council of Learned Societies and the Social Science Research Council is a useful aid to the solution of the language difficulty and the difficulty caused by the heavy dilution of solid information in the Soviet sources.

SOVIET

TEXTBOOKS ON STATE AND LAW

A. A. Askerov, N. D. Durmanov, M. P. Kareva, V. F. Kotok, I. D. Levin, I. P. Trainin, *Sovetskoe Gosudarstvennoe Pravo*, 1948.

Ts. A. Jampolskaja, *Organy sovetskogo gosudarstvennogo upravlenija v sovremenny period*, 1954.

M.P. Kareva and G. I. Fedjkin, *Osnovy sovetskogo gosudarstva i prava*, 1953.

SOURCE MATERIAL

KPSS v rezoljutsijah i reshenijah s'ezdov, konferentsi i plenumov Ts K, 1953 (2 vols.) or 1954 (3 vols.), is indispensable though incomplete.

JOURNALS AND NEWSPAPERS

The principal organs of the Soviet central daily press, particularly the Party paper *Pravda* (seven issues a week), the paper of the soviet system *Izvestia*, the trade-union paper *Trud*, the paper of the youth organisation *Komsomolskaja Pravda*, the paper of the Defence Ministry *Krasnaja Zvezda* (all six issues), the paper of the writers' union *Literaturnaja Gazeta* (three issues), and such journals as the Communist Party's theoretical and political journal *Kommunist* (published eighteen times a year), its organisational journal *Partinaja Zhizn* (fortnightly), and the legal journal published by the Academy of Sciences and the Academy of Juridical Sciences, *Sovetskjoe Gosudarstvo i Pravo* (eight times a year), have long been available abroad. The first three all publish much the same general news, indicating their specialities mainly by emphasis. Even *Literaturnaja Gazeta*, though of different character, extends well beyond the sphere of literature; it appears to specialise in articles working out the implications of new developments in party policy. It has latterly become possible to obtain upon subscription a wider range of the press, including some provincial newspapers and the specialist journals of the several ministries and services. Within their specialised fields these last are useful sources: *Vestnik Vyshej Shkoly*, the journal of the Ministry of Higher Education was, for example, the basis of the appropriate section of the present work.

Otherwise the student of Soviet affairs must rely on the handbooks (*spravochnik*) or textbooks for officials and students in the various branches of the state service which are exported in small quantities from time to time. None is directly to the political scientist's purpose, but much may be quarried from them.

INDEX

Abhazian autonomous republic, 70
Academy of Agricultural Sciences, 102, 226; of Arts, 226; of Juridical Sciences, 226; of Medical Sciences, 226; of Pedagogical Sciences, 226; of Sciences, 225–6; of Social Sciences, 154
Activists, 103–4, 110, 181
Adjarian autonomous republic, 70
Administration: collective, 78–81; party, 176 *et seq.*; tradition of, 23–5, 79–80; units of, 71 *et seq.*
Administrations (*upravlenie*), 131–2, 153, 192
Adygei autonomous region, 70
Agitation, 185, 187–9
Agricultural machinery, 203–4
Agricultural Procurements, Ministry of, 193, 199
Agricultural tax, 239
Agriculture, 29, 80, 198 *et seq.*; collectivisation of, 48–9; Ministry of, 117, 179–80, 193, 198, 203; party and, 179–80
Agro-towns, 201
Alexander II, Tsar, 26, 34
Alexander III, Tsar, 27
Alexei, Tsar, 24
All-Russian Central Executive Committee, *see* Central Executive Committee
All-Russian Congress of Soviets, *see* Congresses of Soviets
All-Union Central Council of Trade Unions, 113, 229–30
All-Union Communist Party, *see* Party
All-Union Congress of Soviets, *see* Congresses of Soviets
All-Union Lenin Communist League of Youth, *see* Komsomol
All-Union Ministries, *see* Ministries
Andreev, A. A., 144–5
April theses of Lenin, 57–8
Arbiters, 210–11
Arbitration tribunals, 210
Area courts, 211
Areas (*okrug*): administrative, 65, 72–4; national, 65, 71, 90
Aristov, A. B., 146, 149, 165

Armenian union republic, 66, 73, 91, 98, 122, 142, 164, 204
Army, 217–20
Artelj, 199
Arts, control of the, 227
Aspirant, 223
Assembly of the Land, 23–4
Assessors, 211–12
Astrahan region, 75
Atomic Energy, Chief Administration on the Use of, 129
Auditing administration, 205–6
Autonomous regions, 65, 70, 90
Autonomous republics, 65, 67, 70, 90–1, 113, 130–1
Autonomy, 64 *et seq.*, 69
Azerbaidjan (union republic), 65–6, 70, 73–4, 91, 113, 134, 165, 209
Azov, Sea of, 191

Bagirov, M. D., 145–6
Baibakov, N. K., 117
Bakunin, M., 40
Ballot papers, *see* Elections
Baltic provinces, 63
Baltic republics, 69, 74
Banking, 206–7
Bashkir autonomous republic, 70, 73–4, 91
Belgorod region, 75–6
Beljaev, 146, 149
Belorussia (union republic), 63, 66, 73, 91, 113, 164, 172
Benediktov, I. A., 117
Beria, L. P., 52, 110, 119, 145, 207–8, 233, 245, 247, 249
Black hundreds, 64
Blanqui, L. A., 40
Boarding schools, 221–2
Bolsheviks, 35–6, 39, 45–6, 58–9, 137, 157–8; administration of, 60; autonomous republics and, 64 *et seq.*; compromises by, 47; discontent with, 46; federation and, 63–4
Bonuses, 178, 197
Bourgeoisie, 29, 35, 249
Brest-Litovsk, treaty of, 41–3
Brezhnev, L. I., 146, 149
Bronstein, *see* Trotski

257

Bubnov, A. S., 144
Budgets, preparation of, 237–8
Budjonni, Marshal S. M., 113
Buharin, N. I., 48
Bulganin, N. A., 104, 106, 119, 145, 148, 151, 197, 235, 244
Bureaucratic centralism, 40
Bureaux: party, 139–40; soviet, 111
Burjat-Mongol autonomous republic, 70, 91
Burjat-Mongol autonomous regions, 71

Candidates (for election), 90 et seq.; (party status), 157, 159
Capital punishment, 245
Catharine II, Tsarina, 25
Caucasus, 21–2, 63, 70
Cells, Communist Party, 138
Central Checking Commission of the party, 140, 149, 219
Central Committee of the party, 51, 52, 80, 83, 136–7, 140, 142–4, 152–3, 219; Praesidium of, 141, 145
Central Electoral Commission, 94
Central Executive Committee, 59, 65–6, 68, 79, 216
Central Statistical Administration, 118
Chairmen of collective farms, 181, 200–1
Charters of collective farms, 199
Chechen-Ingush autonomous republic, 70–1
Che-ka, 47, 207
Cherkassy region, 75–6
Chief administration (*glavnoe upravlenie*), 192; for Counter-Intelligence in the Armed Forces, 218; on the Use of Atomic Energy, 129; Chief Political Administration, 153
China, 17
Chinese Eastern Railway, 23
Chkalov region, 75
Chuvash autonomous republic, 70, 91
Church, Russian Orthodox, 22, 232
Citizens, rights of, 84–5
Civil War in France, The, 56
Coal Industry, Ministry of, 117
Collective farms (*kolhoz*), 72, 74–5, 77, 80, 166, 179–80, 198 et seq.; charters of, 199; homestead plots on, 202; members, earnings of, 202–3, 205; obligations of, 203–4; officials of, 200–1; organisation of, 200–3; quotas of produce of, 204–5
Collectivisation, agricultural, 61–2

Collegiality, 79–80
Collegium, 79, 135
Combines (*kombinat*), 192
Cominform, 190
Comintern, 190
Commerce, Ministry of, 193
Commissariats, People's, 60, 67, 207
Commissars, 60; People's, 60, 79, Councils of, 60, 65, 79, 116, 194, 216; political, 155
Committee of Ministers, 24
Committee of Party Control, 150
Committees of the poor, 61–2
Communism, Russian, 17, 39, 45 et seq., 190
Communist League of Youth, 156
Communist Manifesto, the, 64
Communist Party of the Soviet Union, see Party
Congresses: of Soviets, 46, 59, 61, 66, 82–3, 139, 236; party, 46, 48, 50, 52, 58–9, 72, 79, 136–7, 138–41, 143–5, 147, 150, 156
Constantinople, 22
Constituent Assembly, the, 45–6, 59, 82
Constitutional Democrat Party, 32, 158
Constitutions: nature of, 81; of federated units, 82, 85, 129–31; of Soviet Union, 66–8, 81 et seq., 127
Control: meaning of term, 150 fn.; Commission of Soviet, 206, 215; Committee of Party, 150
Corrective labour camps, 244
Corrective labour colonies, 245
Council of People's Commissars, 60, 65, 79, 116, 194, 216
Council of State, 24, 32
Councils of Ministers, 24–5, 31, 52, 87, 106, 116–20, 207, 211; acts of, 18–19, 88–9, 121; meetings of, 122; powers of, 120–3; Praesidium of, 119, 122; State Commissions, Committees, Councils, etc. of, 118, 120, 129
Councils of the Economy (*sovnarhoz*), 81, 120, 126, 133, 135, 193
Courts of law, 210 et seq.; civil proceedings in, 213–14; criminal proceedings in, 214–16
Creative artists, 226–7
Crimea, the, 22, 71, 105
Criticism, attempts at, 108–9
Culture, Ministry of, 117, 194, 223, 227
Cyrillic alphabet, 68

INDEX

Dagestan autonomous republic, 70, 91
Das Kapital, 32
Decisions (*reshenie*): of soviet executive committees, 124; of councils of the economy, 126
Decree of general nationalisation, 45
Decrees (*postanovlenie*), 86, 105 *et seq.*, 120, 197, 202
Degrees, academic, 154, 223–4
Democracy, acceptance of by Russia, 31
Democratic centralism, 39–40
Department of Propaganda and Agitation, 153, 187, 188
Departments (*otdel*), 126, 131–3, 154–5, 192
Deputies, soviet, 91, 108–10
Deviation, 46
Directives, planning, 236
Director's fund, 242
Directors, in industry, 196–7, 242–3. *See also* Managers
Dispositions (*rasporjazhenie*), 86, 124, 126
Districts (*raion*): administrative, 72–5, 191, 211; economic-administrative, 77. *See also* Councils of the Economy
Drogobych region, 177
Dual subordination, 60, 126
Duma: of boyars, 23–4; state, 31–2; town, 27–8
Dygai, N. A., 177

Economic expansion, 23
Economic motive in politics, 42–3, 48–9
Economic planning, 67, 234 *et seq.*, 242–3
'Economists', 34
Economy, party control of, 176, 236
Edicts (*ukaz*), 86, 93, 104–7, 194–5, 208, 212
Edinonachalie, *see* One-man headship
Education: curricula for, 224–5; higher, 221, 223; system of, 220, *et seq.*
Ehrenburg, Ilja, 170
Elections, 90 *et seq.*
Electrical Engineering, Ministry of, 235
Elementary (*nachalnaja*) school, 220
Employment, conditions of, 194–5
Engels, Friedrich, 33, 38, 64
Esthonia (union republic), 69, 73–4, 91, 96, 98, 113, 164
Executive committees of soviets, 111–15, 123–6

February Revolution, the, 35, 158
Federalism, 64, 67 *et seq.*
Federated units: constitutions of, 85–8; rights of, 85–7
Federation, process of, 63–4, 66–7
Federations (*federatsia*), 192
Ferrous Metallurgy, Ministry of, 235
Finance: control of, 206; government, 238–40; industrial, 196–7, 240
Finland, 63, 70
First World War, Russian losses in, 32
Fishing industry, 191
Five Year Plans, 48, 105, 234–7
Food Products Industry, Ministry of, 198
Food: shortage of, 46; supply, 43
Foreign Affairs, Ministry of, 117
Franco-Prussian War, 56
French Revolution, 42
Fuel Industry, Ministry of (R.S.F.S.R.), 186
Furtseva, Mrs. E. A., 146, 149, 186

Geneva Conference, 104, 106
Georgia (union republic), 66, 70–1, 73–4, 91, 164–5, 204
Glavnoe upravlenie (*glavk*), *see* Chief Administration
Gorki region, 189
Gorkin, A. F., 112
Gorny Badahshan autonomous region, 70–1
Gorny Altai autonomous region, 70
Gosarbitrazh, *see* State Arbitration
Gosplan, *see* State Planning Committee
Governing Senate, 24
Government, *see* Council of People's Commissars, Councils of Ministers
Governors (*gubernator*), 25
Governorships (*gubernija*), 25, 71
Grain Products, Ministry of, 199
Great Britain: political institutions in, 17; Russian view of conditions in, 248
Great Russia, 44, 50
Grishin, V. V., 229
Gromyko, A. A., 117

Hakass autonomous region, 70
Heavy Machine Building, Ministry of, 235
Hegel, G. W. F., 33, 37
Higher Certificating Commission, 224
Higher Education: Minister of, 120; Ministry of, 223
Hitler, Adolf, 82

Housing, shortage of, 242, 243 fn.
Housing and Civil Building, Ministry of (Latvia), 121

Ideology, official, 185, 189
Ignatiev, S. D., 149
Ignatov, N. G., 146, 148
Income tax, 239
Industrial Bank, 196, 207
Industrial conscription, 194
Industrial enterprises, classification of, 191–2
Industrial management, 80–1
Industrialisation, 28–9, 35
Industry: appointments in, 193–5; finance of, 196–7; managers in, 196–8, 242–3; organisation of, 191 *et seq.*; party control of, 178; postings in, 195; recruitment to, 194; taxation of, 239; training for, 194–5
Information, sources of, 16, 18–19, 88–9
Initiative, popular, scope for, 240–1
Instructions (*instruktsia*), ministerial, 134
Intelligentsia, 30, 40, 98–9, 185
Internal Affairs, Ministry of, 117, 207, 216, 218, 245–6
Internal affairs administrations, 208
Internat, 221
Internationale, the, 143
Investment, 242
Ivan IV, Tsar, 23
Izvestia, 104, 120, 125–6, 206, 231

Japan: defeat of Russia by, 31; threat from, 43
Jewish autonomous region, 70
Judges, 211–12, 216–17
Judicial system, 28, 210 *et seq.*
Justice, Ministry of, 208, 210, 212, 245
Justices of the Peace, 28

Kabarda-Balkar autonomous republic, 70, 91
Kaganovich, L. M., 117–19, 146
Kalmyk autonomous region (formerly republic), 70–1
Kalnberzins, Ja. E., 147
Kamchatka, 71; region, 72, 75–6
Kamenev, L. B., 49
Kamensk region, 125
Kara-Kalpak autonomous republic, 70
Karachai-Cherkess autonomous region, 70, 71

Karelian autonomous republic, 70, 91
Karelo-Finnish union republic, 70–1, 73, 90, 106, 112
Kazah union republic (Kazahstan), 69, 73, 91, 98, 101, 106, 108, 113, 129, 134, 142, 157, 165, 201, 204
Kerenski, A. F., 35
Khabarovsk territory, 72–3, 109
Khrushchov, N. S., 50–2, 55, 106, 113, 132, 143–6, 148–9, 151, 166–7, 173, 179, 188, 195, 201, 206, 222, 233, 247
Kiev, 22, 92, 194
Kirgiz union republic (Kirgizia), 69, 73, 91, 164
Kirichenko, A. I., 113, 146, 151
Kirilenko, A. P., 147
Kirov, S. M., 48–9, 161
Kolegialjnostj, 79
Kolhoz, see Collective farms
Kombinat, 192
Komi autonomous republic, 70, 91
Kommunist, 186
Komsomol, 155–6, 163, 218
Kontroljno-revizionnoe upravlenie, see Auditing administration
Korotchenko, D. S., 147
Kosygin, A. N., 118, 119, 144–5, 147, 151
Kozlov, F. R., 146
Krai, see Territories
Krasnojarsk region, 109
Kronstadt, 46
Kropotkin, Prince, 28
Kucherenko, V. A., 118
Kuibyshev, V. V., 147
Kulaks, 61, 82
Kuusinen, O. V., 146, 149
Kuzjmin, I. I., 118–19
Kuznetsov, V. V., 229

Labour books, 194
Labour recruitment, 194
Labour Reserves, 194
Lacis, V. T., 102
Land, ownership of, 29, 198
Land assemblies (*zemstvo*), 27
Language, 68; groups, 65
Latvia (union republic), 69, 73–4, 91, 99–100, 211
Law, training for the, 211–12
Laws (*zakon*), 24, 87, 105–7
Leadership of the party, 52, 54–5
Learned institutions, 225–6
Legal Marxism, 34
Legislation, 24, 88–9, 121
Legislative power, 86–7

INDEX

Lenin (V. I. Uljanov), 34 et seq., 41–2, 45–7, 57–9, 63–4, 80, 92, 144, 157–9, 168, 187
Lenin Draft, the, 159
Leningrad, 111, 124, 194, 210; region, 99, 107, 109, 123, 142
Light Industry, Ministry of, 117
Lihachov, I. A., 116
Lithuania (union republic), 69, 73–4, 91, 98, 164
Lobanov, P. P., 102
Local government, 26–7, 92, 107–9; finance of, 239–40; representation in, 27, 91–2, 105
Lvov, Prince, 35
Lvov, University of, 223
Lysenko, T. D., 226

Machine-Tool Industry, Ministry of, 235
Machine-Tractor Stations, 203–4
Magadan region, 75–6
Malenkov, G. M., 51–2, 106, 117, 119, 142, 145, 148, 151, 164, 181, 233
Malyshev, V. A., 118–19
Managers, 80; illegal practices by, 197–8; incentives to, 197, 242–3; responsibilities of, 196–7
Manpower: allocation of, 180–1; shortage of, 195
Mari autonomous republic, 70, 91
Marx-Engels-Lenin Institute, 152
Marx, Karl, 32–3, 38, 56
Marxism in Russia, 33–4, 36–9, 42–5, 61
Marxist doctrine, 33–6
May Day, 97
Mazurov, K. T., 147
Meat and Dairy Products Industry, Ministry of, 199
Medium Machine Building, Ministry of, 117
Meljnikov, L. G., 117, 146, 151
Mensheviks, 35, 39–40, 59, 158
Merv, capture of, 22
Methods Council, 210
Middle schools, 220
Mihailov, N. A., 117
Mikojan, A. I., 110, 119, 145
Militia, 208
Military service, 217–19
Millerevo, 125
Ministers, 116–20; acts issued by, 134; responsibilities of, 133–5
Ministries, 65, 78, 85–6, 116, 126 et seq.; All-Union, list of, 127;
changes in, 128–30; in autonomous republics, 130–1; industries, control of by, 191–3; internal structure of, 133; Republican, lists of, 129–30; Union-Republican, lists of, 127, 129. *See also individual names of ministries*
Minsk, 141, 170
Mir, the, 26
Moldavian union republic, 70, 73, 91, 98, 164–5, 226
Molotov, V. M., 41, 55, 83, 119, 145, 206
Mordovian autonomous republic, 70, 91
Moscow, 22, 31, 41–2, 56, 100, 109, 111, 141, 194, 210, 235; region of, 73, 75–6, 92, 99, 142
Motor Transport and Highways, Ministry of, 116
Muhitdinov, N. A., 146–7
Myths, political, 249
Mzhavanadze, V. P., 147

Nagorny Karabah autonomous region, 70
Nahichevan autonomous republic, 70
Napoleon I, Emperor, 38
Naselenie, 53
National areas, 65, 71, 90
National character, 30–1
Navy, 217
New Economic Policy, 46–7, 82, 193
Newspapers, 186–7
Nicholas II, Tsar, 35
Nobility, the, 25–7, 30
Nomenklatura, 181–2, 188
Nosenko, I. I., 117
Novgorod, 109

Oblastj, see Region
Officers of armed forces, 218–20
Officials, 44, 53; collective farm, 200–1; party, 138, 147, 166–7, 173–5, 178
O.G.P.U., 207
Oil Industry, Ministry of, 120
Okrug, see Areas
Omsk region, 75
One-man headship (*edinonachalie*), 80, 115, 155
Orgburo, 143–4, 148
Orders (*prikaz*) issued by ministers, 134
Orthodox Church in Russia, 22, 232
Osoboe soveshchanie, 216
Ossetian autonomous area, South, 71

Ossetian autonomous republic, North, 70, 91, 113
Otdel, see Departments

Pages' corps, 222
Paris Commune, the, 56–8
Partijnaja Zhizn, 186
Partorg, 155
Party, the (Communist Party of the Soviet Union): administrative functions of, 176 *et seq.*, 189; admission to, 157–8, 160, 163; advancement in, 151–2, 171–2, 174–5; agriculture and, 179–80; appointments made by, 181–2, 188; armed forces and, 155, 217–18; bureaux of, 139–40; 'cadres' of, 153–4, 180; 'candidates' in, 157, 159; 'candidates' of organs of, 141 *et seq.*; cells of, 138; Central Checking Commission of, 140, 149; Central Committee of, 51, 52, 80, 83, 136–7, 140, 142–4, 152–3, 161, 186, 188, Praesidium of, 141, 144–5, secretaries of, 147–9; character, change in, 163, 165–6; checking commissions of, 138; class discrimination in, 159–60; 162–3; Committee of Party Control of, 150; committees of, 138–40; conferences of, 138, 141; Congresses of, 46, 48, 50, 58–9, 72, 79, 136–7, 139–41, 144, 147, 149, 150, 156, 158–60, 186, meetings of, 140–1, representation in, 140; discipline within, 168; doctrine, attitude to, 197–8; economic activities of, 176, 189, 236; educational activities of, 153–4, 156–7, 186, 188; election practices of, 172; General Secretary of, 147–8; groups, 138, 154; ideological activities of, 184–7, 189; industry and, 178; influence within, 173; intellectuals and, 159; international significance of, 190; judiciary and, 216–17; leadership of, 52, 54–5; membership, advantages of, 171, dangers of, 171, duties of, 167–8, 176, fluctuations in, 157 *et seq.*, obligations of, 169–70, rights of, 168; ministries and, 155; name of, 137; nationalities within, 164–5; offences against, 169; officials of, 138, 147, 166–7, 173–5, 178; organisation of, 138–9, 147; orgburo of, 143–4, 148; peasants in, 158–60, 162; politburo of, 143–4; Praesidium, 141, 145; press, control of by, 186–9; propaganda, control of by, 185–9; publications sponsored by, 186–7; purges of members of, 159, 161; R.S.F.S.R. and, 137; recruitment to, 158–9, 163; representation in, 137–8, 142, 166–7; republican branches of, 102, 136, 147, 164–5; rewards by, 175; rules of, 137; schools of, 153–4, 188; secretaries of (central committee), 147–9, (local), 139–42, 172; soviets, control of by, 176–7; staff organisation of, 152–3; Stalin and, 141, 143, 147–8, 151, 159, 162–3, 168, 173, 183; state, relations with, 167, 176–7, 183–4; structure of, 136–7; supervision by, 177–8; symbolic importance of, 190; sympathisers' groups attached to, 161; trade unions and, 228–9; training for, 153–4; Ukrainian branch of, 143, 147; wartime concessions by, 163; women in, 165; workers in, 158, 160–1; youth and, 156–7
Passports, internal, 194
Patriarch, the, 22
Pavlenko, A. S., 117
Peasants, 25–6, 29–31, 34–5, 46–7, 61–2, 158–60, 162, 247
Penal system, 244–6
Penza district, 180
People's Commissariats, 60, 80; Internal Affairs, 60, 207, 216; Labour, 229; Nationalities, 65–6
People's Courts, 211
Pervuhin, M. G., 118–19, 145–7
Peter II, Tsar (the Great), 22, 24–5
Peter III, Tsar, 25
Petrograd, 41, 141; soviet of, 58–9
Pioneers, the, 156
Planning: directives in, 236; long-term, 235–6; short-term, 235–7
Plekhanov, G. Y., 187
Poland, 63
Police, 28, 47, 205, 207–8
Politburo, 143–4
Political commissars, 155
Political parties: emergence of, 32; lack of opposition by, 249–50
Political system, nature of, 16–17
Polozhenie, 121, 133, 208
Ponomarenko, P. K., 113, 117, 145, 148
Popov, V. F., 142
Population, 23, 75–6, 90–1
Populist movement, 34
Posjolok, see Settlement

Pospelov, P. N., 147, 149
Postanovlenie, see Decrees
Power Stations, Ministry of, 117
Powers, separation of, 86–7
Praesidia, 111–12
Praesidium of Communist Party Central Committee, 141, 145
Praesidium of Council of Ministers, 119
Praesidium of Supreme Soviet, 66, 68, 79, 93–4, 100, 104–7, 112, 122, 194–5, 208, 212; chairman of, 79, 112; responsibilities of, 79; secretary of, 112
Pravda, 59, 146, 149, 176–7, 186–7, 189, 196, 227, 231
Praviteljstvo, 116
Pravlenie, 200
Press, the, 18–19, 173, 178–9, 183, 215, 217; letters to, 231, 241; party control of, 186–9; power of, 231
Prikaz, 134
Primorski territory, 72, 177
Printing, control of, 227
Prisons, 244
Procurator-General, 25, 208, 212–13
Procurator service, 208–10
Procurators of republics, 208–9
Profits, 239, 242
Profsojuz, 228
Proletariat, 29, 35
Propaganda, 185–9
Property-owners, status of, 27
Property, private, 241–2
Publications, periodical, 187
Purges, 46, 49–51; party, 159, 161

Railways, 22–3
Raion, see Districts
Rank, military, 219
Rasporjazhenie, see Dispositions
Reforms, governmental, 31–2
Regional courts, 211
Regions (*oblastj*): administrative, 25, 65, 72–5; autonomous, 65, 70, 88, 90; departments of, 131–3
Representation in Supreme Soviets, 76, 90–1
Republics: autonomous, 70, 90–1, 113, 130–1; industrial control in, 191–3; ministries in, 129–31; officers of, 113; Union, 66–7, 69–70, 90–1
Research, academic, 223, 225
Reshenie, see Decisions
Revenue: local, 239–40; state, 239
Revolution, French, 42

Revolution, Russian: forebodings of, 31; immediate effects of, 37; of 1905, 35; of March 1917, 35, 158; of November 1917, 36, 41–2
River Fleet, Ministry of, 117
Romanov, house of, 24
Rostov, 191
Rumania, 70
Russia: area of, 21; climate of, 21; communications in, 21–3; Communist Party in, see Party; early history of, 22; economic expansion of, 23; Japan and, 31, 43; Marxism in, 33–4, 36–9, 61; natural resources of, 21; population of, 23, 75–6, 90; railway development in, 22–3; territorial expansion by, 22; topography of, 21. *See also* Soviet Union
Russian Orthodox Church, 22, 232
Russian revolutions, 31, 35–7, 41–2
Russian Social-Democrat Workers' Party, 31, 34–5, 56–7, 137, 158
Russian Soviet Federated Socialist Republic (R.S.F.S.R.), 64–6, 72–3, 91, 96, 101, 113, 117, 120, 129–32, 137
Ryzhov, N. S., 117

Saburov, M. Z., 118–19, 145
St. Petersburg, 22, 31, 56, 59
Savings, 242
Schools, 220–2
Science, regard for, 224
Scientists, 226–8
Sectors (*sektor*), 192
Selo, see Villages
Sentences, penal, 216, 244–5
Serfdom, 24–5
Serfs: emancipation of, 26; registration of, 25
Settlements (*posjolok*), 73–6
Seven-year schools, 220
Shashkov, S. A., 117
Shatalin, N. N., 149
Shepilov, D. T., 146, 149
Shkola-internat, 222
Shvernik, N. M., 113, 144–6, 151, 229
Shturmovshchina, 243
Siberia, 21, 22–3, 70–1, 73
Slogans, 58–9
Smolensk region, 166, 181–2
Social Democrats, see Russian Social-Democrat Workers' Party
Social Revolutionary Party, 34–5, 46, 57–9, 158
Societies, control of, 232

Sophia, Regent, 24
Soviet Control, Commission of, 206
Soviet of Nationalities, 66, 83, 90, 94, 102; 106–7
Soviet of the Union, 90
Soviet regime: achievements of, 248–9; periods of, 44 et seq.; problems of, 42–4, 249–50; top-level groups within, 233–4
Soviet Union: armed forces of, 248–9; citizens of, 53, 247–8; constitutions of, 66–8, 81 et seq.; economic basis of, 42–3; economic problems of, 48–9; federalism and, 67 et seq.; foreign communists and, 43; foreign nations and, 43, 248–9; frontier problems of, 43; languages within, 68; legislative power of, 86–7; Second World War and, 50–1; society within, 53–4; territorial expansion of, 50
Soviets, 56, 63; activities of, 60, 107–11; bureaux of, 111; business procedure of, 108–9; chairmen of, 102; Congresses of, 46, 59, 61, 66, 82–3, 93, 137; deputies in, 91, 108–10; early, 56–7; elections to, 90 et seq.; executive committees of, 111–12, 113–14, 123–6, officers of, 113–16; party control of, 176–7; powers of, 62, 77–8; praesidia of, 111–12; rural, 61–2; sessions of, 101; standing commissions of, 103; town, 71, 92, 108, 124–5; use of by Lenin, 57 et seq.; village, 61–2, 71 et seq., 75–8, 92, 101, 103, 108, 114. See also Supreme Soviet, Supreme soviets
Sovnarhoz, see Councils of the Economy
Special Consultation, 216
Stalino region, 76
Stalin, J., 36, 38, 40–2, 50, 51, 55, 63, 65, 70, 80, 82, 84, 88, 95, 97, 110, 204, 234, 249–50; career of, 48 et seq.; Communist Party and, 141, 143–5, 147–8, 151, 159, 162–3, 168, 173, 183
Stalin Constitution of 1936, 82–9
State Arbitration, 210
State Bank, 118, 206–7, 239
State Control, Ministry of, 206
State Economic Commission, 236
State Establishments Administration, 193
State Farms, Ministry of, 193, 198
State farms, 199, 201, 203

State Planning Commission (republican), 120, 130
State Planning Committee (federal), 81, 118, 130, 133, 236–8
State Political Administration (G.P.U.), 207
State Scientific-Technical Committee, (federal), 118, (republican), 120
State Security: Committee of (federal), 118, (republican), 120; Ministry of, 207
Storm, The, 170
Strikes, 30–1
Subordination, 68, 76; industrial, 191–2
Succession to leadership, 47, 51–2
Suffrage, see Elections
Suharevo, village of, 99
Supervision: system of multiple, 122–6, 244; party, 177–8
Supreme Council of the Economy, 67, 80–1
Supreme Court, 38, 210–13
Supreme courts, 211–12
Supreme Soviet of U.S.S.R.: budget commissions of, 238; categories of business of, 105; composition of, 90; elections to, 94; gazette of acts of, 18, 89, 126; legislation by, 52, 104–7; mandates commissions of, 101; meetings of, 100; membership of, 97–100; officers of, 102; Praesidium of, 66, 68, 79, 93–4, 100, 104–7, 112–13, 122, 194–5, 208, 212; representation in, 76, 90; sessions of, 100; standing commissions of, 102–3
Supreme soviets of republics, 91–2; business of, 121–2; mandates commissions of, 101–2; meetings of, 100–1; membership of, 97–100; officers of, 102–3, 112; praesidia of, 112; sessions of, 100–1; standing commissions of, 102–3
Suslov, M. A., 145, 149, 151

Tadjik union republic (Tadjikistan), 69, 71, 91, 96, 120, 135, 142, 204
Tammerfors, 39
Tatar invasion, 22
Tatar autonomous republic, 70, 73–5, 91
Taxation, 239–40
Teachers, 221
Technicum, 221
Terminology, Soviet political, 15, 53, 60, 129, 132, 136

Territorial courts, 211
Territories (*krai*), administrative, 72–3, 75; departments of, 131–2
Territory, losses of, 63
Textbooks, official, 18–19, 95, 100
Third International, 190
Tito, Marshal J. Broz-, 233–4
Titoists, 40
Tjan-Shan region, 101
Town soviets, 71, 92, 108, 124–5
Towns, 27–8, 61, 73, 75–6
Trade unions, 80, 228–30; activities of, 229–30; leaders of, 229
Transcaucasian union republic, 66, 69
Trans-Siberian Railway, 23
Transport and Heavy Machine Building, Ministry of, 117
Transport Machine Building, Ministry of, 117
Trest, 192
Trials, 215–16
Troika, 216
Trotski (L. D. Bronstein), 39, 47–9, 57–8, 141
Trusts, 192–3
Tsar: *Duma* and, 32; institution of, 22; powers of, 24–5, 32; status of, 23, 31
Tula region, 114
Turkestan, 69
Turkmen union republic (Turkmenia), 69, 73, 91, 96
Turnover tax, 239
Tuva autonomous region, 70, 72
Two Tactics of Social Democracy, 35

Udmurt autonomous republic, 70, 71, 91
Uezd, 26–7, 71–2
Ukaz, *see* Edict
Ukraine (union republic), 21, 63, 66, 71, 73, 75, 91–2, 105, 113, 115, 129, 142–3, 147, 164, 177
Uljanov, *see* Lenin
Unified State Political Organisation (O.G.P.U.), 207
Union of Soviet Artists, 226
Union of Soviet Composers, 226
Union of Soviet Socialist Republics, *see* Soviet Union
Union of Soviet Writers, 188, 226
Union of Zemstvos, 35
Union republics, 66–7, 69–70, 90–1, 113; ministries of, 129–31

United States of America, 66–7
Universities, 223–4
Unrest, 30–1
Uprava, 27–8
Upravlenie, *see* Administrations
Urban settlements, 73–4, 76
Urban workers, 28–30
Urbanisation, 76–7, 247
Uzbek union republic (Uzbekistan), 69–71, 73, 91, 113, 142, 165, 235

Village (*selo*) soviets, 61–2, 71 *et seq.*, 75–8, 92, 101, 103, 108, 114
Volga German autonomous republic, 71
Volkov, A. P., 102
Volostj, 26–7, 71–2
Voronezh region, 76, 101, 125
Voroshilov, Marshal K. E., 79, 144–5, 233
Voting procedure, *see* Elections

Wages, 196
War communism, 45, 48
Women in Communist Party, 165
Workers: agricultural, 199, 201–3; in Communist Party, 158, 160–1; industrial, 194–5; urban, 28, 30
Workers' settlements, 73, 75–6
Writers' Union, *see* Union of Soviet Writers

Yakut autonomous republic, 70, 91
Yezhov, N. I., 49
Youth organisations, 156. *See also Komsomol*
Yugoslavia, 195-6
Yugoslavs, 167

Zakon, *see* Laws
Zampolit, 155, 218
Zakonodateljnaja vlastj, 87
Zavenjagin A. P., 117
Zemskaja uprava, 27
Zemski Sobor, 23–4
Zemstvo, 27
Zhdanov, A. A., 48–9, 51, 148, 153, 187
Zhukov, Marshal G. K., 146, 219–20, 233
Zinoviev, G. E., 49, 61